THE PRACTICAL ENCYCLOPEDIA
ASIAN COOKING

THE PRACTICAL ENCYCLOPEDIA OF
ASIAN COOKING

From Thailand to Japan, classic ingredients and authentic recipes from the East

SALLIE MORRIS AND DEH-TA HSIUNG

HERMES
HOUSE

This edition is published by Hermes House, an imprint of Anness Publishing Ltd,
108 Great Russell Street, London WC1B 3NA; info@anness.com

www.hermeshouse.com; www.annesspublishing.com; twitter: @Anness_Books

If you like the images in this book and would like to investigate using them for publishing, promotions or advertising,
please visit our website www.practicalpictures.com for more information.

© Anness Publishing Ltd 2016

A CIP catalogue record for this book is available from the British Library.

Publisher: Joanna Lorenz
Senior Editor: Felicity Forster
Editor: Jenni Fleetwood
Photography: Nicki Dowey (recipes) and Janine Hosegood
Food for photography: Becky Johnson (recipes) and Annabel Ford
Additional recipes: Kit Chan and Masaki Ko
Designer: Nigel Partridge
Production Controller: Pirong Wang

PUBLISHER'S NOTE
Although the advice and information in this book are believed to be accurate and true at the time of going to press,
neither the authors nor the publisher can accept any legal responsibility or liability for any errors or omissions
that may be made nor for any inaccuracies nor for any harm or injury that comes about
from following instructions or advice in this book.

COOK'S NOTES
Bracketed terms are intended for American readers.
For all recipes, quantities are given in both metric and imperial measures and, where appropriate, in standard cups and spoons.
Follow one set of measures, but not a mixture, because they are not interchangeable.
Standard spoon and cup measures are level. 1 tsp = 5ml, 1 tbsp = 15ml, 1 cup = 250ml/8fl oz.
Australian standard tablespoons are 20ml. Australian readers should use 3 tsp in place of 1 tbsp for measuring small quantities.
American pints are 16fl oz/2 cups. American readers should use 20fl oz/2.5 cups in place of 1 pint when measuring liquids.
Electric oven temperatures in this book are for conventional ovens. When using a fan oven, the temperature will probably need to be
reduced by about 10–20°C/20–40°F. Since ovens vary, you should check with your manufacturer's instruction book for guidance.
Medium (US large) eggs are used unless otherwise stated.

CONTENTS

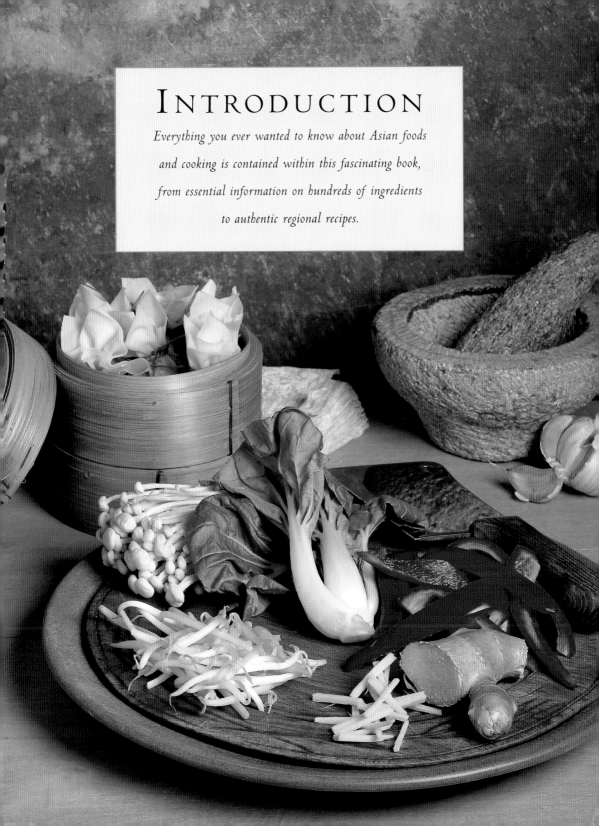

INTRODUCTION

Everything you ever wanted to know about Asian foods

and cooking is contained within this fascinating book,

from essential information on hundreds of ingredients

to authentic regional recipes.

SOME OF THE WORLD'S most exciting cuisines come from the Far East and South-east Asia. From the vastness of China to the island states of Indonesia and the Philippines, food is prepared with pleasure and keen attention to detail. Each of the countries in this broad sweep has its own unique style of cooking, coloured by climate, local crops, cultural mores and the impact of historical events such as invasion or war, but there are common threads too. Throughout this region, the emphasis is always on serving food that is as fresh as possible. Presentation is paramount, particularly in Japan and Thailand, and the sharing of food is so fundamental to the faith of each culture that honoured guests are precisely that.

Rice is the staple food of the whole of this region. Cultivated in southern Asia for over 5,000 years, rice is eaten at every meal, including breakfast, and is the basis of both sweet and

Above: A variety of crops and grains are grown on the terraced fields on river banks in southern China.

Below: A chef preparing a variety of fresh fish, meats, vegetables and herbs at a roadside food stall in Hong Kong.

savoury snack foods, as well as being a source for both wine and vinegar. In Japan, vinegared rice is used to make sushi, those delicious titbits that consist either of shaped rice topped with fish or vegetables, or rice and other ingredients rolled in thin sheets of edible seaweed.

Fish forms an important part of the diet. Every country, with the exception of Laos, has miles of coastline, as well as rivers, lakes and ponds, all of which yield plentiful supplies of fish. The lower reaches of the Yangtze River are traditionally known as the "Land of Fish and Rice", a term that is used to indicate the well-being of the local inhabitants. The first king of Siam expressed similar sentiments when, in 1292, he wrote of the value of having "fish in the water and rice in the field".

The Japanese cooks' skill in preparing and serving fish is legendary. This is partly due to the fact that the country has abundant fish stocks and only limited land for grazing, but is also because for many years, meat was off the menu, due to a government decree that prohibited its consumption by any but the sick, on the grounds that it increased aggression. As a result,

Below: Fresh red chillies, which are used in many South-east Asian dishes, being sold at a market in Myanmar.

Japanese cooks became extremely adept at preparing fish in a wide variety of ways. Very fresh fish is sliced thinly and served raw, or marinated, but this is by no means the only way of preparing it. Fish is also poached, grilled, cooked on skewers and battered and fried in the famous tempura.

In Thailand, too, fish is of enormous importance. As elsewhere in Asia, it is always served as fresh as possible. In restaurants it is usual for diners to choose their own fish from tanks, a

Above: Planting rice in a paddy field in the Mekong Delta, Vietnam. Two crops are harvested each year.

serious business that demands considerable deliberation, and nobody objects to waiting while the grouper or snapper is despatched, prepared and cooked in the manner the host has selected. Fish bought at market is often live and is carried home in a bucket of water for preparation by the cook.

The Asian preoccupation with the freshest possible food, be it animal or vegetable, can be a little disconcerting for the Western visitor. Before enjoying the famous Hong Kong dish Drunken Prawns, for instance, the diner must first watch as the live prawns are marinated in Shao Xing rice wine, then cooked in fragrant stock.

At the other end of the spectrum, salted and cured fish is a valuable source of food throughout the area, but particularly in South-east Asia. All sorts of fish and shellfish are prepared in this way, either in brine or by being dried in the sun. Dried fish and shellfish also furnish the raw material for fish sauce and shrimp paste, essential ingredients that go under various names, and contribute a subtle but unique signature to so many dishes.

Fish sauce is not the only condiment to play a seminal role in Asian cooking. Even more important is soy sauce, which was invented by the Chinese thousands of years ago. Tofu is another soya bean product that was originally peculiar to the region, but is now widely used in the Western world, as are noodles, another valuable food.

As well as having many ingredients in common, the countries of the Far East and South-east Asia share a similar approach to food. All prepare, cook and serve their daily meals according to the long-established principle the Chinese call *fan-cai*. The "fan" is the main part of the meal, usually rice or another form of grain, while the "cai" includes the supplementary dishes such as fish, meat, poultry and vegetables. These elements must be balanced in every meal, as must the ingredients in

Above: The colourful floating market in Bangkok, Thailand, sells a wonderful selection of fresh fruits and vegetables.

every supplementary dish, so that aromas, colours, textures and tastes are all in perfect harmony.

Harmony dictates that all the dishes be served together, buffet style, rather than as separate courses. Guests begin by taking a portion of rice, and then one beautifully served. Thai girls learn the art of fruit carving from a young age, and fruit (and vegetables) are cut into fabulous shapes of birds, flowers and butterflies. They are, of course, fortunate in having such wonderful raw materials. Visit the floating market in Bangkok – or, indeed, any market in this part of the world – and you will marvel at the array of vegetables and fruit on offer, many of them relatively unknown in the West until recently, when Asia became such a sought-after travel destination.

Tourism is one of the major reasons why Asian food has become so popular in Europe, America, Australia and elsewhere. Travellers discovered that Chinese food was not a single cuisine, but many, ranging from Peking cooking

Below: Asia stretches from China, through Japan and Korea, down to the South-east Asian islands of Malaysia, Indonesia and the Philippines.

in the north, to the hot and spicy Sichuan-style in the west and Cantonese in the south. Visitors to Vietnam and Thailand learned to enjoy – and distinguish between – the cuisines of those countries and, when they returned home, they wanted to be able to continue eating the meals that had been so much a part of their holiday. In major cities the world over, it is now possible to enjoy authentic Thai, Vietnamese, Indonesian, Malayan and even Filipino food, and it is only a matter of time before lesser-known cuisines are equally well represented.

Home cooks are eager to experiment with this quick, healthy and sensual style of cooking too. Ingredients such as lemon grass and galangal, which could once be bought only in specialist Asian stores are now readily available in many supermarkets. There's never been a better time to discover or extend your repertoire of Asian recipes, and this book is the very best place to start.

of the supplementary dishes on offer, relishing it on its own before taking another portion of rice and a second choice. Soup is served at the same time as other dishes, and is enjoyed throughout the meal.

Harmony extends to presentation, too, an art which reaches its apogee in Japan, where food is valued as much for its aesthetic appearance as for its flavour. In Thailand, too, food is

EQUIPMENT AND UTENSILS

The equipment in the average Western kitchen will be perfectly adequate for most of the recipes in this book, particularly now that the wok has become an indispensable item in many households. There are some items, however, that will make cooking Asian food easier and more pleasurable. The fact that many of these simple pieces of equipment also look good, and instantly establish you as an adventurous cook in the eyes of your friends is a bonus.

The best way to build up your store of specialist items is to start slowly, with a few basics such as a cleaver, bamboo steamer and wok, then gradually add extra pieces as you experiment with the exciting and different styles of cooking that are explored within these pages. If you enjoy making sushi, for instance, you will need a mat for rolling, and moulds for shaping the rice; if Thai curries are your current favourite, you'll be glad of a rough mortar and a pestle for grinding wet spice mixtures.

Visit an Asian or Chinese store and you'll be amazed at the array of items on sale at very reasonable prices. The design of many utensils has not changed in centuries, and items made from basic materials are often more effective than modern equivalents.

Cleaver

To Western cooks, a cleaver can seem rather intimidating. In reality, cleavers are among the most useful pieces of equipment ever invented. The blade of a heavy cleaver is powerful enough to cut through bone, yet delicate enough in the hands of a master chef to create paper thin slices of raw fish for sushi. The flat of the broad blade is ideal for crushing garlic or ginger, and the same blade can be used to convey the crushed items to the wok or pan.

Cleavers come in several sizes and weights. Number one is the heaviest. The blade is about 23cm/9in long and 10cm/4in wide. It can weigh as much as 1kg/2¼lb and resembles a chopper more than a knife. At the other end of

the scale, number three has a shorter, narrower blade and is only half as heavy as the larger cleaver. It is mainly used for slicing, rather than chopping. Number two is the cook's favourite. This medium-weight cleaver is used for both slicing and chopping. The Chinese name translates

Above: A medium-weight cleaver is a multi-purpose tool.

as "civil and military knife" because the lighter, front half of the blade is used for slicing, shredding, filleting and scoring (civil work), while the heavier rear half is used for chopping with force (military work). The back of the blade is used for pounding and tenderizing, and the flat for crushing and transporting. Even the handle has more than one purpose – the end can be used as a pestle.

Cleavers are made of several types of material. They can be made of carbonized steel with wooden handles, or of stainless steel with metal or wooden handles. Choose the one you are comfortable with. Hold it in your hand and feel the weight; it should be neither too heavy nor too light. One point to remember is that while a stainless-steel cleaver may look good, it will require frequent sharpening if it is to stay razor-sharp. To prevent a carbonized steel blade from rusting and getting stained, wipe it dry after every use, then give it a thin coating of vegetable oil. Cleavers should always be sharpened on a fine-grained whetstone, never with a steel sharpener. The cleaver is user-friendly. It is not as

dangerous as it looks, provided you handle it with care. Learn to regard it as just another kitchen knife, and you will be rewarded with a lot of fun and very satisfactory results.

Chopping block

The traditional chopping block in the East is simply a cross-section of a tree trunk, usually hardwood. The ideal size for use in a domestic kitchen is about 30cm/12in in diameter and about 5cm/2in thick, but you will see much larger blocks being used in restaurants.

Season a new block with a liberal dose of vegetable oil on both sides to prevent it from splitting. Let it absorb as much oil as it will take, then clean the block with salt and water and dry it thoroughly. After each use, scrape the surface with the back of your cleaver, then wipe it down with a cloth. Never immerse a wooden block in water.

A large rectangular cutting board of hardwood can be used instead, but make sure it is at least 5cm/2in thick or it may not be able to take a hard blow from a cleaver. Acrylic boards can obviously be used if preferred, but they will not have the same aesthetic appeal as a traditional wooden one.

Left: A traditional Asian grater made of wood.

Above: The rough surface of a stone mortar and pestle helps grip the ingredients that are being pounded.

Grater

Traditional graters, used for preparing ginger, galangal and mooli (daikon), are made from wood or bamboo, but a metal cheese grater makes a satisfactory substitute.

Mortar and pestle

Asian cooks prefer granite or stone mortars and pestles, since these have rough surfaces which help to grip the ingredients that are being chopped or pounded. Bigger, flat-bowled mortars are good for making spice pastes that contain large amounts of fresh spices, onion, herbs and garlic.

Spice mill

If you are going to grind a lot of spices, a spice mill will prove useful. An electric coffee grinder works well for this purpose,

Right: A double-handled wok is useful for all types of cooking; those with a single handle are particularly good for stir-frying..

but it is a good idea to reserve the mill for spices, unless you like to have your coffee flavoured with cardamom or cloves.

Wok

It is not surprising that the wok has become a universal favourite, for it is a remarkably versatile utensil. The rounded bottom was originally designed to fit snugly on a traditional Chinese brazier or stove. It conducts and retains heat evenly and because of its shape, the food always returns to the centre where the heat is most intense. This makes it ideally suited for stir-frying, braising, steaming, boiling and even for deep-frying.

Although the wok might not at first glance appear to be the best utensil for deep-frying, it is actually ideal, requiring far less oil than a flat-bottomed deep-fryer. It has more depth and a greater frying surface, so more food can be cooked more quickly. It is also much safer than a standard pan. As a wok has a larger capacity at the top than at the base, there is plenty of room to

accommodate the oil, even when extra ingredients are added, and it is not likely to overflow and catch fire.

There are two basic types of wok available in the West. The most common type, the double handled wok, is suitable for all types of cooking. The single-handled wok is particularly suitable for quick stir-frying, as it can easily be shaken during cooking. Both types are available with flattened bases for use on electric cookers or gas cookers with burners that would not accommodate a round base.

The best woks are made from lightweight carbonized steel. Cast iron woks are too heavy for all but the strongest cooks to handle, and woks made from other materials, such as stainless steel or aluminium, are not as good for Asian cooking. They also tend to be a great deal more expensive than the standard carbonized steel wok.

A new carbonized steel wok must be seasoned before use. The best way to do this is to place the wok over high heat until the surface blackens, then wash it in warm, soapy water. Use a stiff brush to get the wok clean, then rinse it well in clean water and place it over medium heat to dry completely. Finally, wipe the surface with a pad of kitchen paper soaked in vegetable oil. After each use, wash the wok under the hot water tap, but never use detergent as this would remove the "seasoning" and cause the wok to rust. Any food that sticks to the wok should be scraped off with a stiff brush or with a non-metal scourer, and the wok should then be rinsed and dried over low heat. Before being put away, a little oil should be rubbed in to the surface of the wok.

Below right: A perforated metal scoop and a wire skimmer

Above: Essential wok tools include a dome-shaped lid, wooden or bamboo chopsticks, a long-handled spatula and a large ladle.

Wok tools

Some wok sets come with a spatula and ladle made from cast iron or stainless steel. These are very useful, particularly the ladle. In addition to its obvious purpose as a stirrer, it can be used to measure small quantities of liquid. A standard ladle holds about 175ml/ 6fl oz/¾cup. A dome-shaped lid is also useful, as is a metal draining rack that fits over the wok. Small items such as deep-fried foods can be placed on the rack to keep warm while successive batches are cooked. Other accessories include wooden or bamboo chopsticks. Short ones can be used at the table or in the kitchen – they are ideal for beating eggs – and the long pair are used for deep-frying, as stirrers or tongs. Finally, a wok stand is handy for protecting your table when serving.

Strainers

Several types of strainer are available, but the two most useful are the perforated metal scoop or slotted spoon, and the coarse-mesh, wire skimmer, preferably with a long bamboo handle. Wire skimmers come in a variety of sizes and are useful for removing food from hot oil when deep-frying.

Below: Bamboo steamers come in several sizes.

Steamers

The traditional Chinese steamer is made from bamboo and has a tight-fitting lid. Several sizes are available, and you can stack as many tiers as you like over a wok of boiling water. The modern steamer is free-standing and made of aluminium, but the food cooked in a metal steamer lacks the subtle fragrance that a bamboo steamer imparts. If you do not have a steamer, you can improvise with a wok and a trivet. Having placed the trivet in the wok, fill it one-third full of water

Above: An authentic clay pot can be used in the oven or, with care, on top of the stove.

and bring this to the boil. Place the food in a heatproof bowl on the trivet, cover the wok with the dome-shaped lid and steam the food until it is cooked.

Clay pot

Also known as the sand-pot or Chinese casserole, this earthenware cooking utensil must have preceded the cast iron pot by thousands of years. Several shapes and sizes are available, and most are glazed on the inside only. They are not expensive and can be bought in

Below: A large pan with a tight-fitting lid is ideal for cooking rice.

Asian or Chinese stores. With care, the pots can be used on top of the stove, where they retain an even heat. They are, however, fairly fragile, and are prone to crack easily.

Rice cooker

Electric rice cookers work extremely well and are worth investing in if you cook rice on a regular basis. However, a good-sized, deep, heavy pan that has a tight-fitting lid is just as suitable for preparing rice.

Mongolian fire pot

Also known as a Chinese hot pot or steamboat (in Singapore), this is not unlike a fondue pot, in that it allows food to be cooked at the table. The design is different from that of a fondue, however, as it consists of a central funnel, which is filled with burning charcoal, surrounded by a moat in which hot stock is placed. The pot is placed in the centre of the table and guests cook small pieces of meat and vegetables in the hot stock. Once these are all cooked and eaten, the stock is served as a soup. There are several different models available, the most expensive being made of brass, while the cheaper ones are made of aluminium or stainless steel.

Japanese omelette pan

To make the rolled omelettes that are so widely used in Japanese cooking, a rectangular omelette pan or *makiyaki-nabe* is useful, but not essential: a large non-stick, heavy frying pan or a flat, heavy griddle could be used instead.

Below: A Mongolian fire pot or steamboat is used for cooking at the table. The central funnel is filled with burning charcoal, and this heats the stock in the surrounding moat.

Sushi equipment

If you are going to make sushi properly, you will need a few simple pieces of equipment. A *makisu,* also known as a *sushimaki sudare,* is essential. This is the bamboo mat (shown below), which is about the size of a table mat, that is used for rolling sheets of nori (seaweed) around vinegared rice and other fillings when making *norimaki.*

Sushi chefs spread the rice on the nori with their fingers, but this is a sticky business and can prove tricky for the uninitiated. A rice paddle or *shamoji* makes the job easier. For pressed sushi, shaped moulds made from wood or plastic are very useful.

INGREDIENTS

This visual directory includes essential information on every
type of Asian food, from the daily staples, such as rice and
noodles, to unusual fruit and vegetables and exotic fish,
and includes preparation, cooking and storing instructions.

RICE

CHINESE: *MI*; THAI: *KHAO*

Rice is the staple grain of the whole of Asia, which is well over half the world's population. It is true that wheat is also grown in northern China and India, but its consumption is rather small in comparison with rice.

Throughout Asia, the importance of rice is underlined by the fact that in Chinese and other Asian languages, there is no single word for rice, but many. The crop, grain, raw rice and cooked rice are all referred to by different terms, and the Chinese character *fan* for cooked rice has acquired a much wider meaning in colloquial speech; it is also synonymous with nourishment and good health. When friends meet, instead of asking "How do you do?" they will often greet each other with the words: "Have you eaten rice?" An affirmative answer indicates that all is well.

Another common Chinese word with more than one meaning is *fan-wan* (rice-bowl). Aside from the obvious, this also means a job or livelihood; so the expression "to lose one's rice bowl" or "to have one's rice bowl broken", suggests that one has been given the sack; similarly, someone described as having an "iron rice-bowl" has probably got a job for life. Paradoxically, the expression *fan-tong,* which means a rice bucket (something that holds a large amount of cooked rice) has become a derogatory expression to describe a person who lacks refinement (a big eater of plain rice).

Rice has been cultivated in southern Asia for over 5,000 years. There are more than 40,000 different strains grown in China alone. Since rice requires a wet and warm climate for its cultivation, some 90 per cent of the world production of rice is grown (and consumed) in the monsoon regions of Asia. A small amount of rice is cultivated on dry land in northern China, but because of the cold climate, only one crop can be grown each year, whereas two crops per annum is the norm in the temperate south.

Above: Thai fragrant rice has a delicate, fragrant scent.

Below: Patna rice is one of the many types of long grain rice.

Freshly harvested rice has a special aroma, and is eagerly sought after in China and Japan, the rice from the autumn harvest (usually in November) being reckoned to taste the best.

TYPES OF RICE

Broadly speaking, rice can be classified as being either *Oryza sativa indica* or *Oryza sativa japonica*. Varieties of both types are cultivated in Asia. Long grained indica *(xian)* rices – of which there are many strains – are the most common. Long grain white rice has had its husk, bran and germ removed, taking most of the nutrients with them and leaving a bland-flavoured rice that is light and fluffy when cooked. Long grain brown rice has had only its outer husk removed, leaving the bran and germ intact, which gives it a chewy, nutty flavour. It takes longer to cook than white rice but contains more fibre, vitamins and minerals.

Patna rice gets its name from Patna in India. At one time, most of the long grain rice sold in Europe came from Patna, and the term was used loosely to mean any long grain rice. The custom persists in parts of America, but elsewhere Patna is used to describe a variety of long grain rice from the Bihar region of India.

Basmati rice is a slender long grain rice that is grown in northern India, in the Punjab, in parts of Pakistan and in the foothills of the Himalayas. After harvesting it is aged for a year, which gives it a characteristic flavour and a light, fluffy texture. The grains are long and slender, and become even longer during cooking. Widely used in Indian cooking, basmati rice has a cooling effect on hot and spicy curries.

Thai fragrant rice has a delicate but distinctive scent of jasmine, and is particularly highly prized.

Short-grained japonica *(geng)* rices are less fragrant, but tend to taste slightly sweeter than indicas. This type of rice is cultivated in northern China, Japan, Korea and surrounding areas. The rices are higher in amylopectin than long grains, and are therefore more starchy. The grains cling together when cooked, which makes them ideal for sushi and similar Japanese dishes.

Glutinous rice – also known as sweet or waxy rice – is even more sticky than Japanese short grain rice. This endears it to South-east Asian cooks, as the cooked rice can be shaped or rolled, and is very easy to pick up with chopsticks. White glutinous rice, with its fat, opaque grains, is the most common type, but there is also a black glutinous rice, which retains the husk and has a nutty flavour. A pinkish-red glutinous rice is cultivated on the banks of the Yangtze River, and a purple black variety has recently been developed. Glutinous rice has a high sugar content, and is used in Japan for making *senbei* (rice crackers) and *mochi* (rice cakes), as well as sweet rice wine.

Right: Short-grained japonica rice is ideal for sushi because, when cooked, the grains stick together.

Above: Basmati rice is considered by many people to be the prince of rice. There are various grades of basmati, but it is impossible to differentiate between them except by trying various brands to discover the best fragrance and taste.

Culinary uses

It is impossible to think of Asian food without rice. Rice is served in one form or another at every meal, including breakfast. Although wheat – in the form of dumplings or noodles – is eaten more often than rice in some parts of Asia, such as northern China, Asians everywhere regard rice as their staple food, with wheaten foods as mere supplements. In some languages the phrase for eating rice is the same as that for eating food.

The most common way of serving rice throughout Asia is simply boiled or steamed; fried rice does not normally form part of an everyday meal, but is either served as a snack on its own, or reserved for a special occasion such as a banquet. Unlike the Indian pilau, the Italian risotto or the Spanish paella, Asian fried rice dishes are never based upon raw rice, but always use ready cooked rice (either boiled or steamed). For the finest results, the rice should be cold and firm, rather than soft.

The universal breakfast in all Asian countries is a creamy, moist rice dish, which is known as congee or rice pudding. Considered to be highly nutritious, it is often given to babies and people with digestive problems as well as the elderly. Coconut milk is used instead of water in many South-east Asian countries, but because it usually takes over an hour to make a smooth, creamy congee, many Japanese cooks (and some Chinese) cheat by simply adding hot water to cold cooked rice.

Below: Black and white glutinous rice

others, and the amount of liquid required varies, too. The general rule is to use double the amount of water by volume to dry rice. However, if the rice has been washed or soaked first, less water will be needed otherwise, when cooked, the rice will be soft and sticky, instead of firm and fluffy.

Asian cooks often add a teaspoon of vegetable oil to the water to prevent the rice from sticking to the bottom of the pan. Whether to add salt or not is a matter of choice. It is usually added when cooking regular long grain rice, but not for Thai fragrant rice. The width, depth and material of the pan used will also make a difference to the result. One of the best ways of cooking perfect boiled rice is in an electric rice-cooker, while some cooks get very good results in the microwave.

Storage

Raw rice should not be kept for too long, or the grains will lose their fragrance. Keep the rice in an airtight container in a dry, cool place, away from strong light, and use it within 3–4 months of purchasing.

Preparation and cooking techniques

There can never be a definitive recipe for cooking plain rice, because each type requires individual treatment.

Some benefit from being rinsed in cold water first, while others should be soaked before use. Some types of rice need to be cooked for longer than

---

Plain boiled rice

Use long grain Patna or basmati rice; or better still, try Thai fragrant rice. Allow 50g/2oz/generous ¼ cup raw rice per person.

1 Put the dry rice in a colander and rinse it under cold running water.

2 Transfer into a large pan, then pour in cold water to come 2cm/¾in above the surface of rice. (In Asia the traditional way of measuring this is with the help of the index finger. When the tip of the finger is touching the surface of the rice, the water level should just reach the first joint.)

3 Add a pinch of salt, and, if you like, about 5ml/1 tsp vegetable oil, stir once and bring to the boil.

4 Stir once more, reduce the heat to the lowest possible setting and cover the pan with a tight-fitting lid.

5 Cook for 12–15 minutes, then turn off the heat and leave the rice to stand, tightly covered, for about 10 minutes. Fluff up the rice with a fork before serving.

FLOURS

The most popular thickening agents in Asia are cornflour (cornstarch), tapioca flour and potato flour. Mung bean flour, water chestnut flour, lotus root and arrowroot are favoured for clear sauces. Gram flour is used to make batters. Rice flour is used as a thickener, and for rice papers, dumplings and cakes.

Cornflour
Also called cornstarch, this fine white powder, made from corn is a useful thickening agent for sauces, soups and casseroles.

Rice flour
More finely milled than ground rice, this is also known as rice powder. The texture is similar to that of cornflour. Rice flour is used for thickening sauces, and to make rice papers and the dough for dumplings. It is often used to make sticky Asian cakes and sweets, but because rice flour has no gluten, the cakes made with it are rather flat. Rice flour can be combined with wheat flour to make bread, but this produces a crumbly loaf.

Gram flour
This very fine flour is also called chickpea flour, or besan. Mainly used in India, where it originated, it also plays a role in Malayan cooking, thanks to Indian immigrants who introduced it.

Wheat flour
Ground from the whole grain, this may be wholemeal (whole-wheat) or white. Hard, or strong wheat flour is high in gluten, making it ideal for adding to rice flour to make bread.

Soya flour
This is a finely ground, high-protein flour made from the soya bean. It is used as a thickener in a wide range of sauces and soups, and is often mixed with other flours such as wheat flour to make bread and pastries. It adds a pleasant nutty flavour.

Left: Japanese rice flour

Far left: Japanese wheat flour

Below: Gram flour

Left: Thai rice flour

Right: Cornflour (cornstarch)

Left: Japanese soya flour

NOODLES

MANDARIN: *MIAN (TIAO)*; CANTONESE: *MEIN*;
THAI: *GUEYTEOW*

Whether Marco Polo actually introduced noodles from China to Italy is a debatable point, but we do know that noodles made from wheat flour appeared in China as early as the first century BC, around the time of the Roman Empire. Noodles rapidly became a popular food, not only in China, but throughout the whole of Asia.

Up to the end of the last century, when modern machinery was first imported from Europe, noodles were always made by hand, and even today, certain types of noodle are still hand-made, most notably, the "hand-pulled" or "drawn" noodles made by chefs in northern China. It takes more than ten years to master the technique, so is beyond the reach of ordinary mortals.

Noodles form an important part of the daily diet in the Far East, ranking second only to rice as a staple food. Unlike rice and steamed buns, however, which are usually served plain to be eaten with cooked dishes, noodles are

Left: Four types of Japanese Udon noodles

usually cooked with other ingredients. For this reason, noodle dishes are seldom served as accompaniments, but are eaten on their own as light meals or snacks. In Vietnam, rice noodle soup is the standard breakfast. In Japan there are restaurants that specialize in noodle dishes such as noodles served solo with dipping sauces; bowls of steaming noodle soup; and noodles cooked with slivered vegetables and seaweed.

Below: Plain Chinese (top) and Thai noodles (bottom)

Below: Bundles of thin, white, Japanese Somen noodles

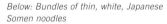

Thailand has its noodle stalls, noodle boats and even noodle meals on wheels available from vendors with ingenious mobile shops mounted on their bicycles. In Asia, you need never be far from a noodle seller.

WHEAT NOODLES

Asian noodles are made from a variety of flour pastes, including wheat, rice, mung bean, buckwheat, seaweed, corn and even devil's tongue, which is a plant related to the arum lily. Some noodles are plain, others are enriched with egg. Dried wheat noodles, with or without eggs, are often called "longevity noodles" because of their association with long life.

Right: Fresh egg noodles

Plain noodles

Made from strong plain (all-purpose) wheat flour and water, these can be flat or round and come in various thicknesses. In Japan, they are known as **Udon** and are available fresh, pre-cooked or dried. **Somen** are thin, delicate, white Japanese noodles. They are sold in bundles, held in place by a paper band.

Egg noodles These are far more common than plain wheat noodles. In China they come in various thicknesses and are sold fresh or dried. **Ramen** are the Japanese equivalent and are usually sold in coils or blocks. Very fine egg noodles, which resemble vermicelli, are called **Yi noodles** in China, after the family that originally made them. They are popular in Hakka-style cooking.

Shrimp noodles These seasoned egg noodles are flavoured with fresh shrimp and/or shrimp roe, They are usually sold dried, in coils of various widths.

Instant noodles Packets of pre-cooked egg noodles are a familiar sight in the West. They come in various flavourings, such as chicken, prawn and beef.

Preparation and cooking techniques

Noodles are very easy to prepare. Some types benefit from being soaked before being cooked, so see individual recipes for advice, read the instructions on the packet or seek advice from someone in the store where you bought them. Both dried and fresh noodles have to be cooked in boiling water before use. How long for depends on the type of noodle, the thickness of the strips, and whether (as is usual) the noodles will be cooked again in a soup or sauce. Dried noodles generally require about 3 minutes' cooking, while fresh ones will often be ready in less than a minute, and may need to be rinsed under cold water to prevent them from overcooking.

After the initial cooking, noodles are then usually prepared and served in one of the following ways:

Noodles in soup Most popular in China, Korea, Japan, Vietnam, Myanmar and Singapore, this usually consists of noodles served in bowls of clear broth with pieces of cooked meat, poultry, seafood and/or vegetables, sometimes with a sharp sauce on the side.

Braised noodles *(lao mein)* The difference between this and noodles in soup is that braised noodles are first cooked in a broth, then served with a thickened sauce.

Fried noodles *(chow mein)* This has to be one of the most popular Chinese dishes in the West (and in South-east Asia, but not so much in north China or Japan). The two basic types of fried noodles are dry-fried (crisp) or soft-fried. Generally speaking, only the fine vermicelli-type of noodles are used for dry-frying; the thicker round or flat noodles are more suitable for soft-frying.

Left: Blocks of dried Japanese Ramen noodles

Above: Instant noodles come in a variety of flavourings.

RICE NOODLES

CHINESE: *MIFEN;* VIETNAMESE:
LAI FAN

Wheat noodles must
have preceded rice
noodles by
several
centuries,
since there
were no written
records of their
existence until
well into the Han
Dynasty in the
third century AD. Not surprisingly,
rice noodles are very popular in
southern China and South-east Asia
where not much wheat is grown.

Unlike most other noodles, which are
made from flour of one type or another,
rice noodles are made from whole
grains of rice, which are soaked and
then ground with water into a paste.
This paste is drained through a strainer
to form a dough, which is divided into
two. One half is cooked in boiling water

*Above: Fine Thai rice noodles are
sometimes referred to as vermicelli.*

for 15 minutes, before it is kneaded
with the raw half to make a firm dough.
The dough is then put through a press,
which cuts it into various shapes and
sizes. The finished strands are blanched
in water, drained and rinsed before
being sold as fresh noodles, or dried
in the sun before packaging.

Types of rice noodles

Although they are known by different
names, the rice noodles sold in
southern China, Thailand and Vietnam
are all similar. Like wheat noodles,
they come in various widths, from the
very thin strands known as rice
vermicelli or *lai fan* (*sen mee*
in Thailand) to rice sticks,
which start at around
2mm/$\frac{1}{16}$in and can be
as wide as 1cm/$\frac{1}{2}$in,
as in the case of *ho fun,* a
special variety from south
China reputedly made with
river water rather than tap
water. In Thailand it is possible
to buy a rice noodle enriched
with egg. Called *ba mee,* it is
sold in nests. A wide range
of dried rice noodles is
available in Asian or
Chinese stores, and
fresh ones can
occasionally be
found in the chiller cabinets.

*Below: Thin and thick Chinese rice
noodles or sticks*

Preparation and cooking techniques

Because all rice noodles are pre-
cooked, they need only be soaked in
hot water for a few minutes to soften
them before use. If they are soaked
for too long, they will go soggy and lose
the texture that is part of their appeal.

Below: Japanese rice noodles

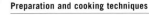

Preparing rice noodles
Rice noodles need only to be
soaked in hot water for a few
minutes to soften them.

Add the noodles to a large bowl
of water that has been recently
boiled and leave for 5–10 minutes,
or until softened, stirring
occasionally to separate the
strands as they soften.

MUNG BEAN (CELLOPHANE) NOODLES

CHINESE: *FENSI;* VIETNAMESE: *BUN;*
JAPANESE: *HARUSAME*

Also known as transparent noodles, bean thread vermicelli or glass noodles, these very fine, rather brittle strands are made from green mung beans, which are the same beans as those used for sprouting. Although very thin, the strands are firm and resilient, and they stay that way when cooked, never becoming soggy, which doubtless contributes to their popularity.

Preparing cellophane noodles
Cellophane noodles are never served on their own, but always used as an ingredient in a dish. Soak them in hot or warm water for 10–15 minutes to soften them.

When they are soft, use a pair of scissors or a sharp knife to chop the noodles into shorter strands for easier handling.

Left: Cellophane noodles

Cellophane noodles are almost tasteless unless cooked with other strongly flavoured foods and seasonings, but they have a fantastic texture. They are not served solo, but are always used as an ingredient in a dish, most notably in vegetarian cooking and in hot pots, as well as in Vietnamese spring rolls. They are only available dried. In Japan, cellophane noodles are called *harusame,* which means "spring rain".

BUCKWHEAT NOODLES

JAPANESE: *SOBA*

The best-known buckwheat noodles are the Japanese soba, which are usually sold dried in bundles of fine strands. Soba are much darker in colour than wheat noodles. There is also a dark green variety called *cha-soba* (tea soba), which is made of buckwheat and green tea. Korean cooks use buckwheat noodles, too, preferring a very thin variety.

Unusual noodles

Shirataki This popular Japanese noodle (*above left*) is made from a starch derived from the tubers of the devil's tongue plant, which is related to the arum lily.
Bijon Made from corn, these noodles (*above right*) are made in South-east Asia.
Canton These Chinese wheat noodles are sometimes enriched with eggs (*above top*).

Storage

Packets of fresh noodles normally carry a use-by date, and must, of course, be stored in the fridge. Dried noodles will keep for many months if kept sealed in the original packet, or in airtight containers in a cool, dry place, but again, the packets have an expiry date.

Below: Soba noodles

PANCAKES AND WRAPPERS

PANCAKES

CHINESE: *BING*

The pancakes of Asia are quite different from their counterparts in the West. For a start, they are almost always made from plain dough, rather than a batter, and they are more often than not served with savoury fillings rather than sweet.

There are two types of pancakes in China, either thin or thick. Thin pancakes *(bobing)* are also known as mandarin or duck pancakes, because they are used as wrappers for serving the famous Peking duck. They are also served with other savoury dishes, most notably, the very popular *mu-shu* or *moo-soo* pork, which consists of scrambled egg with pork and cloud ear (wood ear) mushrooms. Making pancakes demands considerable dexterity, so many cooks prefer to buy them frozen from the Chinese supermarket.

Thick pancakes are made with lard and flavoured with savoury ingredients such as spring onions (scallions) and rock salt. In northern China, they are eaten as a snack, or as part of a main meal, rather like the Indian paratha. Both thin and thick pancakes are sometimes served as a dessert, with a filling of sweetened bean paste.

NONYA SPRING ROLL PANCAKES

These are the exception to the rule that most Asian pancakes are made from dough. Typical of the Singaporean style of cooking known as Nonya, they are made from an egg, flour and cornflour (cornstarch) batter and are traditionally served with a wide selection of fillings.

Above: Thick pancakes are eaten as a savoury snack, or filled with sweet bean paste and served as a dessert.

Below: Thin pancakes are used as wrappers, notably for Peking duck, or served with savoury dishes.

Reheating Chinese pancakes

1 Stack the pancakes, interleaving them with squares of baking parchment.

2 Carefully wrap the stacked pancakes in foil, folding over the sides of the foil so that the pancakes are completely sealed.

3 Put the foil parcel in a steamer and cover. Place the steamer on a trivet in a wok of simmering water. Steam for 3–5 minutes until the pancakes are hot.

SPRING ROLL WRAPPERS

Mandarin: *CHUNJUAN PI*; Cantonese:
SHUEN GUEN PIE

Spring rolls are called egg rolls in the
USA, and pancake rolls in many other
parts of the world. They must be one
of the most popular Chinese snacks
everywhere, including China itself.
While the fillings may vary from region
to region, or even between different
restaurants and fast food stalls, the
wrappers are always more or less
the same. They are made from a
simple flour and water dough,
except in Vietnam, where wrappers
are made from rice flour, water and salt.

There are three different sizes of
ready-made spring roll wrappers
available from the freezers of Asian
stores: small, medium and large.
They are all wafer-thin. The smallest
wrappers, which are about 12cm/4½ in
square, are used for making dainty,
cocktail-style rolls. The standard-size

wrappers measure 21–23cm/8½–9in
square, and usually come in packets
of 20 sheets. The largest, 30cm/12in
square, are too big for general use, so
they are usually cut in half or into strips
for making samosas and similar snacks.

*Above: Small and medium-size spring
roll wrappers. Any unused wrappers
can be returned to the freezer.*

Preparing spring rolls
Use medium-size spring roll
wrappers, which you will find in the
freezer cabinet in Asian or Chinese
stores. They should be thawed before
use. For the filling, use ingredients
such as beansprouts, bamboo
shoots, water chestnuts and dried
mushrooms, with chopped prawns or
finely minced pork. When you have
prepared the rolls, deep-fry them
a few at a time in hot oil for 2–3
minutes, or until golden and crisp.

2 Spoon the spring roll filling diagonally
across the wrapper.

4 Brush the edges of the wrapper with
a little cornflour (cornstarch) paste.

1 Peel off the top spring roll wrapper.
Cover the rest to keep them moist.

3 Fold over the nearest corner of the
wrapper to cover the filling.

5 Fold the edges towards the middle,
then roll up into a neat parcel.

WONTON SKINS

MANDARIN: *HUNTUN PI*;
CANTONESE: *WANTON PIE*

Wonton skins or wrappers are made from a flour and egg dough, which is rolled out to a smooth, flat thin sheet, as when making egg noodles. The sheet is usually cut into small squares, although round wonton wrappers are also available. Ready-made wonton skins are stacked in piles of 25 or 50, wrapped and sold fresh or frozen in Asian or Chinese stores.

Unlike spring roll wrappers, which have to be carefully peeled off sheet by sheet before use, fresh wonton skins are dusted with flour before being packed, This keeps each one separate from the others and so they are very easy to use. Frozen wrappers must, however, be thawed thoroughly before use, or they will tend to stick together. Any unused skins can be re-frozen, but should be carefully wrapped in foil so that they do not dry out in the freezer.

There are several ways of using wonton skins. They can be deep-fried and served with a dip, filled and boiled, steamed or deep-fried, or simply poached in a clear broth. On most Chinese restaurant menus in the West, this last option is listed under soups, which is misleading, as in China and South-east Asia, wonton soup is always served solo as a snack, never as a separate soup course as part of a meal.

Above: Large spring roll wrappers can be cut into strips for making samosas.

Below: Wonton skins can be square or round and come in a variety of sizes.

Preparing wontons

Place the filling in the centre of the wonton skin and dampen the edges. Press the edges of the wonton skin together to create a little purse shape, sealing the filling completely.

RICE PAPERS

VIETNAMESE: *BANH TRANG*

The rice paper used in Vietnamese (and Thai) cooking is quite different from the rice paper that is used for writing and painting in China and Japan, nor does it bear any resemblance to the sheets of rice paper British cooks use as pan liners when baking macaroons. Made from rice flour, water and salt, it is a round, tissue-thin "crêpe", dried on bamboo mats in the sun, which results in the familiar crosshatch pattern being embedded on each sheet.

Rice paper is used for wrapping Vietnamese spring rolls and small pieces of meat and fish to be eaten in the hand. The sheets are rather dry and brittle, so must be softened by soaking in warm water for a few seconds before use. Alternatively, they can be placed on damp dish towels and brushed with water until they are sufficiently pliable to be used. Spring rolls are usually deep-fried, but this is not always the case. Vietnamese cooks also make a fresh version. Cooked pork, prawns (shrimp), beansprouts and vermicelli are wrapped in rice paper, which has been dipped in cold water until it is pliable and transparent. The filling can clearly be seen through the wrappers, and the rolls look very pretty.

Storage

Packaged and sold in 15cm/6in, 25cm/10in and 30cm/12in rounds, rice papers will keep for months in a cool, dry place, provided the packages are tightly sealed. When buying, look for sheets that are of an even thickness, with a clear, whitish colour. Broken pieces are a sign of bad handling, and are quite useless for wrapping, so avoid any packages that look as if they have been knocked about.

Below: Rice papers are dried on bamboo mats, which give them their familiar cross-hatch pattern.

DUMPLINGS

Dumplings are very popular in China, and there is a wide variety of different shapes and sizes, with fillings ranging from pork and vegetables to mushrooms and bamboo shoots. Some enclose the filling in a very thin dough skin *(jiao zi)* while others use a dough made from a glutinous rice flour. There are also steamed buns *(bao zi)* filled with meat or a sweet bean paste.

The best way to experience the diversity and delicious flavours of dumplings is to indulge in dim sum, that wonderful procession of tasty morsels that the Cantonese have elevated to an art form. Although dumplings originated in northern China, it was in Canton that the practice developed of enjoying these snacks with tea at breakfast or lunch time.

Dim sum literally means "dot on the heart" and indicates a snack or refreshment, not a full blown meal. Although the range of dishes available on a dim sum menu now embraces other specialities (spring rolls, wontons and spare ribs, for instance), dumplings remain the essential items.

Below: Grilled dumplings or "pot stickers" and chilli sauce.

What is more, unlike the majority of dim sum, which are so complicated to make that they can only be prepared by a highly skilled chef, dumplings are comparatively simple to make at home. Both *jiao zi* and *bao zi* are available ready-made from Asian or Chinese stores – the former are sold uncooked and frozen, and the latter are ready-cooked and sold chilled.

Preparation and cooking techniques

Frozen *jiao zi* dumplings should be cooked straight from the freezer. There are three different ways of cooking and serving them.

Poaching

The most common way of cooking dumplings in China is to poach them in boiling water for 4–5 minutes – longer if cooking from frozen.

The dumplings are added to boiling water. When the water boils again, a cupful of cold water is added to the pan and the water is brought to the boil again. This is repeated twice more, by which time the dumplings will be ready. They are traditionally served hot with a vinegar and soy sauce dip, chilli sauce or chilli oil.

Cooking Dumplings

1 To poach dumplings, drop them into boiling water. When the water boils again, add a cupful of cold water. Repeat twice more, cooking the dumplings for 4–5 minutes.

2 To steam dumplings, place them on a bed of lettuce or spinach leaves on the base of a bamboo steamer, cover with the lid and cook for 8–10 minutes.

3 To "grill" dumplings, fry in a shallow frying pan until they are brown, then add a little water, cover with a bamboo steamer lid, and cook until the water has completely evaporated.

Above: Plain steamed buns and sweet buns filled with bean paste.

Steaming

The best way to do this is by using a bamboo basket as a steamer. The dumplings are placed on a bed of lettuce or spinach leaves on the rack of the steamer, which is then covered. The dumplings are served hot with a dip.

Grilling

This description is a bit misleading, because the dumplings are not grilled in the conventional sense but are cooked in a flat frying pan. The dumplings are first shallow-fried, then a small amount of boiling water is added to the pan and they are steamed under cover until all the liquid has evaporated. When cooked by this method, the dumplings are crispy on the base, soft on top and juicy inside. They are often called by their popular name, which is "pot stickers".

PEKING DUMPLINGS

These crescent-shaped dumplings contain minced (ground) pork, greens and spring onions (scallions), seasoned with salt, sugar, soy sauce, rice wine and sesame oil. In northern China they are eaten for breakfast on New Year's Day, but are available all year round, often served as snacks or part of a meal.

STEAMED BUNS

Steamed buns are to Asia what baked bread is to the West, and *bao* (filled buns) are the Chinese fast food equivalent of hot dogs, hamburgers and sandwiches. There are two main types of steamed buns, either plain or filled. The plain, unfilled buns made from leavened dough are treated in much the same way as plain boiled rice and are intended to be eaten with cooked food. Then there are filled buns *(bao zi)*. The name literally means "wraps" and these can be savoury or sweet. The sweet ones usually contain either a lotus seed paste or a sweet bean paste filling and are usually eaten cold. Savoury *bao zi* come with a wide range of fillings, the most common being pork, and a very popular type is filled with Cantonese *char siu* (honey-roasted pork). These are available ready-made, and are best eaten hot.

Also available ready-made, but uncooked, are what are known as Shanghai dumplings. These are little round dumplings, much smaller than *char siu bao*, and each consisting of minced pork wrapped in a thin skin of unleavened dough.

Prawn crackers

Also called shrimp chips, prawn crackers are made from fresh prawns (shrimp, starch, salt and sugar. They are very popular as cocktail snacks, and some restaurants serve them while you wait for your meal. The raw crackers are grey in colour. The small Chinese ones are not much bigger than a thumbnail, while those used in Indonesia are much larger, about 15cm/6in long and 5cm/2in wide. Indonesian prawn crackers are more difficult to find in the West. Once deep-fried, both types puff up to four or five times the original size, and become almost snow white. Ready-cooked crackers are also available. They are sold in sealed packets, but do not keep well once exposed to the air, so should be eaten as soon as possible after opening.

VEGETABLES

CHINESE LEAVES/CHINESE CABBAGE

MANDARIN: *DA BAICAI; HUANG YA BAI;*
CANTONESE: *SHAO CHOI; WONG NGA BAK*

There are almost as many names for this member of the brassica family as there are ways of cooking it. In the West, it is generally called Chinese leaves, but it is also known as Chinese cabbage, Napa cabbage (mainly in the USA) or celery cabbage. The alternative Chinese name translates as "yellow-sprouting-white", a description of the crinkled leaves, and the Cantonese call it Peking or Tianjin cabbage in honour of its northern origin.

It is a cool-season vegetable, most abundant from November through to April, but available all year round.

There are three common varieties which all look similar, but differ in length, width and tightness of leaf.

Aroma and flavour

Chinese leaves have a delicate sweet aroma with a mild cabbage flavour that disappears completely when the vegetable is cooked. The white stalk has a crunchy texture, and it remains succulent even after long cooking.

Culinary uses

This is a very versatile vegetable and it can be used in stir-fries, stews, soups or salads. It will absorb the flavours of any other ingredients with which it is cooked – be they fish or shellfish, poultry, meat or vegetables – and yet retain its own characteristic flavour and texture. In Asian or Chinese restaurants, braised Chinese leaves are often served as a flavoursome base for roasted meats or duck.

Preparation and cooking techniques

Discard the outer layer of leaves and trim off the root, then slice off as much you need. Should you wish to wash the leaves (and this is not strictly necessary unless you are using them in a salad), do so before cutting them, otherwise you will wash away much of the vitamins. If you stir-fry Chinese leaves in hot oil, the stalks often develop dark scorch marks. Restaurant chefs blanch the vegetable in boiling stock, which enhances the flavour, before frying.

Storage

Chinese leaves can be stored for a long time without losing their resilience. Keep them in the salad compartment of the refrigerator and they will stay fresh for up to

Left: Chinese leaves have a crunchy texture and a delicate aroma. The mild cabbage flavour disappears when the vegetable is cooked.

10–12 days. Don't worry if there are tiny black specks on the leaves as this is quite normal and will not do any harm.

Preparing Chinese leaves

1 Discard any damaged outer leaves and trim off the root.

2 It is not usually necessary to wash the leaves, simply cut the head of Chinese leaves crossways into thin shreds.

3 You may prefer to wash the leaves, before using in a salad, for instance. Separate the leaves, then wash under cold running water. Shake off any excess water before shredding.

Right: Dark green bok choy tastes similar to spinach. The white stems can be cooked and eaten separately.

PAK CHOI/BOK CHOY

MANDARIN: *XIAO BAICAI;*
CANTONESE: *BOK CHOI*

Another member of the brassica family, pak choi goes by lots of different names. In the West it is sometimes known as bok choy, horse's ear (from the shape of the leaves) or Chinese white cabbage. In Cantonese, the name means simply white vegetable, which is a bit of a misnomer, as the glossy leaves that are a distinctive feature of this vegetable are dark green. The stalks, however, are pale, and range from light green to ivory white. Pak choi is a perennial, and several varieties are available throughout the year.

Aroma and flavour

Although pak choi is less delicate and does not taste as sweet as Chinese leaves, it has a distinctive flavour, which is a sort of cross between a mild cabbage and spinach.

Culinary uses

Pak choi and Chinese leaves are interchangeable in most dishes, even though their colour and flavour are different. Pak choi can be used in soups and stir-fries, and is delicious when quickly braised, but should not be subjected to prolonged stewing.

Preparation and cooking techniques

Pak choi is prepared in much the same way as Chinese leaves, except that the stems are as important (some would say more important) than the leaves. It is a good idea to separate leaves and stems for cooking, as the latter take slightly longer. Baby pak choi can be cooked whole or in halves or quarters. Only when very young and tender can pak choi be eaten raw.

Storage

Pak choi is completely different from Chinese leaves when it comes to storage. Try to use it as soon as you buy it, because the leaves will start to wilt, and the outer leaves will turn yellow, after 2–3 days, much sooner than lettuce and spinach.

Below: Bright green choi sum is easy to prepare.

CHOI SUM

MANDARIN: *YOU CAIXIN;*
CANTONESE: *CHOI SUM*

Choi sum is a Cantonese word, meaning "cabbage heart". A member of the brassica family, it is related to oilseed rape. It has bright green leaves and thin, pale green stalks that are slightly grooved. The bright yellow flowers at the centre are responsible for its common name of Chinese flowering cabbage.

Aroma and flavour

Choi sum has a pleasant aroma with a mild taste, and remains crisp and tender if correctly cooked.

Culinary uses

A very popular green vegetable, choi sum can be used for soups or stir-fries, either solo or with other ingredients.

Preparation and cooking techniques

Little preparation is required, just wash and shake off excess water before cutting the leaves to the required size. Most restaurant chefs leave the stalks whole, simply blanching them in stock for a minute or two before draining them and serving with oyster sauce.

Preparing choi sum
Choi sum is easy to prepare. You
can chop leaves and stalks into
large pieces before cooking, but
they are more often left whole.

Wash choi sum under cold
running water, then shake off the
excess water and separate the
stalks before use.

Storage

Choi sum can be kept in the salad
compartment of a refrigerator for about
3–4 days if bought fresh, but should
ideally be used as quickly as possible.

*Right: Every
part of Chinese
broccoli is edible.*

MUSTARD GREENS

Mandarin: *GAICAI*; Cantonese: *GAI CHOI*

Although this vegetable is related to
choi sum it looks and tastes completely
different. In shape, it resembles a
romaine lettuce. Unlike many Asian
vegetables, which were relatively
unknown outside their country of origin
until recently, mustard greens have long
been cultivated in Europe. However, the
dark green, slightly puckered leaves
were always thrown away; only the
seeds were prized. It took the Chinese
to introduce us to their delicious flavour.
Mustard greens are most abundant
during the winter and spring, especially
from Asian groceries, but also from
specialist producers and farm shops.

Aroma and flavour

Although mustard greens look a bit like
lettuces, there the resemblance ends.
The leaves have a robust, often fiery
flavour. They can taste quite bitter.

Culinary uses

Very young leaves can be eaten raw in
salads; mature leaves are best stir-fried
or simmered in soups. In China, most of
the crop is salted and preserved.

Preparation and cooking techniques

Before being stir-fried, mustard greens
benefit from being blanched in
lightly salted boiling water or
stock; this preserves the
green colour of the
leaves and also gets
rid of some of the
bitter taste.

Storage

Provided that they are fresh when you
buy them, mustard greens will keep
for a few days if stored in the salad
compartment of a refrigerator.

CHINESE BROCCOLI

Chinese: *GAILAN*

Chinese broccoli has more in common
with purple sprouting broccoli than
the plump, tight heads of Calabrese
broccoli familiar to Western shoppers.
The Chinese version has long, slender
stems, loose leaves and can be
recognized by the tiny white or yellow
flowers in the centre.

Aroma and flavour

As its Chinese name *gailan* (mustard
orchid) implies, Chinese broccoli
belongs to the same family as mustard
greens, but is more robust, both in
terms of texture and of taste. There
is a definite cabbage flavour.

Culinary uses

Every part of this beautiful vegetable
is edible – the flower, leaves and stalk
– and each has its own individual
flavour and texture. Chinese broccoli is
often served on its own as a side dish,
but it can also be combined with other
ingredients that have contrasting
colours, flavours and textures.

Preparation and cooking techniques

Discard the tough outer leaves,
then peel off any tough skin from
the stalks. Leave each stalk whole
if it is to be served on its own, or cut
into two to three short sections if it
is to be cooked with other ingredients.
Before stir-frying it is usual to blanch
the vegetable briefly in salted boiling
water or in stock, which will enhance
the flavour.

Storage

Chinese broccoli will keep for only
2–3 days even if it is very fresh when
bought; after that the leaves will start
to wilt and go yellow, and the stalks
are liable to become tough.

AUBERGINE/EGGPLANT

MANDARIN: *QIEZI*; CANTONESE: *NGAI GWA*

There are numerous varieties of this wonderfully versatile vegetable, which is technically a fruit. Although it belongs to the same family as bell peppers and tomatoes, which originated in America, the aubergine is actually native to tropical Asia, where it has been cultivated for more than 2,000 years.

The most common type in Asia – the Asian or Japanese aubergine – is tubular rather than ovoid in shape and is usually straight or slightly curved. As a rule, Asian aubergines tend to be much smaller and more slender than Western varieties, and some are tiny.

Below: Purple and green aubergines from Thailand

Right: Thai baby aubergines

In Thailand, there are aubergines that are not much bigger than peas. Aubergines come in a wide range of colours, from black through purple, orange and green to the white egg-shaped vegetables that inspired the vegetable's American name of eggplant.

Aroma and flavour

Whatever its shape, size or colour, the aubergine has a unique flavour that is almost impossible to describe. Some object to its smoky, subtly bitter taste, others prize it for the same reason.

Culinary uses

Aubergine absorbs the flavours of other ingredients like a sponge, and therefore benefits from being cooked with strongly flavoured foods and seasonings. It can be stir-fried, deep-fried, stuffed and baked, braised, steamed, or served cold, but seldom eaten raw except in Thailand, where strips of very young aubergine are served like crudités, with spicy dips.

Preparation and cooking techniques

Wash and remove the stalk, then cut into slices, strips or chunks. It is seldom necessary to peel an aubergine, and the smooth skin not only adds a beautiful colour, but also provides the dish with an interesting texture and flavour.

Some recipes advise layering aubergine slices with salt before cooking. This is not essential if the vegetables are young and tender, but in older specimens this is done to reduce bitterness and to prevent the slices from absorbing excessive amounts of oil during cooking. If you do salt an aubergine, be sure to rinse and dry it thoroughly afterwards.

Another method that stops the aubergine from drawing up too much oil, but which has the advantage of retaining the succulent texture, is to dry-fry the strips or slices over medium heat for 4–5 minutes before cooking them in hot oil.

Storage

Aubergines from various parts of the world are available all year round. Select small- to medium-size firm aubergines with a uniformly smooth skin that is free from blemishes. Large specimens with a shrivelled skin are overmature and are likely to be bitter and rather tough.

When bought in prime condition, aubergines will keep for 3–4 days in the salad compartment of the refrigerator.

CHAYOTE

CANTONESE: *FAT SAU GWA*

There are several names for this pear-shaped marrow, vegetable pear being one, and custard marrow being another. In the Caribbean they know it as christophine, but in other parts of the world it is *choko, shu-shu* or *chinchayote*. The Chinese call it "Buddha's fist", because it resembles hands clasped in prayer, with the fingers folded inside.

Aroma and flavour

Chayote has a smooth, pale green skin with a subtle aroma. The taste is delicate, and the texture is fairly firm, not unlike that of courgette (zucchini).

Culinary uses

Because of the religious connotations of its shape, chayote is often used as an offering during Buddhist festivals. It can be eaten raw or cooked, and in Asia is usually stir-fried or simmered in soups.

Preparation and cooking techniques

Wash but do not peel the vegetable, cut it open and remove the stone (pit) from the centre, then cut into thin slices or strips. Since chayote has a mild taste, Asian cooks often cook it with strong seasonings such as garlic, ginger, onion and/or chillies.

Above: Chayote can be eaten raw, stir-fried or cooked in soups.

Storage

Chayote is a quite good keeper. If it is hard and smooth, it will stay fresh for up to a week if stored in the salad compartment of the refrigerator.

MOOLI/DAIKON

MANDARIN: *LUOBO;* CANTONESE: *LOH BAK;* VIETNAMESE: *LOBAC;* MALAY: *LAPHUG*

This large, thin cylindrical vegetable looks rather like a carrot, but with a smooth, white skin. A member of the radish family, it is sometimes known as the oriental radish.

Left: Raw mooli has a delicious, crisp and crunchy texture.

Believed to be a native of China, the mooli is now widely cultivated in many parts of the world.

Aroma and flavour

Mooli has an unmistakable, pungent smell of radish. The texture is crisp and crunchy and it tastes quite mild, with a juicy, sweet flavour similar to turnip.

Culinary uses

Mooli can be eaten raw or cooked. Both the Chinese and the Japanese also pickle it. Cantonese cooks use it to make a stiff pudding with rice flour, which is often served as part of the dim sum selection in a restaurant. At home, mooli is usually braised with meat such as pork or beef, but it is also delicious in a stir-fry. Add it for the last few minutes of cooking so that the slices stay crisp and juicy.

Preparation and cooking techniques

Like carrots, mooli should be scraped or peeled, then cut into slices or chunks before cooking. The beauty of this vegetable is that it withstands long cooking without disintegrating, and absorbs the flavours of other ingredients, but also tastes good raw.

Storage

Buy mooli with firm, unblemished skin. Stored in a cool, dark place or in the salad compartment of the refrigerator, it should keep for 3–4 days.

BITTER MELON

MANDARIN: *KUGUA;* CANTONESE: *FOO GWA*

Also called "bitter gourd", this warty-skinned vegetable originated in Southeast Asia, and is popular in Indonesia, the Philippines and Thailand, where it is used as the basis for a delicious curry. The plant resembles a wild grape vine, and is grown in the West mainly as an ornament, for its attractive foliage and strange-looking fruit.

Aroma and flavour

As the name implies, the flesh of this vegetable tastes quite bitter, especially when it is green and immature, but it has a rather sweet and fragrant smell. The flavour mellows somewhat as the vegetable ripens and turns first pale green and then yellow-orange (when it is past its prime).

Culinary uses

Bitterness may be an acquired taste, but it has a cooling effect in a hot climate, and is highly regarded in Asia. The flesh readily absorbs other flavours and its bitter tang can provide a wonderful accent in a dish.

Preparation and cooking

Since the odd-looking skin is a special feature of this vegetable, it is never peeled. Just wash it, slice it in half lengthways, remove and discard the seeds, then cut into slices or chunks. Blanch these in lightly salted boiling water for about 2 minutes to remove excess bitterness, then drain before stir-frying or adding to soups.

Right: In China and Thailand winter melon is made into a soup and served in the shell.

Storage

Firm, green bitter melon will keep for 3–4 days (and should be allowed to ripen a little before use), but a soft yellowish one should be used within a day or two.

WINTER MELON

CHINESE: *DONG GUA*

This is one of the largest vegetables grown in Asia, or anywhere else. They can grow to 25cm/10in in diameter, and weigh more than 25kg/55lb. Thankfully for the cook, there are small ones, and the larger melons are normally sliced and sold in sections.

Above: Despite its name, bitter melon has a sweet smell.

Aroma and flavour

Winter melon has a subtle, delicate smell, and tastes rather like courgette (zucchini).

Culinary uses

Despite its name, winter melon is really a warm season vegetable, and since more than 90 per cent of it is water, it is popular in hot weather as it is juicy yet not too filling. It is always cooked before being eaten.

Preparation and cooking

Winter melon is prepared in much the same way as pumpkin. The rind must be cut off and the seeds and coarse fibres at the centre scooped out before the flesh is cut into thin strips or wedges. It tastes good in stir-fries or soups. Winter melon readily absorbs other flavours, and is often cooked with strongly flavoured ingredients such as dried shrimps, ham and dried mushrooms.

Storage

A whole winter melon will keep for days if not weeks, but if it has been sliced open, it should be eaten as soon as possible as the exposed surface will deteriorate rapidly.

ONIONS

MANDARIN: *YANG CONG*; CANTONESE: *YUN TS'UNG*

The common onion so widely used in the West is known as "foreign onion" in Asia, where shallots and spring onions (scallions) are generally preferred. They come in a wide range of sizes and colours from huge golden-skinned globes to smaller, milder red and white onions.

Aroma and flavour

There is no mistaking the strong aroma and flavour of the onion. It is used as a flavouring ingredient throughout Asia, but is seldom served on its own as a side vegetable.

Culinary uses

The onion is a very versatile vegetable. It can be eaten fried, boiled, steamed or raw, and it is an essential component of a great number of sauces and dishes, such as curries and stews. Fried onions are a popular garnish, especially in South-east Asia.

Above: Small and large onions

Preparation and cooking techniques

Peel the onions and remove the papery skin, then slice and chop as required. A good tip for avoiding irritation to the eyes when cutting an onion is to leave the root in place until the last minute, and, when the root is exposed, to press it down on the surface of the chopping board rather than expose it to the air.

Storage

If you buy firm onions with smooth, unmarked skins, and store them in a cool, dry place, they will keep for several weeks. If any show signs of sprouting, use them immediately.

SHALLOTS

MANDARIN: *FEN CONG*; CANTONESE: *TS'UNG TAU*; THAI: *HOM DAENG*

Although they belong to the same family as garlic, leeks, chives and onions – and look suspiciously like baby onions – shallots are very much their own vegetable. Sometimes called bunching onions, they have bulbs that multiply to produce clusters joined at the root end.

Aroma and flavour

Shallots tend to be sweeter and much milder than large onions. Some Thai varieties are sweet enough to be used in desserts.

Above: Small red onions

Culinary uses

Indispensable in South-east Asian kitchens, shallots are far more popular than both regular onions and spring onions for everyday use. Minced with garlic, ginger and other aromatics, shallots form the standard marinade and are also an essential ingredient in curry pastes and satay sauce. Dried shallots *(hanh huong)* are a popular alternative in Vietnam.

Preparation and cooking techniques

Top and tail the shallots, peel off the skin, then prize the bulbs apart. Leave these whole for braising, or chop as required. Thinly sliced shallot rings are sometimes dry-fried until crisp, then used as a garnish.

Storage

Shallots will keep for several months in a cool, dry place.

SPRING ONIONS/SCALLIONS

MANDARIN: *QING CONG*; CANTONESE: *TS'UNG*; JAPANESE: *NEGI*

Spring onions, also known as green onions or scallions in the West, have been cultivated in China and Japan since time immemorial. The leaves are tubular, and are always sold with the small white onion bulb attached. Japanese spring onions are larger than the European variety and have blue-green stems.

Aroma and flavour

Spring onions have a more subtle smell than onions and the taste can vary from fairly mild to really pungent. Smaller bulbs generally have a milder flavour.

Left: Spring onions

How to make spring onion curls

1 Trim off most of the green leaves from the spring onion bulbs to leave a 7.5cm/3in length.

2 Finely shred the spring onions to within about 1cm/½in of the root end.

3 Place the shredded spring onions in a bowl of iced water and chill for 15–20 minutes or until the shredded ends have curled.

Culinary uses

In Asia, spring onions are served as a vegetable as well as being used as a flavouring agent. The vegetable forms a yin-yang pair when used in combination with ginger. Spring onions are yin, and ginger is yang.

Preparation and cooking techniques

Trim off the roots from the bulbs and discard any wilted outer leaves, then separate the green and white parts, and cut these into short lengths or shreds. Recipes sometimes stipulate that only the white parts are used. If spring onion green is used in a recipe, it is usually added at the last moment (the white part takes longer to cook) or is simply used raw, as a garnish.

Storage

It is best not to keep spring onions in a plastic bag, but instead to store them loose in the salad drawer of the refrigerator to allow them to "breathe". They should stay fresh for up to 4–5 days if bought in prime condition.

CHINESE CHIVES

MANDARIN: *JIUCAI*; CANTONESE: *GAU CHOI*

Although they belong to the same family, Chinese chives are quite different from the Western variety, both in their appearance and taste. Two species are available: one has long, flat green leaves like a small, thin leek, the other has long, tubular stalks with a single bud at the tip.

Aroma and flavour

Chinese chives have a much stronger aroma

Right: Chinese chives

than the ones grown in the West. They don't really taste of onions, but have a flavour that resembles a cross between garlic and leek.

Culinary uses

Chinese chives are seldom used as a garnish, but are either served as a vegetable in their own right, or used as an ingredient in cooked dishes, especially with seafood or meat. A very popular Chinese vegetarian dish features chopped chives cooked with scrambled eggs and tofu. This is not only colourful, but tastes delicious.

Preparation and cooking techniques

Chinese chives are always sold as leaves only, without the bulb. Uniformly dark green leaves are good, and any that are turning yellow should be discarded. Wash well, drain, then chop or slice into short sections. Cantonese cooks often blanch chives in boiling water or stock for a minute or two before stir-frying.

Storage

Fresh chives in an airtight box in the refrigerator should keep for 4–5 days.

POTATOES AND SWEET POTATOES

MANDARIN: *PENSHU;* CANTONESE: *FAN SHUE*

Although potatoes and sweet potatoes are unrelated, this was not appreciated when they first reached Asia, and they were both given the same Chinese name. In northern China white potatoes are a staple food, although not as important as noodles; in southern China they are far less significant. Sweet potatoes are popular in the Philippines.

Aroma and flavour

Several varieties of both regular potatoes and sweet potatoes are grown in the East, so tubers vary in size, shape and colour, as well as in taste and texture. The sweet potatoes have a red skin and flesh that varies from pale white to yellow-orange in colour.

Culinary uses

Where potatoes are used, they generally form part of a braised dish, or are served as a side dish or snack. Potato flour is a popular thickener.

Preparation and cooking techniques

Both regular potatoes and sweet potatoes are prepared in the same way: after peeling, they are sliced or diced, then stir-fried or braised with seasonings or spices. Thai cooks make a very sweet dessert based on deep-fried sweet potatoes.

Above: Potatoes and sweet potatoes

Storage

Potatoes should always be stored in a cool, dark, dry place. Because of their high sugar content, sweet potatoes do not keep well.

TAROES

MANDARIN: *YUTOU;* CANTONESE: *WOO TAU*

These tubers grow in tropical areas and are widely used throughout South-east Asia. There are two basic varieties: the big, barrel-shaped one with the hairy brown skin is the most common, but there is also a smaller variety which is known in the West as eddo or dasheen. The flesh is white, with purple flecks.

Aroma and flavour

Cooked taro has a subtle flavour that has been described as resembling floury water chestnuts.

Culinary uses

Taroes can be substituted for potatoes in most dishes. They take up a great deal of liquid, so are good in stews. Asian cooks often include taro when cooking belly pork or duck as it absorbs the excess fat.

Above: A barrel-shaped taro

Preparation and cooking techniques

It is essential to cook taroes as there are toxins just below the skin. These are eliminated when the vegetable is boiled. Peel the vegetables thickly, wearing gloves, or cook them in their jackets.

Storage

Store in a cool, dark, dry place. Taroes have a thick skin, so they keep well.

YAMS

MANDARIN: *SHANYAO;* CANTONESE: *SA GOT*

Yams are believed to have originated in China, but are now grown in all tropical regions. The Chinese yam has fine whiskers and the flesh is creamy white.

Aroma and flavour

Yams do not have a pronounced flavour, but are mildly sweet and quite juicy.

Culinary uses

Like taroes, yams can be used instead of potatoes. Asian cooks often use them as a substitute for bamboo shoots.

Preparation and cooking techniques

Peel yams thickly, removing both the outer skin and the layer underneath. Like taroes, they contain a toxin that is eliminated when boiled. Slice or dice the flesh and put into salted water.

Storage

As for taroes.

LOTUS ROOT

MANDARIN: *LIAN OU*; CANTONESE: *LEEN NGAU*

Lotus root, also known as *renkon*, is used throughout Asia and is particularly popular in China and Japan. Raw lotus root looks like a string of fat sausages covered in black mud. Clean, peel and slice it, however, and a beautiful pattern emerges in each cross-section, the result of narrow channels that run through the root. Fresh lotus roots can sometimes be purchased from Asian stores. Canned lotus root is readily available, and dried slices are popular for serving in soups.

Aroma and flavour

The root has very little aroma, but the flavour is mild and subtly sweet. It has a wonderful crunchy texture.

Culinary uses

Apart from the root being used as a vegetable, the seeds of the lotus are eaten as a delicate fruit when fresh, or used as a dessert in dried form. They can also be puréed and blended with sugar to make a filling for cakes and buns. Dried lotus leaves are used for wrapping food in a number of famous Asian dishes.

Preparation and cooking techniques

Fresh lotus roots must be scrubbed. Chop them into sections, discarding the tough "necks" between, then peel off the outer skin. The sliced flesh is usually

Above: Lotus root and seeds

sliced or cut into large chunks, but whole roots can also be stuffed. Japanese cooks often soak the slices in water acidulated with rice vinegar for 5 minutes before boiling them. They cook quickly and make a pretty garnish. Dried lotus roots are sold sliced, and should be soaked in water for 1–2 hours before using in soups or stews. Canned lotus roots are ready for use.

Storage

Fresh lotus root should keep for about 4 days if bought in good condition. Select firm and unblemished roots. If the surface is punctured, dirt will have penetrated inside, which makes the roots difficult to clean. Dried roots will keep almost indefinitely if stored in a dry, cool place.

DRIED LILY BUDS

MANDARIN: *HUANG HUA; JINZHEN*
CANTONESE: *GUM JUM*

Also known in Chinese as "yellow flower" or "golden needles", these dried buds of the tiger lily are popular throughout China and South-east Asia.

Aroma and flavour

Tiger lily has a unique fragrance, which intensifies when the buds are dried. They have a mild sweet taste and a pleasant crunchy texture.

Culinary uses

In Chinese cooking, dried lily buds are often combined with dried black fungus to create an interesting contrast in colour, flavour and texture. The buds are also a popular ingredient in Buddhist vegetarian cooking.

Preparation and cooking techniques

Dried lily buds must be soaked in warm water for 30 minutes or so, then drained and rinsed in cold water until clean. Once the hard ends have been cut off, the buds can be used whole, or cut in half.

Storage

Dried lily buds keep almost indefinitely if stored in an airtight jar, away from strong light, heat or moisture.

Below: Lily buds are never used fresh, but always dried.

the canned ones, but need more preparation. They must be soaked in water for 2–3 hours before use.

Storage

Fresh shoots will keep for up to a week in winter, but only 2–3 days in summer. Unused shoots from a can will keep in the refrigerator for several days if stored in a jar of fresh water that is changed daily. Dried shoots will keep almost indefinitely in a cool, dry place.

BEANSPROUTS

MANDARIN: *DOUYA;*
CANTONESE: *DAU NGA CHOI*

Several types of bean can be sprouted, but the ones most often used in Asian cooking are the small "green" sprouts from mung beans and the larger "yellow" or soya bean sprouts. The fresh sprouts are widely available in supermarkets, health food shops and markets, or you can sprout the beans at home. Avoid canned beansprouts, which are limp and tasteless.

BAMBOO SHOOTS

MANDARIN: *ZHUSUN;* CANTONESE: *CHUK SUN;*
JAPANESE: *TAKENOKO*

Bamboo is one of the most important plants of eastern Asia, and several species are grown, of varying sizes. The shoots used as a vegetable are dug just before they come above ground. Fresh bamboo shoots are difficult to come by outside Asia, but canned shoots are readily available. Vietnamese cooks are fond of pickled bamboo shoots.

Aroma and flavour

The aroma of bamboo shoots is quite delicate. Lovers of this vegetable – and they are legion – claim that the mild sweet flavour changes subtly with the seasons. Therefore winter bamboo shoots are more highly prized.

Culinary uses

In China, where bamboo shoots have been eaten for well over a thousand years, they are regarded as the queen of all vegetables. The shoots not only taste delicious of themselves, but also complement the flavours of other ingredients with which they are cooked.

Above: Chunks of raw bamboo shoot and canned slices

Preparation and cooking techniques

If you are lucky enough to locate fresh bamboo shoots, it is vital to parboil them before cooking, as they contain an acid that is highly toxic. Remove the base and the hard outer leaves, then cut the core into large chunks. Boil these in salted water for 20–30 minutes, then drain, rinse in clean water and drain again. Cut into slices, shreds or cubes for further cooking. Canned bamboo shoots are ready cooked, so they just need to be rinsed and drained before using them. Dried bamboo shoots have been dried in the sun, so they are tastier than

Right: Mung bean sprouts (in bowl) and soya bean sprouts

Aroma and flavour

Soya bean sprouts have a stronger flavour than mung bean sprouts, but both are relatively delicate, with a pleasant crunchy texture.

Culinary uses

Stir-frying, with or without meat, is the most popular way of cooking beansprouts. Mung bean sprouts can be eaten raw in salads, while soya bean sprouts are often used in soups.

Preparation and cooking techniques

Wash the beansprouts in cold water to remove the husks and tiny roots. Some restaurants actually top and tail each individual shoot, which turns this humble vegetable into a luxury dish. Since the sprouts are largely composed of water, overcooking will render them limp and fibrous, and the characteristic crisp texture will be lost.

Storage

In order to preserve their lily-white translucence, keep beansprouts in water in a covered box in the refrigerator. They will stay fresh for 2–3 days.

WATER CHESTNUTS

MANDARIN: *BIQI*; CANTONESE: *MA TAI*

Water chestnuts are popular throughout Asia, cropping up in Chinese, Japanese, Korean and South-east Asian recipes. The name is slightly misleading as they do grow in water (and are actually cultivated in paddy fields) but they certainly aren't nuts. Instead, they are corms, which are about the size of walnuts. There are several varieties, but the Chinese type, which are dark brown and look a bit like small daffodil bulbs, are the most widely available outside Asia. They have a soft skin which, because they grow in water, tends to be covered in dried dirt. Fresh water chestnuts are superior to canned.

Aroma and flavour

The best thing about water chestnuts is their texture. The snow-white flesh is crunchy and juicy, and stays that way,

no matter how long they are cooked for. This, coupled with their pleasantly sweet taste, makes them irresistible.

Culinary uses

Water chestnuts can be eaten raw in both savoury and fruit salads. In many Asian countries they are eaten as a snack food, in much the same way as peanuts are eaten in the West. Cooked water chestnuts taste wonderful in stir-fries or braised dishes. The flesh is also made into a flour, which is used both as a thickening agent and in cakes.

Preparation and cooking techniques

Fresh water chestnuts are not very appealing, especially as they are usually covered in dried mud, but once they are washed and peeled, they do not look very different from the canned variety. Water chestnuts can be left whole, sliced or diced, and are sometimes minced (ground) with fish or meat.

Storage

Fresh, unpeeled water chestnuts will keep well if stored in a paper bag in the vegetable crisper in the fridge. Once peeled, however, fresh water chestnuts must be kept in water in a covered container in the refrigerator and should be used within a week.

Below: Canned water chestnuts (in bowl) and fresh water chestnut corms, which look a little like small daffodil bulbs.

MANGETOUTS/SNOW PEAS

MANDARIN: *XUEDOU;* CANTONESE: *HOH LAN DAU*

Also known as snow peas, mangetouts must be one of the best known and best loved of all Asian vegetables, yet its Cantonese name, meaning Dutch bean, suggests that at some point in its long history it was perceived as being of Western origin. The French name – *mangetout* – means "eat all" and is an apt description, for the vegetable is valued for its pods, not the peas, which never mature. Sugar snap peas are similar, but have slightly plumper pods.

Aroma and flavour

Freshly picked mangetouts have a fresh aroma. The flavour is slightly sweet. The best way to appreciate these delicate, tender pods is to stir-fry them, when they will prove perfect partners for prawns (shrimp), scallops and other shellfish.

Preparation and cooking techniques

Mangetouts need very little by way of preparation. Simply wash, then top and tail the pods. It should not be necessary to string them if the pods are young and tender. Leave whole if small; snap in half if large. Stir-fry on their own, or with other vegetables such as carrots, spring onions (scallions) and baby corn cobs, over high heat for a short time, and do not use too much seasoning.

Storage

Young, crisp and unblemished mangetouts with thin skins will keep fresh for up to 4–5 days in the salad compartment of the refrigerator.

SNAKE BEANS

MANDARIN: *DOUJIAO* CANTONESE: *DAU GOK*

Also called yard-long beans, asparagus beans or Thai beans, these resemble green beans but are much longer. There are two varieties:

Above: Snake beans are also known as yard-long beans.

a pale green type, and a darker green one that is considered to be better. Thinner beans are best.

Aroma and flavour

These exceptionally long beans smell and taste rather like their Western cousins, but the flavour is not identical. When young they are slightly sweeter and more tender, but the mature beans can be tough, and may need slightly longer cooking than green beans.

Culinary uses

Snake beans are usually stir-fried, either on their own or with other ingredients, or served cold as a salad after blanching. They are also delicious blanched and tossed in sesame oil.

Preparation and cooking techniques

Having washed the beans, cut them into 5cm/2in lengths. They go particularly well with shredded pork, chicken or prawns (shrimp), and should only be lightly seasoned. In Sichuan, they are used for a dish called *kan shao* (dry-frying), with strongly flavoured seasonings such as garlic, ginger or chillies.

Storage

Try to use snake beans within about 3 days of purchase before they turn yellow and become stringy.

Right: Mangetouts (top) and sugar snap peas

LUFFA

MANDARIN: *SIGUA;*
CANTONESE: *SZE GWA*

Also known as angled luffa, silk gourd, silk squash or Chinese okra, this vegetable looks like a long, skinny courgette (zucchini) or a very large okra pod. The most common variety is ridged down its length and is dark green. Although not so common, smooth luffa is larger and the shape is more cylindrical, with a thicker base. It is much heavier than ridged luffa, and is lighter in colour.

Aroma and flavour

Luffa has a mild, delicate taste, very similar to that of cucumber and the two are interchangeable in most cooked dishes.

Culinary uses

Used mostly in stir-fries and soups, luffa goes well with foods that will not overwhelm its delicate flavour, such as chicken, fish and shellfish. It is also a popular ingredient in all kinds of vegetable dishes.

Preparation and cooking techniques

If the luffa is young, all you need to do is wash and slice it. Luffas seldom need peeling, but sometimes the ridges toughen as the vegetable ripens, in which case remove the ridges but leave

Above: A whole luffa and slices

the skin between, so that the luffa is striped green and white. If the skin is very tough, it is best to peel it completely. Like cucumber, luffa should not be overcooked, but unlike cucumber, it is never eaten raw.

Storage

Keep fresh luffa in the vegetable compartment of the refrigerator, but do not store it for too long as within two or three days of purchase it will start to go limp.

BABY CORN COBS

MANDARIN: *YUMI SUN;*
CANTONESE: *YOOK MY SON*

Baby corn cobs are available both fresh and canned. The canned ones can be quite large, and are not as tender and delicate as the smaller, fresh cobs.

Aroma and flavour

Baby corn has a lovely sweet fragrance and flavour, as well as an irresistible crunchy texture.

Culinary uses

The baby cobs can be used in salads, stir-fries and soups. In stir-fries, they add colour as well as flavour, and are good combined with carrots, bell peppers, broccoli and mangetouts (snow peas).

Preparation and cooking techniques

Wash the cobs. Large ones can be halved lengthways or sliced in thick diagonal chunks, but small ones are best left whole. Asian cooks blanch them in lightly salted water for 1 minute before stir-frying. Drain and rinse canned cobs before use. Do not overcook them.

Storage

Fresh baby corn cobs will keep for up to a week in the salad compartment of the fridge, but they are best eaten soon after purchase.

Above: Crunchy-textured baby corn cobs make a colourful addition to stir-fries.

FRESH AND DRIED MUSHROOMS

SHIITAKE

MANDARIN: *XIANG GU*; CANTONESE: *HUNG GWO*; JAPANESE: *SHIITAKE*

Fresh shiitake mushrooms used to be a rarity in the West, but are now cultivated and are freely available in supermarkets. They resemble large, brown button (white) mushrooms in appearance, but are actually a type of fungus that grows on hardwood logs in their native Japan. Shiitake mushrooms are frequently dried (see Dried Black Mushrooms, overleaf) and are also canned.

Aroma and flavour

These meaty mushrooms taste slightly acidic, and have a decidedly slippery texture. They contain twice as much protein as button mushrooms. When shiitake are dried the flavour intensifies.

Culinary uses

Although small mushrooms can be eaten raw, cooking brings out their flavour. They are used in soups, stir-fries and braised dishes. They are a popular ingredient in vegetarian dishes, and go well with noodles and rice. They are good combined with less strongly flavoured food.

Below: Fresh and dried shiitake mushrooms

Preparation and cooking techniques

The stems of fresh shiitake mushrooms are usually removed before cooking. Whole or sliced caps can be sautéed, used in stir-fries, cooked in braised dishes or added to soups. Because of their robust texture, shiitake need a slightly longer cooking time than button mushrooms, but they should not be cooked for too long or they may begin to toughen. To serve shiitake mushrooms in a salad, boil

Left: Oyster mushrooms

them briefly in water or stock, then cool them slightly and toss in a French dressing before serving.

Storage

Store fresh shiitake mushrooms in a paper bag in the fridge. Eat within three days of purchase.

OYSTER MUSHROOMS

MANDARIN: *BAOYU GU*; CANTONESE: *HOWYOO GWO*; JAPANESE: *SHIMEJI*

In the wild, oyster mushrooms grow in clumps on rotting wood. The caps, gills and stems are all the same colour, which can be pearl grey, pink or yellow. Once thought of exclusively as wild mushrooms, they are now grown commercially and are widely available in Western supermarkets.

Aroma and flavour

The flavour is fairly mild, with a slight suggestion of seafood.

Culinary uses

Oyster mushrooms are popular in soups and stir-fries, and they are also used in noodle and rice dishes.

Preparation and cooking techniques

Oyster mushrooms seldom need trimming. Large ones should be torn, rather than cut into pieces. The soft texture becomes rubbery if they are overcooked, so always add them to cooked dishes at the last moment.

Storage

Buy oyster mushrooms that smell and look fresh, avoiding any with damp, slimy patches and those that have discoloured. Store in a paper bag in salad compartment of the refrigerator, and use as soon as possible after purchase. They do not keep for more than 2–3 days.

ENOKI MUSHROOMS

MANDARIN: *JINZHEN GU;* CANTONESE: *GUM JUM GWO;* JAPANESE: *ENO ITAKE*

Also called *enokitaki,* these are slender and exceedingly delicate mushrooms with long thin stems and tiny white caps. The Chinese name – "golden needle mushrooms" – is the same as that given to the dried tiger lily buds which they resemble. Fresh enoki mushrooms are popular in both China and Japan. Avoid canned ones.

Aroma and flavour

Enoki mushrooms have a delicate sweet and almost fruity flavour, and a deliciously crisp texture.

Culinary uses

The delicate flavour of enoki mushrooms is best appreciated if they are added raw to salads or lightly cooked and used as a garnish for soups or hot dishes.

Preparation and cooking techniques

The mushrooms are harvested in clumps, attached to a spongy root base which is cut off before use.

Above: Enoki mushrooms have pretty, tiny caps on elegant long stalks.

The mushrooms are then ready for use. They rapidly toughen if overcooked, so are usually added to soups or braised dishes shortly before serving. They are good in stir-fried dishes, too, but should not be cooked for longer than 1 minute.

Storage

If bought fresh, enoki mushrooms will keep for 4–5 days in the salad compartment of a refrigerator. Avoid any that have damp, slimy patches and those that have discoloured.

STRAW MUSHROOMS

MANDARIN: *CAOGU;* CANTONESE: *TSO GWO*

These small, grey-brown mushrooms are grown on beds of rice straw, hence the name. A native of China, they were introduced to South-east Asia by Chinese immigrants.

Aroma and flavour

Fresh straw mushrooms are not readily available in the West, but dried ones can sometimes be found in Asian or Chinese stores. Straw mushrooms have an even stronger aroma than Chinese dried black mushrooms. Canned straw mushrooms are widely available in Asian stores; they have a delicate, silky surface with a subtle, sweet taste and an unusual slippery texture.

Culinary uses

Because they have an almost neutral flavour, straw mushrooms can be combined with all sorts of ingredients in stir-fries, braised dishes and soups. They are an essential ingredient in many Chinese dishes, and they are also used for making mushroom soy sauce.

Preparation and cooking techniques

Canned straw mushrooms must be drained and thoroughly rinsed before use. They are usually cut in half lengthways. This not only reveals the rather attractive "umbrella" pattern, but

Below: Sliced straw mushrooms, showing their attractive "umbrella" pattern.

it also makes them much easier to pick up with chopsticks. Like all mushrooms, straw mushrooms must not be overcooked, especially the canned ones, as they have been cooked already.

Storage

Fresh straw mushrooms are difficult to store, which explains why they are not often seen outside Asia. Dried ones can be stored almost indefinitely, though they may lose some of their flavour.

DRIED BLACK MUSHROOMS/ FRAGRANT MUSHROOMS

Dried black mushrooms are widely used throughout Asia, and are exported around the world. Although they are frequently labelled as "Chinese", to distinguish them from other dried mushrooms, and have come to be widely known as such, the majority of dried black mushrooms sold in Asian stores actually come from Japan, which produces and exports far more dried black mushrooms than does China.

Aroma and flavour

There are generally three different grades of dried black mushrooms, with caps that range in colour from dark grey, to brown-black or tan. The cheapest of these have quite thin caps, may be sold with or without stalks, and may well be labelled "fragrant mushrooms", which is the generic term for shiitake mushrooms. Next come the "winter mushrooms" which have thicker caps and taste more fleshy. The most expensive type are called "flower mushrooms". These are the best of the winter mushrooms. The caps are so thick that they crack, revealing the flower pattern that earned them their name. All three have a dusky aroma with a fragrant flavour, which is much intensified by the drying process.

Above: Dried black mushrooms are also known as fragrant mushrooms and are the dried form of shiitake mushrooms.

Culinary uses

These mushrooms are wonderfully versatile as they can be stir-fried, braised, steamed and used in soups. They form an important part of the vegetarians' diet, and are an ideal partner for bamboo shoots, as they offer a harmonious contrast in colour, aroma, flavour and texture. For non-vegetarians, they can be cooked with seafood, poultry and meat, and, of course, other vegetables.

Preparation and cooking techniques

Dried mushrooms must be soaked in water under cover until supple, before use. The best way is to soak in cold water for several hours or overnight, depending on the thickness of the caps. When time is short, they can be soaked in warm water for 30 minutes, but should not be soaked in hot water, as much of the fragrance will be lost. Do not discard the soaking water; it will enrich the flavour of the dish.

After soaking the mushrooms squeeze them dry and discard the stalks, if any. Small mushrooms can be left whole, but larger ones should be halved, quartered or coarsely chopped. The thinner dried mushrooms are usually either thinly sliced or shredded, but thicker ones, particularly the pretty "flower mushrooms" are generally left whole to show off their attractive shape.

Storage

Dried black mushrooms should keep for a very long time (over a year) if stored in a dry, dark and cool place.

Using dried mushrooms

Dried mushrooms have a rich, intense flavour and are a useful store-cupboard stand-by for adding to Asian dishes. Once they have been reconstituted they can be stir-fried, braised, steamed and used in soups. Dried mushrooms often require longer cooking than fresh ones.

To reconstitute dried mushrooms, soak them in boiling water for 20–30 minutes, depending on the variety and size of mushroom, until tender. Drain and rinse well to remove any grit and dirt.

CLOUD EARS/WOOD EARS

MANDARIN: *MU'ER;* CANTONESE: *WAN YEE;*
VIETNAMESE: *MOC NHI*

Also known as wood ears, tree
mushrooms or simply dried black
fungus, these are widely used in
China, Thailand and Vietnam. The
dried fungi are thin and brittle, and
look like pieces of charred paper.

Aroma and flavour

There is a slightly smoky smell when
cloud ears are first removed from the
packet, but this disappears once they
have been soaked. They are almost
tasteless, but have an intriguing
texture, which is slippery yet crisp.

Culinary Uses

Cloud ears are used in stir-frying,
braising and soups; the fungus is
traditionally paired with dried tiger lily
in several Chinese dishes, including
the popular hot-and-sour soup.

Preparation and cooking techniques

The fungus expands to six or eight
times its volume after soaking, so
use plenty of water in a

*Right: Cloud ears are
also known as wood
ears, tree mushrooms
or dried black fungus*

large bowl. As a guide, a piece of
dried fungus that would fit in a
tablespoon would require at least
250ml/8fl oz/1 cup water. Cover the
bowl and leave the fungus to soak for
about 30 minutes, then drain, rinse well
and drain again. Discard any hard roots
and sandy bits. Do not cut the fungus
into small pieces, just separate the
larger clumps into individual
"ears" in order to
preserve the pretty
wavy shape.

Storage

Dried fungus
will keep almost
indefinitely if stored
in a dry, cool place;
once soaked, keep
it in clean water in
a covered bowl in
the refrigerator.
It will keep for
2–3 days.

*Left: Silver ears,
or dried white
fungus*

SILVER EARS

MANDARIN: *YINER;* CANTONESE: *PAK
MOOK YEE*

Also known as dried white fungus, this
earned its Chinese name of "silver ear"
partly because of its rarity, and partly
because of the high price it fetches on
account of its medicinal value. It is
regarded as being an excellent tonic,
and is also used for the relief of
insomnia and lung and liver diseases.

Aroma and flavour

Silver ears do not belong to the same
genus as wood ears. Although the
texture is similar, white fungus has a
sweeter flavour.

Culinary uses

While cloud ears are regarded as
everyday ingredients, silver ears are
reserved for special occasions. Besides
being cooked with other vegetables in
vegetarian dishes, silver ears are often
cooked and then served on their own,
as one of the many dishes that
comprise a banquet.

Preparation, cooking techniques
and storage

Dried silver ears should be prepared,
cooked and stored in the same way as
dried cloud ears.

SEAWEED

KOMBU

CHINESE: *HAIDAI*; JAPANESE: *KOMBU*

Several types of seaweed are used in Asian cooking, especially in Japan and Korea. The most common variety is the giant seaweed known as kelp in English. It is only available in dried form in the West, usually labelled with the Japanese name of kombu or konbu.

Aroma and flavour

Kombu is full of vitamins and minerals, and is particularly rich in iodine. It has a strong "sea" flavour and a crunchy texture.

Culinary uses

This type of seaweed is mainly used in soups in China, but is served poached or stewed as a vegetable in Japan, as well as being used to flavour the fish stock known as dashi.

Left: Kombu has a strong sea flavour.

Preparation and cooking techniques

Kombu has a pale powdery covering that contributes to its flavour, so do not wash it off; just wipe the seaweed with a damp cloth, then cut it into pieces of the required size. Soak these in cold water for 45–50 minutes. Both the seaweed and soaking water are used.

Storage

Kombu keeps for a long time if stored in a dry, cool place away from strong light.

NORI

JAPANESE: *NORI*

This is the wafer-thin, dried seaweed that is mainly used as a wrapping for sushi. It is sold in sheets that are dark green to black in colour, and almost transparent in places. The sheet should be grilled (broiled) lightly on one side for making sushi, or on both sides until crisp if it is to be crumbled for a topping. Ready-toasted sheets known as yaki-nori are available from Asian stores. These are seasoned with ingredients such as soy sauce, salt and sesame oil. Ao-nori is dried seaweed that is crumbled so finely it looks like powder.

Dashi

This stock, based on kombu and dried bonito flakes, is the basis of most Japanese soups; it can also be used instead of water in any dish that requires a delicately flavoured stock.

MAKES 800ML/27FL OZ/3½ CUPS

10cm/4in square of kombu
900ml/1½ pints/3¾ cups water
40g/1½oz katsuobushi (dried
  bonito flakes)

2 Place the pan over medium heat. Just before the water boils, lift out the seaweed (shred and use for soup).

1 Wipe the kombu with a damp cloth; cut it into three to four strips and put in a pan. Pour over the water, making sure that the seaweed is submerged, and soak for an hour.

3 Stir in the bonito flakes, bring to the boil, remove from the heat and leave to stand until the flakes have sunk to the bottom. Strain through a strainer lined with muslin (cheesecloth).

WAKAME

JAPANESE: *WAKAME*

This young dark-coloured seaweed has a delicate flavour and soft but crisp texture. It is available shredded, fresh (vacuum-packed) or dried, and is used in soups and salads. Dried wakame should be soaked in tepid water for 10–15 minutes until it softens and the fronds turn green. At this stage it should be drained, blanched in boiling water for about 1 minute, then refreshed under cold water and drained again. Use as directed in recipes or cool and chop to use in a salad.

HIJIK

JAPANESE: *HIJIK*

This Japanese seaweed – sometimes called hijiki – is similar to wakame. It is available dried and finely shredded, and should be reconstituted as for wakame.

AGAR-AGAR

CHINESE: *DONGFEN; YANGCAI;* JAPANESE: *KANTEN*

This is the gelatinous substance obtained from the seaweed known as "rock-flower vegetable" in Chinese. Available from Asian stores as long dried strips or as a fine white powder sold in tubs, it is a very popular setting agent, especially for vegetarians seeking an alternative to gelatine.

Aroma and flavour

Agar-agar has no aroma and is entirely flavourless, but will absorb the seasonings with which it is prepared for serving.

Culinary uses

Asian cooks sometimes use soaked strips of agar-agar in a salad, just as they would any other form of seaweed, but it is more often used as a setting agent, usually to make sweet jellies.

Right: Agar-agar is sold in thick and thin strips and as a powder that is used as a setting agent.

Above: Wakame (in bowl), hijik (on top) and nori seaweeds

Preparation and cooking techniques

To use agar-agar in a salad, soften the strips in lukewarm water for about 20–25 minutes, then drain and dry them on some kitchen paper. Separate the strips and cut them into short lengths. Combine the agar-agar with the other salad ingredients, add a dressing and toss to mix.

To use agar-agar to set a jelly, dissolve it slowly in water over very low heat, which may take up to 10 minutes. Heat some milk and sugar, with a flavouring such as almond essence, in a separate pan, then mix with the agar-agar solution. Leave the mixture to cool, then chill in the refrigrator for 3–4 hours until set. Agar-agar varies in strength, so check the packaging to see how much you should use. As a guide, 5ml/1 tsp powder will set 300ml/½ pint/1¼ cups of liquid.

Storage

Agar-agar, both in strips and in the powdered form, will keep almost indefinitely if stored in a cool, dry place.

FRUIT

DURIAN

CHINESE: *LIU LIAN;* THAI: *THURIAN*

This tropical fruit originated in Malaysia or Borneo, and is very popular in South-east Asia. Round or oval, it has a dull green shell-like skin covered with pointed spines that turn yellow as the fruit ripens. A typical durian weighs about 2kg/4½ lb, but they can grow even larger, up to 4.5kg/10lb.

Aroma and flavour

Durian has a very unpleasant smell, often likened to the stench of raw sewage. The ripe flesh, however, is as delicious as the odour is awful: sweet and creamy, with a hint of strawberries.

Culinary uses

The fruit is eaten raw, and the seeds are often roasted and eaten like nuts.

Preparation

Each fruit consists of three, four or five segments. Using a sharp knife, slit the hard shell of the durian at the segment

Below: A durian and its large seeds

Right: Mangosteen can be eaten on its own or added to a fruit salad.

joints, then press the segments out. Take care not to let the juice drip on to your clothes, as it stains. The soft, creamy flesh can be eaten with a spoon, or puréed, either for serving as a dessert or as an accompaniment to a curry. Some Asian cooks soak the durian segments in coconut milk for 10–12 hours before eating them, as they claim this eliminates the unpleasant smell.

Storage

This is not recommended, as the smell will soon pervade your home, however carefully you store the fruit. When buying, look for perfect, undamaged specimens, and get them home as quickly as possible. Don't attempt to take them on public transport; most carriers ban them!

MANGOSTEEN

CHINESE: *SANZHU GUO;* THAI: *MANG KHUT*

The only thing mangosteens and mangoes share in common, aside from being tropical fruits, is the first five letters of their names. Mangosteens are small, apple-shaped fruits with leathery brown skin that turns purple as they ripen. The flesh looks similar to that of a lychee, but tastes completely different. They are native to South-east Asia and are cultivated in Thailand.

Aroma and flavour

The tough skin surrounds delicious white flesh, which is divided into segments, each with a large seed. The pearly white flesh is fresh and fragrant. Some say it tastes like grapefruit.

Culinary uses

Mangosteens are always eaten raw, but the related kokum, which has a pleasant sour taste, is used as a souring agent in Indian cooking.

Preparation

Cut the fruit in half and remove the segments, taking care not to include any of the dark pink pith. Serve the segments solo or in a fruit salad.

Storage

Mangosteens keep well. If not over-ripe when bought, they should remain in good condition for up to 8–10 days.

LYCHEES

MANDARIN: *LIZHI;* CANTONESE: *LA-EE-TZEE;* THAI: *LIN-CHI*

Indigenous to subtropical areas of southern China and Thailand, lychees grow in clusters on small trees. The ripe fruit is about the size of a small plum, with a beautiful, scaly red skin or "shell". Once this is removed, the pearly white fruit, which surrounds a large inedible seed, is revealed. Fresh lychees are seasonal. When they are not available, canned fruit can be used instead, but it lacks the subtlety of the fresh fruit. Choose the ones in natural juice rather than syrup.

Aroma and flavour

Peeled lychees have a delicious perfume. The flesh has a wonderful, clean taste, somewhat like a grape, but much more scented.

Culinary uses

Lychees and their close relatives, longans, "dragon's eyes", are said to boost fertility. In some parts of China it is traditional, when a young person reaches puberty, to celebrate the event with a meal composed of a young cockerel cooked with dried lychees or longans. On most occasions, however, lychees are eaten fresh, and are good for cleansing the palate after a rich meal. They are also used in fruit salads and for making sorbets.

Preparation

Lychees are very easy to prepare. The brittle skin parts readily, and you can either eat the fruit as is, nibbling the flesh off the seed, or the fruit can be pitted and sliced before being added to a fruit salad or similar dessert.

Storage

Store lychees in the refrigerator, as they taste best chilled. They will stay fresh for up to a week.

RAMBUTANS

CANTONESE: *HONG MAO TANG;* THAI: *NGO*

These small tropical fruits originated in Malaysia, but they are also grown in the Philippines and Thailand. They belong to the same family as lychees and longans, and they have a similar taste and texture, but look very different. The reddish-brown skins are covered with fine green-tipped hairs. Inside, the flesh is white, and hides an oblong seed.

Aroma and flavour

Rambutans are not as strongly scented as lychees. The delicate flesh tastes a little sharper.

Culinary uses

Rambutans are usually eaten in the hand, served on the bottom half of the shell, with the top half cut off to expose the flesh. They are used in fruit salads, but are seldom cooked.

Preparation

Make a cut around the equator of the rambutan, then remove half or all the skin. The flesh tends to stick to the seed, so they are more difficult to pit than lychees.

Storage

Like lychees, rambutans are best stored in the refrigerator, where they will keep for at least a week.

Above: Canned and fresh rambutans

Right: Canned and fresh lychees

MANGOES

CHINESE: *MANG GUO*; THAI: *MA-MUANG*

One of the world's favourite fruits, mangoes originated in India and are now widely cultivated throughout South-east Asia, as well as in other tropical and sub-tropical countries. There are thousands of different varieties. Most are oval in shape, with green, gold or red skin and succulent orange flesh, which can be quite fibrous, although modern varieties are usually smooth and velvety. Canned and dried mangoes are also available.

Aroma and flavour

The aroma of a ripe mango is quite unique. Some people say it reminds them of a pine wood in springtime. The juicy flesh is highly scented and tastes deliciously sweet.

Culinary uses

Apart from being eaten fresh as a fruit, mangoes are used extensively for making chutneys and pickles. Asian cooks also use them in savoury dishes,

Above: A selection of some of the many different varieties of mangoes

and when stir-frying a rich meat such as duck, will often add mango instead of pineapple. Mango ice cream is legendary, and Thai cooks make a wonderful dessert from glutinous rice, coconut milk and mangoes.

Preparation

To prepare a mango for eating, first cut off both sides of the fruit, on either side of the stone (pit), then scoop the flesh out of the skin with a spoon. After that, strip the skin off the remaining central part and suck the stone clean. This may sound rather messy, but in Asia it is the traditional way of eating a mango. If you are fastidious, you can always peel the mango first, slice the fruit off the stone and then slice it neatly. Finally – and this appeals to children – you can cut two large slices from either side of the stone, cross hatch the flesh on the skin, then press the skin down so that the pieces of mango pop up to make a mango "hedgehog".

Storage

Mangoes are usually picked just before they are ripe, and then they are packed in straw and shipped by air to the West. Fruit that is bought when it is still firm can be ripened at home. One of the easiest ways of doing this is to wrap the mango in newspaper, lay it in a box and cover with more newspaper. Colour is not necessarily an indication of ripeness, but touch is. Ripe fruit will just yield when lightly pressed. Eat mangoes as soon as they are ripe.

Preparing mangoes

Mangoes can be difficult to prepare because they have a large, flat stone (pit) that is slighty off-centre, and they are very juicy.

1 Cut off both sides of the fruit in thick slices, keeping as close to the central stone as possible.

2 Scoop the flesh out of the skin using a small spoon. Peel the skin off the remaining central part and slice the fruit off the stone.

PAPAYAS

MANDARIN: *FAN MUGUA*; CANTONESE: *MUK GWA*; THAI: *MALAKO*

Papayas – or paw paws as they are sometimes known – are native to tropical America. It was not until 1600 that they were introduced into Asia, but they rapidly became extremely popular so that today they are one of the most common and most important fruits in all tropical and sub-tropical countries.

Papayas can be small and round, but are more often pear-shaped. When ripe, the skin turns from green to yellow, and the flesh, which can be deep salmon pink or glorious orange, becomes soft and juicy. The small grey seeds are not usually eaten, although Asian cooks use them as a garnish.

Aroma and flavour

The flavour of a ripe papaya is sweet and delicately perfumed. It can be sickly, but this can be counteracted by lemon or lime juice. The flesh of under-ripe papaya is pale green, and nowhere near as sweet.

Culinary uses

In South-east Asia, papaya is eaten both as a fruit and a vegetable. When ripe, the flesh is usually eaten as it is, sometimes with a squeeze of citrus, but it is also used in fruit salads and other desserts. Papayas that are not too ripe can be added to soups, curries or seafood dishes. Unripe green papayas are served raw in vegetable salads, especially in Thailand, and can also be made into pickles. Papaya contains an enzyme called papain, which is an excellent tenderizer. Both the juice and skins are used to tenderize meat.

Preparation and cooking techniques

Slice lengthways in half and scoop out the seeds. To serve papayas raw as a table fruit, slice in wedges, sprinkle with lemon or lime juice, and either cut the flesh off the skin, slicing it into bitesize

Right: Papayas are one of the most popular tropical fruits.

chunks, or provide spoons for scooping. To serve papaya raw in a salad, peel slightly unripe fruit, shred the flesh and combine it with carrots and lettuce or cucumber, then toss with a spicy dressing. Thai cooks often add dried shrimps, which give a salty tang.

Storage

Green papayas are not often available outside their country of origin but, if located, can be kept in a refrigerator for up to a week. In the West, ripe fruit is much easier to come by. Look for fruit that is yellow all over, and which has a delicate perfume. If the fruit is not quite ripe, check the skin around the stem end and only buy if this is yellow. If it is green, the fruit will never ripen. Fruit that is almost ripe will soften if kept at room temperature for a few days, but should not be left for too long.

Dragon fruit

These brightly coloured fruits are widely grown in Vietnam. They come in pink and yellow varieties. The pink ones are about 10cm/4in long, and are covered with pointed, green-tipped scales. The yellow ones are smaller and look more like prickly pears. The flesh is sweet and refreshing, and is best eaten chilled, sprinkled with a little lemon juice.

NUTS AND SEEDS

PEANUTS

CHINESE: HUASHENG MI

Also known as groundnuts or monkey nuts, peanuts are thought to have originated in South America, and were introduced into Asia in the 16th century. Today, peanuts are an important world crop, being rich both in oil (40–50 per cent) and protein (about 30 per cent).

Aroma and flavour

Raw peanuts don't have much of a smell, but once cooked – they are usually roasted – they have a powerful, unmistakable aroma, a crunchy texture and a distinctive flavour.

Culinary uses

Peanuts play an important role in Asian cuisine. The smaller ones are used for making oil, while the larger, less oily nuts are widely eaten, both as a snack food and as ingredients in salads and main courses. In Indonesian and Malayan cooking, roasted peanuts, pounded to a paste, are the basis for satay sauce, as well as for a salad dressing in the classic gado-gado salad.

Above:
Raw and
shelled peanuts

Preparation and cooking techniques

Strictly speaking, the peanut is not a nut, but a legume. Its outer shell is the dried fibrous pod of the plant, and contains the seeds or "nuts", which in turn are coated with a thin layer of reddish skin. This skin has to be removed before the nut can be used as a food, and the easiest way to do that is to roast or fry the peanuts, then, when they are cool enough to handle, rub off the brittle skins with your fingers. When the nuts are processed commercially, a fan is used for winnowing, or the nuts are left outside to allow the wind to do the job.

Storage

Raw peanuts in their shells will keep for many months if stored properly. Shelled peanuts will only keep for 7–10 days, even if stored in an airtight container.

GINKGO NUTS

CHINESE: BAIGUO; JAPANESE: GINGKO BILOBA

The ginkgo tree is native to China, and has been grown for many centuries in Japan, where it is called the maidenhair tree.

Aroma and flavour

Ginkgo nuts resemble lotus seeds in appearance and taste, but have a smoother and firmer texture and are somewhat less sweet.

Culinary uses

Ginkgo nuts play an important role in vegetarian cooking in Asia, particularly in China and Japan. They feature in the popular Buddha's delight (a vegetarian casserole) and are used in several Japanese vegetable and rice dishes. When cooked, ginkgo nuts have a viscous texture.

Left: Canned
ginkgo nuts

Preparation and cooking techniques

These nuts do not travel well. The flesh inside the shells tends to dry up or rot after a time, so only dried and canned ginkgo nuts are available in the West. Dried nuts need soaking in water for several hours. Drain before adding to stir-fries, casseroles and soups.

Storage

Any unused soaked or canned ginkgo nuts can be stored in fresh water in the refrigerator for 2–3 days.

ALMONDS

MANDARIN: XINGREN;
CANTONESE: HANG YAHN

These nuts come from the kernel of a fruit closely related to the apricot, but the fruit of the ripe almond is leathery, dusky green and quite inedible.

Aroma and flavour

Almonds have a unique aroma quite unlike that of any other nut. There are bitter and sweet varieties, both with a pleasant, crunchy texture.

Culinary uses

In Asia, sweet almonds are mostly used as garnishes and in desserts and cakes. Bitter almonds contain prussic acid. They must not be eaten raw, but their essence is distilled and used as a flavouring for sweet dishes.

*Above: Shelled
almonds*

Preparation and cooking techniques

Whole kernels should be soaked to
remove the thin red skin. This is seldom
necessary in the West, however, as
shelled almonds are readily available,
whole, sliced, as thin slivers or ground.

Storage

Almonds have a high fat content, so
they become rancid if stored for too
long. Keep unopened packets in a
sealed container in a cool, dry place,
and use within 2–3 months. Nuts
bought loose, or in packets that have
been opened, should be used as soon
as possible.

SESAME SEEDS

CHINESE: *ZHIMA*

The sesame plant probably originated in
Africa, but has been cultivated in India
and China since ancient times. Today,
it is grown all over the world in tropical
and sub-tropical countries. Sesame
seeds are small, flat and pear-shaped.
They are usually white, but can be
cream to brown, red or black.

Aroma and flavour

Raw sesame seeds have little aroma
and are almost tasteless until they have
been roasted or dry-fried, when their
nutty aroma becomes very pronounced
and their flavour is heightened.

Culinary uses

Sesame seeds are about 50 per cent oil,
and processed sesame oil is used in
Asian cooking for flavouring. The seeds
are used in a number of popular

Chinese dishes, most notably
in Chinese honeyed apples
and bang-bang chicken.
They also feature in
Singaporean, Malayan
Indonesian and
Japanese cooking, and
are often toasted then
sprinkled over salads and
other dishes just before serving.

Preparation and cooking techniques

Sesame seeds are frequently roasted
before being used. Place them in a
wok or pan over medium heat. They
burn readily, so shake the pan
constantly to keep them moving
and do not leave them
unattended at any time. If
ground seeds are required,
this can be done in a
mortar with a pestle, or,
as in Korea, between
two flat plates.
Japanese cooks use
a device rather like a
pepper mill, which grinds the

roasted sesame seeds as finely or as
coarsely as needed. The finely ground
seeds are called *irigoma*.

Storage

The high oil content
means that sesame
seeds do not keep
well. Store them
in a cool, dry
place and
observe the
"use by"
dates on
packets.

*Above: White and black
sesame seeds*

Other nuts

Candle nuts Native to Indonesia,
these nuts are similar to macadamia
nuts, which can be used as a
substitute. In Asia, the pounded
nuts are used as a thickener.
They are slightly toxic
when raw, and
should always
be cooked.
Cashew nuts Both
raw and roasted
cashews are used in
Asian cooking.

Chestnuts These have a robust
flavour and meaty texture, which
makes them a popular addition to
a variety of vegetarian dishes. They
are particularly delicious
stir-fried with pak choi
or other leafy
vegetables.

*Above: From left, cashew nuts,
candlenuts and chestnuts*

TOFU AND GLUTEN

TOFU/BEANCURD

MANDARIN: *DOUFU*; CANTONESE: *DAU FOO*;
JAPANESE: *TOFU*

Made from soya beans, tofu (also commonly known in the West as beancurd) is one of China's major contributions to the world as a cheap source of protein. Highly nutritious and low in fat and sugar, it is a much healthier food than either meat or fish, at a fraction of the cost.

The soya bean plant is a legume that has been cultivated in China for thousands of years. A number of bean by-products constitute an important element in the Chinese diet. Soy sauce is one of them, and tofu is another, as well as miso, the fermented soya bean paste that is essential to Japanese cooking. Written records indicate that fermented bean sauces were in use well over 2,000 years ago, but no one knows precisely when tofu was invented. All we know for certain is that it was introduced to Japan during the Tang dynasty in the 8th century AD, along with Buddhism.

The process of making tofu is not unlike making cheese, only much less time-consuming. The soya beans are soaked, husked, then pounded with water to make soya milk. This mixture is then filtered, boiled and finally curdled with gypsum.

There are two basic types of fresh tofu widely available in the West: soft or silken tofu (called *kinu* in Japan); and a firm type, which Japanese cooks know as *momen*. Both are creamy-white in colour and are either packed in water or sold in vacuum packs. The firm type is usually sold in cakes measuring about 7.5cm/3in square and 2.5cm/1in thick. Also available, often only from Asian stores, are marinated tofu, deep-fried tofu and pressed tofu.

Aroma and flavour

The quality of fresh tofu is largely dependent upon the water used to make it. Good quality tofu should smell fresh with a faint, pleasant "beany" aroma. On its own, it is quite bland, but the beauty of tofu is that its soft, porous texture will absorb the flavour of any other ingredient with which it is cooked.

Culinary uses

The nutritional value of tofu cannot be stressed too highly. As a vegetable protein, it contains the eight essential amino acids plus vitamins A and B. It is free from cholesterol, and is regarded as an excellent food for anyone with heart disease or high blood pressure. In addition, it is very easy to digest, so is an ideal food for infants, invalids and the elderly.

Tofu is very versatile and, depending upon the texture, it can be cooked by almost every conceivable method, and used with a vast array of ingredients, both sweet and savoury.

Preparation and cooking techniques

Soft or silken tofu is mainly steamed or added to soups, since its light and delicate texture means that it will disintegrate if handled roughly. It makes a refreshing sweet dessert and is also used to make "ice cream".

Firm tofu is the most common type, and also the most popular for everyday use. Although it has been lightly pressed, and is more robust than silken tofu, it still needs to be handled with care. Having been cut to the required size and shape – cubes, strips, slices or triangles – the pieces are usually blanched in boiling water or briefly shallow-fried in oil. This hardens them and prevents them from disintegrating when stir-fried or braised. Yaki tofu is tofu that has been lightly grilled (broiled) on both sides.

Because tofu is bland, it is important to cook it with strongly flavoured seasonings such as garlic, ginger, spring onions, chillies, soy sauce, oyster sauce, blachan, fermented black beans, salted yellow beans,

Above: Clockwise from top, deep-fried tofu, silken tofu, and cubes of fresh tofu. All these types of tofu absorb the flavours of the other ingredients with which they are cooked.

or sesame oil. Although its primary purpose is as a vegetarian ingredient, tofu also tastes very good with meat. It is often cooked with either pork or beef, but seldom with chicken. It goes well with fish and shellfish, too. One of the most popular tofu dishes is the world-famous *ma po doufu* from Sichuan, in which cubed tofu is first blanched, then braised with minced (ground) beef, garlic, spring onions (scallions), leeks, salt, Sichuan pepper, rice wine, chilli bean paste, fermented black beans and sesame oil.

Left: Pressed tofu

Storage

Buy tofu from an Asian store, if possible. Fresh tofu submerged in water in a plastic box will keep for several days in the refrigerator. Vacuum-packed fresh tofu bought from health food stores and supermarkets will keep for slightly longer, but is unlikely to taste quite as good. Tofu is also available as a powder mix. This has a long shelf life, making it a useful item for the store cupboard.

DEEP-FRIED TOFU

MANDARIN: *YOUZHA DOUFU*; CANTONESE: *DAU FOO POK*; JAPANESE: *ABURAGE*

This is fresh, firm tofu that has been cut into cubes, squares or triangles, then deep-fried until light brown. Deep-fried tofu has an interesting texture. It puffs up during cooking, and underneath the crispy brown skin the flesh is white and soft. It sucks up seasonings and the flavours of other ingredients like a sponge.

Culinary uses

Deep-fried tofu can be used in the same way as fresh tofu in soups, stir-fries, braised dishes or casseroles. As it has been fried in vegetable oil, it is suitable for vegetarian cooking. Non-vegetarians stuff the larger squares or triangles of tofu with minced pork, chicken, fish and prawns (shrimp), then

braise them in a sauce. The Japanese version of deep-fried tofu, known as *aburage*, is a popular addition to a wonderful hotpot called *oden*, which is sold from street stalls during the winter.

Preparation and cooking techniques

Unlike fresh tofu, which is very delicate, deep-fried tofu can be handled fairly roughly without disintegrating. Even though the crisp crust is porous, it is best to chop up the larger pieces a little to allow the seasonings to penetrate more easily.

Storage

Cakes of deep-fried tofu are sold in plastic bags from the chiller or freezer in Asian stores. They usually have a "use by" date stamped on them, and will keep for much longer than uncooked fresh tofu. They can be frozen for up to a year or more.

PRESSED TOFU

MANDARIN: *DOUFU GAN*; CANTONESE: *DAU FOO GONN*

Pressed tofu is fresh tofu that has been compressed until almost all the liquid has been squeezed out, leaving a solid block with a smooth texture. It is usually marinated in soy sauce and seasoned with Chinese five-spice powder, so is

pale brown on the surface, but still creamy white inside.

Culinary uses

Pressed tofu is cut into thin slices, cubes or fine shreds, then stir-fried with meat and vegetables. It offers a contrast in both texture and flavour when it is combined with other ingredients.

Storage

Pressed tofu can be bought in vacuum-packed plastic bags from Asian stores, and will normally keep for several weeks in the refrigerator. Check the "use-by" date on the packaging, and do not freeze it, as this would alter the texture of the tofu.

DRIED TOFU SKINS

MANDARIN: *FUZHU*; CANTONESE: *FOO PI*; JAPANESE: *YUBA*

Dried tofu skins are made from soya milk. The process is simple, but requires considerable skill: a large pan of soya milk is gently brought to the boil, the thin layer of skin that forms on the surface is skimmed off with a stick in a single swoop, and this is hung up. When it dries, it forms a flat sheet. Dried tofu sticks are made by rolling the skin up while still warm, then leaving the sticks to dry.

Culinary uses

Fermented tofu is either served on its own with rice congee at breakfast, or used as a seasoning in marinating and cooking.

Storage

Fermented tofu is available in cans and jars from Asian stores. Once opened, store the contents in the refrigerator.

Below: Fermented tofu

Above: Dried tofu skins have no discernible flavour or aroma.

FERMENTED TOFU

MANDARIN: *DOUFU NAI*; CANTONESE: *FOO YU*; THAI: *TAO-HOO-YEE*

This is made by fermenting fresh tofu on beds of rice straw, then drying the curd in the sun before marinating with salt, alcohol and spices. Finally, it is stored in brine in sealed earthenware urns and left to mature for at least six months before being packaged and sold.

Aroma and flavour

Fermented tofu is definitely an acquired taste. It is no coincidence that it is sometimes referred to as Chinese cheese, because it smells very strong indeed, and the flavour is pretty powerful as well. There are two types of fermented tofu readily available in the West: the red type is coloured on the surface only, and the white one can be quite hot and spicy.

Aroma and flavour

Like fresh tofu, dried tofu skins have neither aroma nor flavour until they are cooked, when they will absorb the flavours of the seasonings and other ingredients in the dish.

Culinary uses

The flat skins are used in soups, stir-fries and casseroles, and are sometimes used as wrappers for spring rolls. The sticks are used in vegetarian dishes, and are also cooked with meat in braised dishes and casseroles.

Preparation

Dried tofu skins need soaking before use: the sheets only require an hour or two, but the sticks need to be soaked for several hours or overnight.

Storage

Dried tofu sheets and tofu sticks will keep for a very long time. Store them in their packet or in a sealed plastic bag in a cool and dry place.

*Above: Tempeh has a
firmer texture than tofu.*

TEMPEH

INDONESIAN: *TEMPEH*

This Indonesian speciality is made by fermenting cooked soya beans with a cultured starter.

Aroma and flavour

Tempeh is similar to tofu but has a nuttier, more savoury flavour.

Culinary uses

It can be used in the same way as firm tofu and also benefits from marinating. Its firm texture means that it can be used as a meat replacement.

Storage

Tempeh is available chilled or frozen. Chilled tempeh can be stored in the refrigerator for up to a week. Frozen tempeh can be left in the freezer for 1 month. Defrost before use.

MISO

JAPANESE: *KOME MISO, MUGO MISO AND HACHO MISO*

This thick paste is made from a mixture of cooked soya beans, rice, wheat or barley, salt and water. Miso is left to ferment for up to 3 years.

Aroma and flavour

There are three main types: kome, or white miso, is the lightest and sweetest; medium-strength mugi miso, which has a mellow flavour and is preferred for everyday use; and hacho miso, which is a dark chocolate colour, and has a thick texture and a strong flavour.

Culinary uses

Miso can be used to add a savoury flavour to soups, stocks, stir-fries and noodle dishes, and is a staple food in Asia.

Storage

Miso keeps very well and can be stored for several months, but it should be kept in the fridge once it has been opened.

Left: Hacho miso

Gluten

MANDARIN: *MIANJIN;* CANTONESE: *MING GUN;* JAPANESE: *FU*

Also known as "mock meat", gluten is another source of vegetarian protein. It is made from a mixture of wheat flour, salt and water, from which all the starch has been washed out. What remains is a sponge-like gluten. Its Chinese name literally means "muscle or sinew of flour".

Like tofu, gluten has no aroma nor flavour of its own, but it has a much firmer texture than tofu, and can be shaped, coloured and flavoured to resemble meat, poultry or fish.

Unlike tofu, which is often cooked with meat and fish, gluten is regarded as a pure Buddhist ingredient, and as such, no non-vegetarian item may be mixed with it. This does not prevent accomplished Asian cooks from using a bit of sleight of hand, however, and gluten is often used with tofu to produce dishes such as "mock chicken", "mock abalone", "vegetarian duck" or "Buddhist pork" – which are all said to look and taste very much like the real thing.

Although gluten can be made at home, the task is too time-consuming to contemplate. Flavoured and cooked gluten is available in cans from Asian stores. It only needs to be reheated before being served.

Once opened, it will keep in the refrigerator for up to a week.

DRIED FISH AND SHELLFISH

SALTED FISH

MANDARIN: *YAN YU*; CANTONESE: *GON HAHM YU*

Many different types of fish, both freshwater and saltwater, are salted and cured for general use in South-east Asia. They range from tiny whitebait to large croakers, and they are generally preserved in salt or brine, although some are dried in the sun. In Japan, sun-dried young sardines, known as *niboshi*, are eaten as snacks, and are also used for making stock.

Aroma and flavour

To say that salted fish is an acquired taste is an understatement. It smells so pungent and has such a strong flavour that some people may find it positively disagreeable. It is, however, very popular throughout South-east Asia.

Culinary use

Salted fish has two basic functions. It is either eaten on its own with rice, or used as a seasoning for vegetables and meat in steamed dishes, casseroles or soups.

Preparation and cooking techniques

Soak the salted fish in water before use, to remove the excess salt. Large fish are usually sold without the heads.

Storage

Preserved fish in brine is seldom seen in the West, but salted and dried fish are both available from Asian stores. Salted and dried fish will keep almost indefinitely if stored in a cool, dry place.

Left: Dried anchovies

Above: Bonito flakes or shavings (top) and powder

DRIED ANCHOVIES

MALAY: *IKAN BILIS*

Dried anchovies, which are known as *ikan bilis*, are a Malayan speciality. For some unknown reason, anchovies are seldom eaten fresh in South-east Asia, they are either used for making fish sauce, or are salted and dried. Fishing for anchovies is a huge industry in Malaysia. Having located the schools of fish with the aid of electronic fish finders and echo sounding equipment, the fishermen haul in their catch and immediately boil the fish in salted water for about 5 minutes. Back on shore, the fish are dried, graded and packed.

Aroma and flavour

Dried anchovies have an overpowering aroma and a very strong flavour.

Culinary uses

Dried anchovies can be used as a flavouring, as an ingredient in a composite dish, or as a snack food. A favourite Malayan recipe involves steaming and filleting the fish, then serving them with a sauce made from preserved black beans that is flavoured with fresh chillies and lime juice and sweetened to taste with sugar. Dried anchovies are also often deep-fried until they are crunchy and served either at parties as a snack to eat with drinks, or as an appetizer. They also make a tasty accompaniment to spicy curries and chicken rendang.

Storage

Dried anchovies will keep for a very long time if stored in a dry and cool place, but make sure that their container is airtight, or you will attract all the neighbourhood cats.

BONITO FLAKES

JAPANESE: *KATSUOBUSHI*

Bonito is the name given to several different kinds of fish in different parts of the world. For instance, the Atlantic bonito is a relative of mackerel, and is known as Spanish mackerel in Europe, while the Pacific bonito is a small tuna, much used in Japanese cooking.

Aroma and flavour

The Pacific bonito has a much stronger flavour than regular tuna, particularly when it is dried.

Culinary uses

In Japan, where dried bonito is widely used, the flakes come in various thicknesses. Fine shavings are one of the main ingredients in the basic stock known as *dashi,* and are also used as a topping or garnish. Powdered bonito flakes are used as a seasoning.

Storage

Dried bonito flakes will keep almost indefinitely if stored in an airtight jar .

DRIED SHRIMPS

MANDARIN: *XIAMI;* CANTONESE: *HA MY;* THAI: *GUNG HAENG*

Dried shrimps are popular throughout Asia, especially in China and Thailand.

They are pale pink in colour, having been boiled before being spread out in the sun to dry. There are several different sizes, from tiny shrimp not much bigger than grains of rice (hence the Chinese name, "sea rice") to large ones, which are still less than 1cm/½in long. The larger ones are usually sold shelled and headless, while the tiny ones are sold whole, heads and all.

Aroma and flavour

Dried shrimps have a very strong smell, so strong that it can be detected through the plastic bags in which they are sold. The smell dissipates with cooking. The flavour is sharp and salty.

Culinary uses

Because of their strong taste, dried shrimps are usually used as a seasoning rather than as an independent ingredient. They are often used as a garnish in salads and also feature in the popular "eight-treasure stuffing", when they are combined with dried mushrooms, bamboo shoots, glutinous rice and other ingredients.

Preparation and cooking techniques

Dried shrimps must be soaked for an hour or so before use, either in water or rice wine. The soaking liquid is saved and often added to the dish during cooking.

Storage

Dried shrimps keep well in airtight containers if they are stored in a dry, cool place. Their colour is a good indication of freshness as older shrimps tend to fade. Any shrimps that look grey,

Left: Dried shrimps

*Above:
Dried
scallops*

or start to turn grey while being stored, will be past their prime. Stored dried shrimps may become a bit moist. If this happens, spread them on baking sheets and dry them briefly in a hot oven.

DRIED SCALLOPS

MANDARIN: *GANBEI;* CANTONESE: *GONG YU CHU*

Another Asian delicacy, dried scallops are very expensive because the most sought-after varieties are so scarce. The Chinese variety known as *conpoy,* for instance, is only found in the inland sea called Po Hai, and then only during a short summer season. The best scallops are round and golden, with a delicate, sweet flavour. Japan produces fine dried scallops, including the variety *aomori.*

Aroma and flavour

Before being dried, scallops are cooked in their shells in boiling water. The flesh is then removed and cleaned. Dried scallops have quite a distinct aroma with a highly concentrated flavour.

Culinary uses

Dried scallops are seldom used on their own, but are combined with other ingredients in soups and stuffings.

Above: Dried squid has a subtle fishy aroma, but a strong flavour.

Preparing dried squid

1 Soak the dried squid in warm water for 30 minutes or so, then drain and wash in fresh water.

2 Score the squid on the inside in a criss-cross fashion, then cut it into small pieces.

Dried and fresh scallops are sometimes used in the same dish. Dried scallops are the classic garnish for crispy seaweed, but when this dish is served in Chinese restaurants overseas, ground fried fish is often used as a substitute.

Preparation and cooking techniques

The scallops must be soaked in boiling water for at least an hour before use, then drained.

Storage

For some inexplicable reason, dried scallops seem to be available only in large boxes in the West. Should you acquire any, transfer them to jars, close

the lids tightly and store them in a cool, dry place. They will keep indefinitely.

DRIED SQUID

MANDARIN: *YOUYU*; CANTONESE: *YOW YU*

In inland China and other parts of Asia that are far from the coast, where fresh seafood was for a long time unobtainable, dried squid and cuttlefish have always been regarded as delicacies.

Aroma and flavour

Dried squid is pale brown in colour and has a subtle fishy aroma, but a very strong taste. Some people find the

texture rather tough when compared to fresh squid, but others like the chewiness of the dried version.

Culinary uses

In Asia, dried squid is mainly used in soups or meat stews. The stronger texture and flavour provides an interesting contrast to fresh squid, and the two are often stir-fried together in a popular dish that is known as "two-coloured squid-flowers".

Preparation and cooking techiques

Before using them for cooking, dried squid must be soaked in warm water for at least 30 minutes, then drained and cleaned in fresh water. If the dried squid is to be stir-fried, it is the normal practice to score the inside of the flesh in a criss-cross pattern, then cut it into small pieces. Cooking causes the cuts to open up so that each piece of squid resembles an ear of corn, which is how they came to be called "squid flowers".

Storage

Dried squid will keep almost indefinitely if they are wrapped tightly and stored in a dry, cool place.

FISH MAW

CHINESE: *Yu Du*

Fish maw is the swim bladders or stomachs of certain types of large fish and eels, which have been dried in the sun for several days, then deep-fried. It is considered a delicacy in both China and Thailand.

Aroma and flavour

Fish maw has little aroma, nor does it have a distinctive flavour.

Culinary uses

Fish maw is mainly valued for its texture, which is slippery.

Preparation and cooking techniques

The maws must be soaked in a large bowl of cold water for 24 hours before use. They will float at first, so will need to be kept submerged with the aid of a plate or dish. As they absorb the water, the maws will swell to four times the original size and slowly sink to the bottom of the bowl. Before use, drain but do not dry the maws, then slice or cube them as required.

Below: Dried jellyfish

Dried jellyfish
Sheets of dried edible jellyfish are sold in plastic bags in some Asian stores. This Chinese delicacy is valued for its crunchy yet elastic texture. To prepare, soak the sheets in cold water for several hours, changing the water frequently, and squeezing the jellyfish each time to get rid of as much of the fishy smell as possible. Drain, give the jellyfish sheets a final squeeze to remove the excess water, then cut them into strips. Strips of dried jellyfish are often added to a stir-fry, but they must be tossed in at the last moment; if they are overcooked, they will become rubbery.

Left: Dried sea cucumber, which is actually a type of sea slug and not a vegetable at all.

Dried sea cucumber Sold as *iriko*, *trepang* or *bêche-de-mer*, this is not a vegetable, but a marine animal, also known as a sea slug. Before use, dried sea cucumber must be soaked in cold water for at least 24 hours, during which time it will double in bulk and become quite gelatinous. It is mainly used in soups, stews and braised dishes.

Above: Fish maw

PRESERVED MEATS AND EGGS

CHINESE SAUSAGES/ WIND-DRIED SAUSAGES

MANDARIN: *XIANG CHANG*; CANTONESE: *LOP CHONG*

Although these are always described as Chinese sausages, wind-dried sausages are made throughout South-east Asia, and are widely available in the West. There are basically two types: a pink and white sausage, which is made from pork and pork fat, and a darker sausage, in which the pork is mixed with duck liver. The sausages are about 15cm/6in long and about 2cm/¾in wide, and are sold in pairs, tied together with string.

Aroma and flavour

The dried sausages do not have any aroma, but as soon as they are cooked, they become really fragrant and taste deliciously sweet.

Culinary uses

Chinese sausages are very versatile. They can be eaten on their own, combined with milder meats such as chicken, or used as the main ingredient in a vegetable dish.

Preparation and cooking techniques

Unlike salami, Chinese sausages must be cooked before eating them. The best way of cooking them is to cut them diagonally into thin slices, then steam them on top of rice for 10 minutes or so. Alternatively, the whole sausage can be steamed for 10 minutes, then skinned and sliced before adding to dishes such as fried rice.

Storage

As the sausages are cured and contain preservatives, they will keep for several months in the refrigerator, and almost indefinitely in the freezer.

Right: Chinese sausages are popular throughout South-east Asia.

Above: Pork crackling

PORK CRACKLING

MANDARIN: *SAI YUDU*; CANTONESE: *JA YUHK PEI*

Also known as chicaron, pork crackling is made from pork rind that has been deep-fried, forming crisp puffy crackers. It is served as a crunchy contrast alongside curries, or sliced in salads.

Aroma and flavour

The deep-fried rind has a meaty aroma with a subtle flavour. It has a very interesting firm yet spongy texture that absorbs other strongly flavoured ingredients.

Wind-dried belly pork

This is a Chinese speciality, found principally in Hunan province but available all over China. It must be cooked before eating. Wind-dried belly pork can be bought in Asian stores.

Culinary uses

Pork crackling is used in soups, stews, hot pots and casseroles.

Preparation

Pork crackling is simply sliced if it is to be used as a crunchy topping for salads, otherwise it needs to be soaked before use, partly to soften it and partly to rid it of excess fat. It is usually soaked in hot water for about 35 minutes before being drained and chopped.

Storage

Pork crackling should keep for several months if well wrapped and stored in a cool, dry place. It will become rancid if kept for too long.

PRESERVED EGGS

MANDARIN: *YANDAN; PIDAN;* CANTONESE:
HAHAM DON; PEI DON

In China, and among the
Chinese communities
throughout South-east
Asia, preserved eggs
are a very popular
delicacy. There are
two main types, and
both use duck eggs.
This is partly because
duck eggs are bigger
and have a stronger
flavour than hen's eggs,
but also because the
yolk of a duck egg
contains more fat than a
hen's egg. The more common type,
much favoured in southern China, is the
salted duck egg. The other, which has
more universal appeal, is the famous
thousand-year-old egg.

Both types of preserved egg are
made by a similar method; it is the
materials used in the process that are
different. Basically, salted eggs are
made by coating raw duck eggs in a salt
and mud paste, then rolling them in
rice husks until they are completely
covered. At this stage the eggs are
packed into an earthenware urn, which
is tightly sealed and stored in a cool,
dark place for 30–40 days. Thousand-
year-old eggs are nothing like as old as
their name suggests. They are raw duck
eggs that have been covered with a
mixture of wood ash and slaked lime
and left for up to a hundred days. By
the time they are used, the egg
whites will have turned to
pale brown jelly and the
yolks will be creamy and
tinged green.

Aroma and flavour

The two types of
preserved egg smell and
taste quite different. As
might be expected, the
former are quite salty.
Thousand-year-old eggs
taste milder, but still have
a definite aroma and flavour.

*Above: The solid whites and yolks of
thousand-year-old eggs are eaten raw.
The eggs only require peeling.*

Culinary uses

Salted eggs must be cooked. They are
often eaten on their own, or used as
part of the filling in cakes for festivals.
Thousand-year-old eggs need no
cooking. Sliced and seasoned with soy
sauce and sesame oil, they are often
served as an appetizer, or chopped
and added to congee and eaten

at breakfast time. They can also be
used in a delicious omelette, with pork
and fresh hen's eggs.

Preparation and cooking techniques

Both types of egg must have
their outer coating
removed and then they
should be thoroughly
washed. Salted eggs
can then be boiled
or steamed before
removing the shells.
The whites and yolks of
thousand-year-old eggs
will have solidified, so
all that is required is to
carefully remove the shell
before cutting the eggs into
quarters or eighths for serving.

Storage

Since these eggs are preserved, they
should keep for a long time in the
refrigerator. The salted eggs will keep
for about a month, and the thousand-
year-old eggs will keep for 4–6 months.

*Left: Throughout Asia thousand-
year-old eggs (front) and salted
duck eggs (back) are a very
popular delicacy.*

POULTRY

CHICKEN

The chicken is a descendant of a South-east Asian jungle fowl that was domesticated over 4,500 years ago. Today chicken features in almost every cuisine. Its universal popularity is due to the fact that the flesh combines happily with a huge variety of different ingredients. Nowhere is this more amply illustrated than in Asia, where it is used in soups, salads, stir-fries, curries, roasts and braised dishes. Every part of the bird is utilized, including the liver, gizzard, heart and even the feet, which are used to make a delicious stew in South-east Asia.

Preparation and cooking techniques

Chicken can be cooked whole, jointed, or taken off the bone and chopped or cut into thin strips – this is the usual practice if the meat is to be stir-fried. In China, chicken breasts on the bone are sometimes cut into as many as 20 pieces before being stir-fried. The ability of the Chinese to pick up these

---

Game birds
Small game birds are eaten in China and South-east Asia, but most are caught in the wild. Only quail and pigeon are farmed.

---

tiny pieces of chicken with chopsticks and to remove the meat from the bone in the mouth is a marvel of dexterity.

Serving meats and other foods in manageable morsels is the norm in Asia, where knives are viewed as weapons, and therefore inappropriate for such enjoyable communal activities as meals. Chopsticks are widely used, except in Thailand, where it is more common to find a spoon and fork at each table setting.

In Japan, chicken is the most important meat on the menu, second only to fish in terms of popularity. Chicken breast is the favourite cut, largely because it cooks so quickly and remains beautifully tender in dishes such as the famous *yakitori* or *teriyaki*. Skinless, boneless chicken breast fillets are readily available in Japan, unlike in the rest of Asia, where it is more usual for cooks to buy chickens whole, as portions are regarded as wasteful, or simply as too expensive.

Throughout the East, frugality is a virtue, so one chicken might be used in three dishes: the breast fillets sliced in strips for a stir-fry; the rest of the meat braised in a red cooked dish or a curry; and the carcass used to make stock.

The skill that is exhibited by Asian cooks with the simplest equipment is testament to their creative love of food. Using a cleaver and a small sharp knife, a chicken can be chopped into appropriate portions in no time at all.

DUCK

Ducks symbolize happiness and fidelity, which doubtless contributes to their popularity in the Chinese cuisine. Duck is central to celebratory meals, and is served in countless imaginative ways. At Chinese New Year, for instance, duck is an essential part of every banquet.

How to joint a chicken
This method will give you eight good-sized portions of chicken.

1 Place the chicken breast side up on a chopping board. Ease one of the legs away from the body, and using a sharp knife make an incision to reveal the ball of the thighbone as you pull the leg further away from the body. When the thigh socket is visible, cut through the bone to release the drumstick and thigh in one piece. Repeat with the other leg.

2 Trim off the end of the leg bone, then locate the knee joint and cut the leg portion in half at this joint. Repeat with the other chicken leg.

3 Cut through the breastbone so that the carcass is in two halves. Cut and separate each breast and wing from the backbone.

4 Cut both of the wing and breast pieces into two portions.

COOK'S TIPS
• Use the backbone to make stock, adding onion, celery and a piece of bruised root ginger if appropriate.
• If more pieces of chicken are required, say for stir-fries, the portions can be further divided. Deft Asian cooks will cut the breast and wing portions into as many as ten pieces, the legs into four pieces and the thighs into six pieces.

Right: In Asia, every part
of the chicken is used
– even the feet.

Duck is also popular in
Vietnam,Thailand and Indonesia,
but is seldom served in Japan.

Preparation and cooking techniques

The most famous duck dish has to be
Peking duck. The classic way of making
this universally popular restaurant dish
involves hanging the prepared birds in a
windy place to dry before roasting them
in a special oven. At one time only the
skin was eaten, but it is now more usual
to eat the succulent meat as
well. This is wrapped in a
Mandarin pancake
which has been
spread with a
little plum
sauce and
sprinkled
with a few

pieces of shredded spring onion
(scallion) and slivers of cucumber. This
dish is so popular that is now possible
to buy packages of Peking duck, with
all the trimmings, in the West.

The Chinese technique for preparing
duck for roasting involves pricking
the skin lightly all over
with a fork, placing
the bird on

a trivet in the sink,
then pouring a kettle
of freshly boiled water
over the top. The bird is then drained
well, and the cavity wiped with kitchen
paper, before being suspended from
duck hooks or butcher's hooks and left
to dry overnight. Once the bird is dry,
the skin is sprinkled with a little salt.
The bird is then placed on a trivet in a
roasting tin and roasted in a hot oven
until the skin is quite crisp and golden
brown and the bird is fully cooked.

If the duck is to be jointed the same
procedure can be used as for chicken.

COOK'S TIP

To make duck sauce to serve with
Peking duck, heat 30ml/2 tbsp sesame
oil in a small pan. Add 90ml/6 tbsp
yellow bean sauce and 30ml/
2 tbsp soft light brown sugar
and stir until smooth.
Leave to cool
before serving.

Right: An oven-
ready duck

MEAT

PORK

This is as popular as chicken in China and in other parts of Asia with large Chinese communities. Like chicken, it blends happily with a wide range of ingredients, from vegetables to shellfish, and is equally at home with salted and pickled foods.

Wherever there are Muslim communities, however, pork is off limits and either beef or lamb is served instead. This is the case throughout Malaysia, the only exception being the Nonya style of cooking. This came about because of the intermarriage of Chinese merchant men with Malayan women who then started to cook pork dishes for their husbands. Nonya cooking is popular in Singapore, the west coast of Malaysia around Malacca and on the island of Penang.

Pork seldom features in Indonesian cuisine, except where cooked by members of the Chinese communities on the thousands of islands of the archipelago. Bali is an exception. The population of this island are mainly Hindu and therefore pork is permissible and widely used.

Throughout Asia, therefore, the choice of meat is greatly influenced by religious beliefs and habits. Almost all Chinese except those who have converted to Islam love pork. Thais find the smell of lamb and mutton offensive; and Indians would never touch beef, because for them the cow is sacred. Poultry has none of these taboos.

Preparation and cooking techniques

For stir-frying, fillet, lean leg or belly are the preferred cuts, along with the meaty parts of chops or spare ribs. The meat is cut into thin shreds so that it responds to really quick cooking over high heat, which is economical in the use of fuel.

For casseroles and braised dishes shoulder, spare ribs or belly pork might be used, and the meat is often cooked for so long that it forms a luscious jelly-like mixture.

OTHER MEATS

Beef has only relatively recently been eaten in China and Asia, because cattle were considered beasts of burden and highly valued as such. The buffalo, too, has always been used widely, mainly in the paddy fields to plough the land prior to planting by hand. Beef and lamb are traditionally eaten only in the north of China and in places such as Malaysia where there are Muslim communities. However, because of the proximity of Beijing to the northern provinces and the number of Chinese Muslim restaurants in the capital, lamb and beef are becoming increasingly popular there, too.

Lamb is cooked in the famous Mongolian hotpot, while beef is used in many different types of recipes, mainly as a substitute for pork. It is generally thinly sliced and used for dishes where a quick method of cooking such as stir-frying is required. Because it has a stronger flavour than pork, it works best in dishes that contain aromatic flavouring ingredients, such as garlic and onions.

Above: Lean leg steaks, fillet and spare ribs are the preferred cuts of pork.

FISH

There is an old Thai saying that suggests that all is well when "there is fish in the water and rice in the field". The main source of protein in the Thai diet is fish, which is hardly surprising when you take a look at the map and see the immense coastline in addition to the rivers, canals, lakes and flooded paddy fields. Along these waterways local people catch their daily supply of fish using simple fishing poles or nets. The fish is steamed, grilled with local spices or herbs, served in soups or curries, or added to salads or omelettes.

The Cantonese word for fish is "yu" which sounds the same as the word for abundance or bounty. A whole fish is traditionally served at the Chinese New Year banquet as a symbol of hope that the family will enjoy a plentiful supply of food during the coming year. Serving a fish whole, as opposed to cutting it into portions, has great appeal in Asia, as the fish is aesthetically pleasing and complete. Also, by cooking the fish whole the juices are retained and the prized morsel that is the fish cheek can be served to the guest of honour.

Fish – nature's bounty – is exploited and enjoyed all over the East. With a coastline of over 3,000 miles China has an abundant and varied supply of saltwater fish, some of which are familiar to Westerners, such as bass and sea bass, halibut, mackerel, sea bream, sole, plaice, tuna, cod, salmon, sardines and herring. China also has majestic rivers and lakes, which are a source of freshwater fish, including the ubiquitous carp.

Indonesia, the Philippines and Japan are all island nations, so it is not surprising that fish plays an important role in their cuisines. This is especially so in Japan, where an early moratorium on meat eating was one of the factors

Above: Freshwater carp, mackerel and grey mullet

that led to the Japanese expertise in preparing this popular food. Sashimi – very fresh fish that is finely sliced and served raw – is a delectable treat that is now appreciated well beyond the shores of the country that invented it. Trout, mackerel, tuna, salmon and herring are popular in Japan, as well as more exotic varieties, such as parrot fish or pomfret.

The most important requirement when buying and preparing is that it be as fresh as possible. This goes for all of Asia, but particularly Japan.

Buying fish

When buying fresh fish, the following indicators should be considered:
• The eyes of the fish should be bright and clear, not sunken.
• Gills should be clean and bright red/coral in colour.
• The skin should be firm and fresh with a sheen and, when held, the fish should feel almost springy, as if it could swim away at any moment.
• Freshness can also be detected in the smell. It is difficult to disguise the odour of a fish that is past its prime.

Cooking fish

Steaming and simmering in clear stock are typical Asian cooking methods, along with deep-frying, pan-frying, stir-frying and braising.

Steaming Choose a very fresh whole fish. It should not be too large (about 675g/1½lb). Rub the skin with salt and sprinkle the fish with shredded fresh root ginger. Pour over a mixture of Chinese rice wine, soy sauce and sugar, then steam immediately over rapidly boiling water. For the best results remove the fish from the steamer when the fish is almost, but not absolutely cooked. The flesh should have just begun to flake when tested with the tip of a sharp knife, but should still be beautifully moist. Serve with the cooking juices poured over.

Clear simmering This method is usually reserved for larger fish (about 1.5kg/3lb). Use a fish kettle, if you have one. Pour in 1.75 litres/3 pints/7½ cups water and add salt to taste. Slice a 4cm/1½in piece of root ginger and add the slices to the kettle. Bring the water to the boil. Meanwhile slip a wide strip of foil under the fish to act as a strap. Lift the fish into the kettle, placing it on the trivet. Allow the water to return to

Right: Snapper, parrot fish and pomfret

the boil, then lower the heat and simmer for about 4 minutes. Lower the heat again, until the water barely bubbles, and cook the fish for 6–8 minutes. Lift the fish out of the fish kettle and let it drain before transferring it to a heatproof serving dish. Heat 75ml/5 tbsp groundnut (peanut) oil and pour this over the hot fish to complete the cooking. This is a finish also used in Vietnamese cuisine, but they would sprinkle the fish with shredded spring onion (scallion) before pouring over the hot oil.

Frying Fish can be stir-fried, deep-fried or pan-fried, and whichever method is used, the fish is always cooked quickly to retain its shape and flavour.

Braising Used for whole fish, which is first fried in garlic and ginger oil. Soy sauce, Chinese mushrooms and other flavourings are added, then the pan is covered tightly and the fish is cooked very briefly.

TYPES OF FISH

Carp A freshwater fish that is believed to have originated in Asia thousands of years ago. It is extensively farmed and thrives in ponds, lakes and flooded paddy fields. There are several varieties. Ask the fishmonger to remove the large scales and strong dorsal fins. The flesh is meaty and moist. Bake carp whole. Like grey mullet, it needs a stuffing with a distinctive flavour.

Cod A handsome fish with greenish bronze skin dappled with yellow, cod can vary in size from 1kg/2¼lb to 30kg/66lb. When properly cooked the flesh is moist and will break into large flakes. It is ideal for grilling, baking or frying, and is excellent in fish curries, but only add the cubes of pearly white fish at the very end of cooking so that they keep their shape.

Grey mullet This fish has dark stripes along the back, thick scales and a heavy head. The flesh is soft and rather coarse but responds well to distinctive flavours. Try it baked, with a stuffing of minced (ground) pork and prawns (shrimp) with ginger and spring onion or chopped Chinese mushrooms, or moisten it with fish sauce and steam it.

Halibut This is a rather chunky flatfish and can reach an enormous size. It has a brownish skin on one side and is pearly white underneath with two eyes on the bridge of the snout. The smaller type, called a chicken halibut, weighs under 1.5kg/3lb and is ideal for poaching or baking.

Mackerel Mackerel and bonito are from the same family. The fish is easy to recognize, thanks to the wavy dark blue markings which run part of the way down to a silvery green side and pale underbelly. The inside of the mouth is black. Mackerel is an oily fish, with soft, pinkish flesh, and is ideal for grilling or poaching with miso. Serve mackerel with wedges of lemon or lime. It is also excellent in a *laksa* or a Thai fish soup.

Parrot fish Either blue or brightly coloured, these are striking to look at and delicious to eat.

Plaice Easy to recognize, this flatfish has dark brown skin with orange spots and a white underside. The flesh is soft and moist. Cook plaice whole, either deep-fried or poached. If filleted, make a stock from the bones with bruised ginger, onion and seasoning.

Pomfret Held in high regard by Malay and Thai cooks, the pomfret is a fisherman's dream as it is very easy to net. So easy that at one stage these fish were almost fished out. A type of flatfish, pomfret is silver grey with a pearly white underside. The ideal way to preserve the delicate flavour of this fish is to steam it with a few simple flavourings, such as ginger, spring onion, light soy sauce and seasoning. It is good grilled and fried, too.

Salmon Often called the king of fish, the finest wild salmon makes delicious sashimi. Farmed salmon makes a very reasonable and good buy for a vast array of cooked dishes. The skin on a salmon's back is steely blue going down to a silver body. The flesh is oily, an attractive shade of pink, and firm. It is best clear simmered or poached in a fish kettle or wrapped in foil and baked. Cutlets can be cooked on a barbecue and served with Thai salad or used to make the Filipino dish, escabeche.

Sea bass The family of sea bass also includes the groupers (sometimes called garoupas). Sea bass is silver in colour with a dark back and white underbelly. The flesh is delicate in flavour and holds its shape when cooked. The fish can be grilled, steamed, baked or barbecued whole, or cut into fillets or steaks before being cooked. It is expensive but worth it.

Sea bream Look for the gilt head with a gold spot on each cheek and squat compact body. Sea bream must be scaled before being cooked. The flesh is rather coarse but remains moist if not overcooked. Slash each side two or three times so that the thicker part of the fish will cook more evenly. Sea bream is best baked whole in an oiled or buttered foil parcel with ginger, spring onion (scallions) and seasoning. It is good served with a sweet and sour sauce.

Above: Tuna steaks and salmon cutlets

Snapper The red snapper is perhaps the best known but there other colours, too, such as grey, silver and even a silver-spotted grey. The red colour is quite distinctive. The fish has large eyes and very strong dorsal fins which should be removed before cooking. The flesh is moist and well flavoured. Small to medium snappers are good for steaming or baking whole.

Sole Another member of the flatfish family, sole has rough brown skin on top and a long lozenge-shaped body. The flesh has superb texture and a delicate flavour. Sole is best grilled or fried whole. It can be sold filleted, in which case ask for the bones to make stock for a fish soup.

Squid Asian cooks are fond of squid. In the West, this cephalopod usually comes ready cleaned, but if you should you come across squid in the unprepared state here is what to do: Pull the tentacles out from the body sac. Squeeze the tentacle in the centre gently to remove the hard central bone or "beak". Trim the tentacles from the head and set aside. Using fingers pull the quill and innards from the body cavity and discard. Pull off the mottled outer skin, it should come away quite easily. Wash the squid well inside and out. It is now ready for stuffing. When it is two thirds full, pop the tentacles back into the sac. Secure the tentacles and the top of the squid body with a cocktail stick (toothpick).

If the squid are to be stir-fried, further preparation will be necessary: Slit the sac from top to bottom and turn it inside out. Flatten it on a board and score the inside surface lightly with a knife, pressing just hard enough to make a criss-cross pattern. Cut lengthways into ribbons. These will curl when cooked.

Tuna These enormous fish are the big brothers of the mackerel family. Tuna swim enormous distances at speed and this causes the muscles to fill with blood, which explains the deep red colour of the fresh fish. The skipjack and the albacore are much sought after by the Japanese for making **sashimi** and **sushi.** When grilling or cooking tuna on the barbecue, marinate the fish first and then baste it to keep it moist throughout the cooking. It is also good pan-fried.

SHELLFISH

Asian cooks have access to a wonderful assortment of shellfish, not only from the ocean, but also – in the case of crabs and shrimps – from freshwater lakes, rivers and canals. In Asia it is considered essential that shellfish be as fresh as possible when cooked. This isn't always possible for the Western cook, who often has no option but to resort to using good quality frozen shellfish. In this case, the shellfish should be thawed slowly, and dried before being cooked. The cooking period should be kept to a minimum to preserve the delicate flavour and texture of the shellfish. In Asia, favoured cooking methods for shellfish are steaming, deep-frying and stir-frying, but they are also used in soups, and made into dishes such as crab cakes.

Abalone This large shellfish has a particularly pretty shell, lined with what looks like mother-of-pearl. The flesh of abalone can be tough, and it is usually beaten to tenderize it before cooking. Frozen abalone is available from some Asian markets, and it is also possible to buy canned abalone. This is yellow brown in colour and has a savoury flavour. The texture tends to be rubbery, so canned abalone is seldom served solo, but is usually combined

Above: Mussels and clams

with other ingredients. The can juices can be used in soups and sauces. Dried abalone is an expensive and much sought-after delicacy.

Clams There are many different types of clam. In Japan, the giant clam and the round clam are both used for making sushi, and in China clams with black bean sauce are a favourite treat. When buying clams, check that none of the shells are broken. Wash them well in running water, then leave in salt water before steaming for 7–8 minutes or until the shells open. Serve clams simply, with a dipping

Above: Canned abalone

Mussels and clams in coconut cream

Mussels and clams can be steamed, but here they are cooked Thai-style in coconut cream and flavoured with lemon grass, kaffir lime leaves and Thai green curry paste.

SERVES 4–6

1.75 kg/4 – 4¹/₂lb mussels
450g/1lb baby clams
120ml/4fl oz/¹/₂ cup dry white wine
1 bunch spring onions
  (scallions), chopped
2 lemon grass stalks, chopped
6 kaffir lime leaves, chopped
10ml/2 tsp Thai green curry paste
200ml/7fl oz/scant 1 cup
  coconut cream
30ml/2 tbsp chopped fresh
  coriander (cilantro)
salt and ground black pepper

1 Scrub the mussels, pull off the beards and remove any barnacles. Discard any mussels that are broken or which do not close when tapped sharply. Wash the clams thoroughly.

2 Put the wine in a large pan with the spring onions, lemon grass, lime leaves and curry paste. Simmer gently until the wine has almost evaporated. Add the mussels and clams to the pan, cover tightly and steam the shellfish over high heat for about 6 minutes, until they open.

3 Using a slotted spoon, transfer the mussels and clams to a warmed serving bowl and keep hot. Discard any shellfish that remain closed. Strain the cooking liquid into a clean pan and simmer to reduce to about 250ml/8fl oz/1 cup.

4 Stir in the coconut cream and coriander, with salt and pepper to taste. Heat through. Pour the sauce over the mussels and clams.

is often pan-fried or cooked in a pot of rice where it releases a delicious, delicate flavour.

Lobster This luxury shellfish is usually served as a restaurant dish. To cook a live lobster, put it in a pan of ice cold water, cover the pan tightly and bring the water to the boil. The shell will turn bright red and the flesh will be tender and succulent when the lobster is cooked. If you buy a ready-cooked lobster the tail should spring back into a curl when pulled out straight. One of the best ways of eating lobster is with a simple dip of soy sauce with grated ginger.

Scallops Prized for their tender, sweet flesh, scallops are popular throughout Asia. The delicate flesh needs the briefest possible cooking. A good way of cooking scallops is to marinate them in a mixture of Chinese rice wine, sugar and soy sauce for 30 minutes, then steam them with the marinade and slivers of ginger and spring onion (scallion).

Above: Lobster and scallops

sauce based on hoisin sauce, plum sauce or soy sauce with ginger. Clams are also very good in soups.

Mussels Another shellfish that is widely used in Asian cooking. Farmed mussels are now readily available and have the advantage that they are usually relatively free of barnacles. They are generally sold in quantities of 1kg/2¼lb, sufficient for a main course for two or three people. Look for good-size specimens with glossy shells. Discard any that are not closed, or which fail to shut when tapped. Use the back of a short stout knife to scrape away any barnacles, pull away the hairy "beards", then wash the shellfish thoroughly. The best way to cook mussels is to steam them in a small amount of flavoured liquor in a large lidded pan for about 3–4 minutes until the shells open. Use finely chopped ginger, lemon grass, a few torn lime leaves and some fish sauce to add flavouring to the mussels.

Crabs are eaten with great relish all over the East. There are many different species which are exclusive to Asia. Travellers to Thailand and Hong Kong

will doubtless have seen – and enjoyed – blue swimming crabs. This species obligingly moults its shell so that the crab can be eaten whole. The meat

Below: Blue swimming crabs

Fantail or phoenix prawns

This way of serving prawns (shrimp) comes from China. The cooked prawns, with their bright red tails, are supposed to resemble the legendary phoenix, which is a symbol of dignity and good luck. Large prawns are used.

1 Remove the heads from the prawns and peel away most of the body shell. Leave a little of the shell to keep the tail intact.

2 Make a tiny incision in the back of each prawn and remove the black intestinal cord.

3 Hold the prawns by the tails and dip them in seasoned cornflour (cornstarch), and then in a frothy batter before cooking them in hot oil until the tails, which are free from batter, turn red.

Left: Cooked prawns

Shrimps and prawns Both shrimps and prawns can be caught in either fresh water or the sea. The names tend to be used indiscriminately in Asia. Shrimps can be small or large and the same holds good for prawns. Buy fresh raw shellfish where possible, choosing specimens that are a translucent grey colour tinged with blue. If using frozen shrimps and prawns, it is preferable to buy raw shellfish, thaw them slowly and dry them well before using. Further preparation will depend upon the chosen recipe. The shells may be left on or removed, or the shrimps or prawns may be shelled, with the tails left intact.

Butterfly prawns

Prawns (shrimp) prepared this way cook quickly and curl attractively.

1 Remove the heads and body shells of the prawns, but leave the tails intact. Pull out the intestinal cords with tweezers.

2 Make a cut through the belly of each prawn.

3 Gently open out the two halves of the prawn so that they will look like butterfly wings.

Left: Raw prawns

HERBS, SPICES AND AROMATICS

Above: Garlic

GARLIC

MANDARIN: *SUAN;* CANTONESE: *SUEN;*
THAI: *KRATIAM*

Garlic is a member of the lily family, which is the same genus as leeks and onions. It is believed to have originated in Asia, and is mentioned in Chinese texts that date back over 3,000 years. The ancient Egyptians valued it for food and also accorded it a ceremonial significance. Garlic's curative qualities are well documented, and in many cultures it is used to ward off evil.

Aroma and flavour

There are several varieties of garlic, from tiny heads to the aptly named elephant garlic. The colour of the skin varies from white through to pink and purple, and the flavour can be anywhere from mild to extremely pungent. The most common variety in the Far East has a purple skin, a distinctive aroma and a fairly strong flavour with a hint of sweetness. In South-east Asia, cooks use a miniature variety of garlic. There are only four to six cloves in each bulb, and both the aroma and the flavour are much more concentrated. Thai cooks favour small garlic bulbs whose cloves have such thin skins that it is seldom necessary to remove them for cooking. The cloves are simply smashed with a cleaver, then added to the pan, where the skins dissolve to become part of the dish.

Culinary uses

Garlic forms a trinity of flavours with spring onion (scallions) and ginger in thousands of dishes in Chinese cooking, particularly in Beijing and Sichuan. It is a basic ingredient in much of Asia, including Korea, but is less popular in Japan, where it is used mainly for medicinal purposes. Vietnamese cooks use a great deal of garlic, and in Thailand a mixture of crushed garlic, coriander root and pepper is the foundation of many dishes. Garlic is an essential ingredient in the famous Thai curry pastes, too. Throughout Asia, garlic is also used to flavour oil for frying, partly because of the aromatic flavour it imparts, and also because it cuts down on the "oiliness".

Raw garlic is often used in dips, marinades and dressings.

Preparation and cooking techniques

Except in a few rare instances, when whole cloves of garlic are roasted or packed inside a chicken, garlic is always peeled before use. One of the easiest ways of doing this is to place it on a chopping board and crush it with the flat blade of a Chinese cleaver. The skin will separate from the flesh, and can easily be removed before the garlic is crushed completely, again with the flat of the blade. Although both cleaver and board will need to be washed afterwards, this is a lot easier than using a garlic press.

For whole cloves of garlic, or slices, just cut off the root end of the clove and remove the peel with your fingers.

If the garlic is to be used in a spice mix, as is often the case in South-east Asia, put the whole clove in a mortar and give it a blow with a pestle to release the skin. This can then be removed and the garlic crushed with the other ingredients. Recipes indicate whether garlic is to be sliced, chopped or crushed, but as a general rule, crushed garlic is used for overall flavour, the amount determining the intensity. Slices are used for accent, and are sometimes added early in the cooking process, and then removed once they have imparted a subtle flavour to the dish.

Apart from buying whole cloves of garlic, Asian cooks appreciate the convenience of minced garlic in jars. Dried garlic is also available, either as granules or flakes. Flakes need to be reconstituted in water before stir-frying, but can be added directly to braised dishes with plenty of liquid. Garlic purée is available in tubes in the West but is not widely used in Asia.

Storage

Look for firm, plump garlic bulbs with clear, papery skins. Avoid any that are beginning to sprout. Garlic bulbs (also called heads) keep well if stored in a cool, dry place. If it is too warm, the cloves will dry out and become powdery.

Making garlic oil

1 Heat 120ml/4fl oz/½ cup oil in a small pan. Add 30ml/2 tbsp crushed garlic.

2 Cook gently for about 5 minutes until the garlic is pale gold, stirring occasionally. Do not let it burn or the oil will taste bitter. Cool, strain and use as required.

GINGER

MANDARIN: *JIANG;* CANTONESE:
GEUNG; THAI: *KHING;* JAPANESE:
SHOGA

Ginger is believed to
be indigenous to the
tropical jungles of
South-east Asia, and
was introduced into
China by way of India
more than 2,000 years
ago. The portion of
the plant popularly
called root ginger
is actually a
rhizome or
underground stem. The
colour ranges from pale
pink (when very young) to
a golden beige, with a dry,
papery skin. Ginger is highly
valued throughout Asia, not
only as an aromatic, but also
for its medicinal properties. It is
believed to aid digestion, check
coughs and quell nausea.

Aroma and flavour

Fresh root ginger has a refreshing
scent, reminiscent of citrus, and a
pleasant, sharp flavour. Young ginger is
tender and mild enough to be stir-fried
as a vegetable, while older roots
become fibrous and more pungent.
Root ginger is available dried, but tastes
quite different from fresh. It is used
mainly as a pickling spice and Asian
cooks would not consider it an
acceptable substitute for the fresh root.
Ground ginger tastes different again;
in Asia its use is limited to mixing with
other ground spices such as when
making curry powder.

Culinary uses

Root ginger is an indispensable
ingredient in Eastern cooking. In China,
it is usually paired with spring onions
(scallions) to create a harmonious
yin-yang balance in a wide variety of
dishes; the cool spring onion providing
the yin and the hot ginger the yang.
Together they complement (and
sometimes tame) the dominant flavours

*Above: Fresh root ginger, ground ginger
and bottled ginger paste*

of certain meats and seafood. Ginger is
also used on its own to cut the oily flavour
of some cooking oils and marinades.
In Thailand, sticks of young ginger are
often served as dippers with a spicy
sauce, while Indonesians make a
wonderful sambal by grinding chillies,
shallots and garlic with ginger, and
stirring in sugar, salt and rice vinegar.
Pickled ginger also plays an important
role in Asian cooking. It can be served
solo as a side dish, or combined with
other ingredients such as beef or duck.
One of the most popular items on a
Chinese restaurant menu is duck with
pineapple and pickled ginger. Chinese
pickled ginger is packed in sweetened
rice vinegar, and is quite hot. Japanese
pickled ginger has a more delicate
flavour. The pale pink type called *gari* is
always served with sushi or sashimi to
refresh the palate between mouthfuls.

Preparation and cooking techniques

Fresh root ginger is usually peeled
before being used. The thin, tough skin
is quite easy to scrape or cut away, and
the flesh is then thinly sliced, grated,
shredded or finely chopped. When the
ginger is intended
purely for use as
a flavouring, and
is discarded after
cooking, it should be
bruised using the
flat blade of a knife
or cleaver.

Storage

It used to be
difficult to get
really juicy fresh
root ginger in
the shops, but
it is now readily
available. Look for firm
pieces with smooth skin. If
bought really fresh, root ginger will keep
well for up to two weeks in a cool, dry
place, away from strong light. Root
ginger can also be frozen. It can be
grated straight from the freezer and
will thaw on contact with hot food.

*Below: Japanese pink, pickled ginger is
also known as* gari.

Preparing fresh root ginger

1 Thinly peel the skin using a sharp knife or vegetable peeler.

2 Grate the peeled root finely.

3 Alternatively, cut thin slices of ginger into matchstick strips, or coarsely chop the strips.

4 Bruise the root for use in dishes where the ginger will be removed.

GALANGAL

CHINESE: *LIANG JIANG;* THAI: *KHAA;* VIETNAMESE: *CU GIENG*

Like root ginger, galangal is a rhizome that grows underneath the ground. The finger-like protruberances of galangal tend to be thinner and paler in colour, but the two look similar and are used in much the same way. Fresh galangal used to be virtually unobtainable in the West (although it was widely used in medieval Europe), but is now almost as easy to come by as ginger. There are two types. Greater galangal, also known as *lengkuas,* is a native of Indonesia, while lesser galangal originated in southern China. It is not as widely used as its larger relation, but is popular in Thailand, where it is known as *krachai.*

Laos powder is dried galangal that has been ground. Although it does not taste the same as fresh galangal, South-east Asian cooks appreciate its convenience and you will find it in many South-east Asian recipes. As a guide, 5ml/1 tsp of laos powder is equivalent to 1cm/½in fresh galangal, which has been peeled and chopped.

Aroma and flavour

Greater galangal has a pine-like aroma with a correspondingly sharp flavour; lesser galangal is more pungent and the flavour has been likened to a cross between ginger and black pepper. The rhizome is usually used fresh, but is also dried and powdered.

Culinary uses

Galangal is an essential flavouring agent in South-east Asian cooking, particularly in seafood and meat dishes. It is often pounded with shallots, garlic and chillies to make a spice paste for dips or curries. In Thailand, slices of galangal are added to soups, with shreds of lemon grass and lime leaves, while Vietnamese cooks add it to a peanut and lime sauce used to dress meat and vegetable salads.

Preparation and cooking techniques

Fresh galangal should always be peeled. It is usually thinly sliced or cut into matchsticks for cooking. Because it is harder than ginger, you will need to slice it before attempting to crush it, and slices or shreds need to be cooked for somewhat longer than ginger if they are to be tender.

Storage

Fresh galangal will keep for up to 2 weeks if stored in a cool, dry place. It can be stored in the refrigerator, but it must be well wrapped in baking parchment to keep it moist.

Right: Fresh and dried galangal

CHILLIES

MANDARIN: *LAJIAO;* CANTONESE: *LAT JIU;*
THAI: *PRIK*

Chillies are native to tropical
America. Christopher
Columbus introduced
them to Europe,
having come across
them in Mexico while
searching for peppercorns.
Their fame spread rapidly,
and soon they were
being cultivated in
Africa, India and the
Far East, where they rapidly
became an integral part
of the cuisine. There is,
however, a wild variety grown in China's
Sichuan province known as "Towards
Sky Cannon" or "Peacock's Eye Chilli"
(*Capsicum sinense*) which appears to
be native to China. Hot chillies and
sweet bell peppers belong to the same
genus, capsicum. There are scores of
varieties, but the ones most commonly
used in Asia are the Indian *kalyanpur,*
kovilpatt and *kesanakurru* chillies,
the Japanese *honka* or *hontaka,* the
Korean chilli and the family of Thai
chillies, which includes the fiery bird's
eye. Like bell peppers, many chillies
start out green and ripen to red, while
others change from yellow to

*Below: Green
chillies*

*Below: The same
type of chilli can
come in various
colours.*

*Right: Red
chillies*

Chilli paste

Ready-made chilli
paste is sold in
jars, however, it is
easy to make at home.
Simply halve and
seed fresh
chillies, then place them in the
bowl of a food processor and
purée to make a smooth paste.
A chopped onion can be added to
the processor to add bulk to the
paste. Store small amounts of
the paste in the fridge for up
to 1 week, or spoon into small
containers, cover and freeze for
up to 6 months. *Sambal oelek,* an
Indonesian chilli sauce, is made
in a similar way, but first the
chillies are blanched.

red and finally to brown or even black,
so what might appear to be a basket
of assorted chillies could turn out to
be the same type of chilli in varying
degrees of ripeness. In size, they range
from tiny pods not much bigger than a
pea to 30cm/12in monsters. Although
Asian cooks tend to use them fresh,
chillies are also available dried.

Aroma and flavour

Although heat is the quality most closely
associated with chillies, flavour is
important too, and aficionados use
terms such as sweet, smoky and
piquant to describe their favourite
types. The degree of heat varies from

*Left: Medium
red chillies*

blisteringly hot.
Chillies grown
in hot climes
also tend to
be hotter
than those
grown in
cooler conditions.

skin, they actually promote cooling. In
many Asian countries, they are eaten
out of hand, as snacks, and cooks
seeking to determine the strength of a
chilli before buying will often do so by
nibbling a sample from a market stall.
Chillies are used fresh, in sauces and
salads, and are essential ingredients
in Indonesian sambals. They also find
their way into a huge variety of cooked
dishes, including stocks, soups,
braised dishes and stir-fries, either

very mild to
positively explosive, but can
be moderated somewhat if the seeds
and pithy membrane (where most of the
heat resides) are removed. The shape
and colour give no sure indication of the
hotness, for instance, some large green
chillies are very mild, while others are

Culinary uses

That chillies and
other spicy foods are
perfect for hot climates is a bit
of a paradox, but because
they encourage
blood to rush to
the surface of the

*Above: Neither the colour nor
the size of chillies gives a sure
indication of their hotness as some
green chillies are hotter than red ones,
and some large chillies are hotter than
small ones.*

with or without the seeds. Where just
a hint of heat is required, chillies are
sometimes added whole to a dish, then
removed again just before serving.

Thailand is one of the world's major
producers of fresh chillies, so it is
not surprising that Thai cooks have
developed some of the most exciting
and innovative chilli recipes. A favourite
way of serving whole chillies is with
a pork and prawn (shrimp) stuffing.
The chillies are steamed, then fried.

In Chinese cooking, hot chillies are
used not to paralyse the tongue but
to stimulate the palate. The regional
cuisines of Hunan, Jiangxi, Guizhou
and Yunnan all feature chillies, although
not as strongly as does the province of
Sichuan, which is famous for its spicy
food. Even in Sichuan, however, chillies
are used with discretion and at least a
third of Sichuan dishes do not contain
any chillies at all. Even the Cantonese
use chillies in some of their dishes, and
chilli sauce and chilli oil are popular
condiments on Cantonese tables.

Preparing fresh chillies

1 Remove the stalks, then slice the
chillies lengthways.

2 Scrape out the pith and seeds
from the chillies, then slice, shred
or chop the flesh as required. The
seeds can be either discarded or
added to the dish, depending on
the amount of heat that is required.

Preparing dried chillies

1 Remove the stems and seeds and
snap each chilli into 2–3 pieces.

2 Put these in a deep bowl, pour
over hot water to cover and leave
to stand for 30 minutes. Drain,
reserving the soaking water if it can
usefully be added to the dish, and
use the pieces of chilli as they are,
or chop them more finely.

Making chilli flowers

Thai cooks are famous for their beautiful presentation, and often garnish platters with chilli flowers. These are quite simple to make.

1 Holding each chilli in turn by the stem, slit it in half lengthways.

2 Keeping the stem end of the chilli intact, cut it lengthways into fine strips.

3 Put the prepared chillies in a large bowl of iced water, cover and chill for several hours.

4 The cut chilli strips will curl back to resemble the petals of a flower. Drain well on kitchen paper and use as a garnish. Small chillies may be very hot, so don't be tempted to eat the flowers.

Right: Dried chillies

Using dried chillies

Dry roasting heightens the flavour of dried chillies. Heat a heavy frying pan without adding oil. Press the chillies on to the surface of the pan to roast them, but don't allow them to burn, or their flavour will become bitter. Once the chillies are roasted, remove them from the pan and leave to cool, then crush or grind them in a mortar with a pestle before adding to dishes.

Preparation and cooking techniques

Chillies must be handled with care. They contain capsaicin, an oily substance which causes intense irritation to sensitive skin. Get capsaicin on your hands, or worse, transfer it to your eyes by rubbing, and you will experience considerable pain. It is therefore very important to wash your hands immediately after handling chillies, and to use plenty of soap, as the oil does not dissolve in water alone. Some cooks prefer to wear latex gloves when preparing chillies, and some become extremely adept at using a knife and fork, and avoid touching the chillies at all, but whichever method you use, remember that it is also essential to wash cutting boards and implements.

Storage

Look for firm, unblemished fruit, avoiding any chillies that are soft or bruised. Some types look wrinkled even in their prime, so do not let this put you off fruit that otherwise appears to be in good condition. The best way to store chillies is to wrap them in kitchen paper, place them in a plastic bag and keep them in the salad compartment of the refrigerator. They will keep well for a week or more, but it is a good idea to check them occasionally and discard any that begin to show signs of softening. If you intend to use them solely for cooking, they can be frozen. There is no need to blanch them if you plan to use them fairly quickly. To dry your own chillies, thread them on a string, hang them in a warm place for a week or two until they are dry, then crush them in a mortar with a pestle.

Below: Pickled chillies are available in jars. They are mainly used as a relish.

LEMON GRASS

MANDARIN: *NINGMENG CAO;*
CANTONESE: *XIANG MAO;*
MALAY: *SERAI;* THAI: *TAKRAI;*
VIETNAMESE: *XA*

Few ingredients have seized the Western imagination quite so dramatically as has lemon grass in recent years. At one time this scented grass was little known outside South-east Asia; today it is to be found in nearly every supermarket. Lemon grass is a perennial tufted plant with a bulbous base. It grows in dense clumps in tropical and subtropical countries and is commercially cultivated on a grand scale. The cut stems are about 20cm/8in long, and look a little like fat spring onions (scallions) or very skinny leeks.

Aroma and flavour

It is only when the stems are cut that the distinctive citrus aroma can be fully appreciated. This is matched by the clean, intense lemon flavour, which has a hint of ginger but none of the acidity associated with lemon or grapefruit.

Below: Dried lemon grass

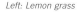

Left: Lemon grass

Lemon rind is sometimes suggested as a substitute, but it lacks the intensity and liveliness of fresh lemon grass, and will give disappointing results. Ground dried lemon grass, also known as serai powder, can be used instead of fresh. As a guide, about 5ml/1 tsp powder is equivalent to 1 fresh stalk. Whole and dried chopped stalks are also available in jars from Asian stores and larger supermarkets, as are jars of lemon grass paste.

Culinary uses

Lemon grass is widely used throughout South-east Asia, in soups, sauces, stir-fries, curries, salads, pickles and marinades. It is a perfect partner for coconut milk, especially in fish, shellfish and chicken dishes. Thai cooks often start a stir-fry by adding a few rings of lemon grass and perhaps a little grated or chopped fresh root ginger or galangal to the oil. This not only flavours the oil, but also fills the room with a glorious aroma. A favourite Vietnamese dish consists of sea bream coated in a lemon grass paste, which is left to stand until the flavour penetrates the fish, and then fried.

Preparation and cooking techniques

There are two main ways of using lemon grass. The stalk can be bruised, then cooked slowly in a soup or stew until it releases all its flavour and is removed, or the tender portions of the lemon grass (usually the lower 5cm/2in of the bulbous end of the stem) can be sliced or finely chopped,

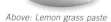

Above: Lemon grass paste

then stir-fried or used in a salad or braised dish. Often one stalk will serve both purposes, the tougher top end is used for background flavouring while the tender portion forms the focal point of a dish. For basting food that is grilled (broiled) or cooked on a barbecue, the upper portion of the lemon grass stalk can be used. The fibrous end is flattened with a cleaver or pestle to make a brush.

Storage

Store lemon grass stalks in a paper bag in the salad compartment of the refrigerator. They will keep for 2–3 weeks.

Making a lemon grass brush
Instead of discarding the dry stalk, make it into a basting brush.

Trim off the bottom 5cm/2in of the lemon grass stalk to use in a recipe, then flatten the cut end of the remaining stalk using a cleaver or pestle to produce a fibrous brush.

KAFFIR LIMES

THAI: *BAI MAKRUT;* INDONESIAN: *DAUN JERAK;* VIETNAMESE: *CHANH SAC;* MALAYSIAN: *LIMAU PURUT;* MYANMAR: *SHAUK-NU*

These fruit are not true limes, but belong to a subspecies of the citrus family. Native to South-east Asia, they have dark green knobbly skins, quite unlike those of their cousins, the smooth-skinned limes or lemons. The fruit is not edible. The rind is sometimes used in cooking, but it is the leaves that are most highly prized. Kaffir limes yield very little juice, and what there is is very sour. Thai and Malaysian cooks occasionally use it to heighten the flavour of dishes with a citrus base. Vietnamese women use the juice as a hair rinse.

Japanese citron peel

In Japan, very thin slices of citron peel *(yuzu)* are used to garnish soups. The ground peel is used to flavour miso.

Aroma and flavour

The scented bouquet is unmistakably citrus, and the full lemon flavour is released when the leaves are torn or shredded.

Culinary uses

Kaffir lime leaves are synonymous with Thai cooking, and are also used in Indonesia, Malaysia, Myanmar and Vietnam. The leaves are torn or finely shredded and used in soups (especially hot and sour soups) and curries. The finely grated rind can be added to fish or chicken.

Storage

Fresh kaffir limes and leaves are obtainable in Asian stores. They will keep for several days, or can be frozen. Freeze-dried kaffir lime leaves are also available. These are used in much the same way as bay leaves, and do not need to be soaked in water first. Stored in a sealed container in a cool, dry place, the dried leaves will keep their flavour for only a few months.

ORANGE OR TANGERINE PEEL

MANDARIN: *CHEN PI;* CANTONESE: *CHAN PEI*

Both oranges and tangerines originated in China, where they were held in high regard for centuries before traders introduced them to the West. The sun-dried peel of both these citrus fruits is used as a spice, particularly in the cooking of Sichuan and Hunan.

Left: Dried orange peel

Above: Kaffir limes and kaffir lime leaves

Aroma and flavour

The dried peel is dark brown and brittle, but retains a strong citrus fragrance. When it is used in cooking, it imparts a tangy flavour to the food.

Culinary uses

Originally, dried citrus peels were mainly used medicinally. Today, they are a popular seasoning and are often combined with star anise and cinnamon when braising meat or poultry.

Preparation and cooking techniques

In braised dishes, pieces of dried peel are used in much the same way as star anise, and are discarded after cooking. When peel is used in a stir-fry, however, it is first soaked in water until soft, and the pith is scraped off before the peel is shredded or sliced.

Storage

Orange and tangerine peel are sold in plastic bags in oriental stores. Once opened, the bags should be resealed and kept in a cool, dry, dark place. The peel will keep for many months.

Left: Dried curry leaves

CURRY LEAVES

INDONESIAN: *DAUN KARI*; THAI: *BAI KAREE*; MYANMAR: *PINDOSIN*

These are the shiny green leaves of a hardwood tree that is indigenous to India. They are widely used in Indian cooking, especially in South India and Sri Lanka, and were introduced into Malaysia by Tamil immigrants. The spear-shaped leaves grow on a thin stem. They are slightly serrated, with a pale underside, and are not unlike small bay leaves.

Aroma and flavour

Curry leaves have an intriguing warm fragrance, with just a hint of sweet, green (bell) pepper or tangerine. The full flavour is released when the leaves are bruised. When added to curries or braised dishes, they impart a distinctive flavour. Dried curry leaves come a very poor second to fresh, and rapidly lose their fragrance.

Culinary uses

The leaves are used whole or torn in Indian, Malay and Indonesian curries. Fried in ghee, with mustard seeds, they make a good addition to dhals.

Preparation and cooking techniques

Rinse the leaves and then strip from the stems. Use the leaves whole or chopped as directed in recipes.

Storage

Fresh curry leaves can be bought from shops selling Indian and Gujerati produce. They will keep for several days in the refrigerator, but should be closely wrapped to prevent their distinctive flavour from being transferred to other items. Alternatively – and this is more convenient – open freeze the leaves, then transfer them to a plastic box. Dried leaves do not have much taste, unless you can locate the vacuum-packed variety, which have better colour and flavour.

MINT

CHINESE: *PAK HOM HO*; INDONESIAN: *DAUN PUDINA*; THAI: *BAI SARANAI*; VIETNAMESE: *HUNG QUE*

Mint originated in the Mediterranean region, but it spread rapidly throughout the world. There are many types grown in Asia, but the most commonly used is a tropical variety of spearmint, which has grey-green oval leaves.

Aroma and flavour

Mint has a fresh, stimulating aroma. The Asian variety is much more strongly flavoured than most European types, and is slightly sweet tasting, imparting a cool aftertaste.

Culinary uses

Mint is an essential ingredient in Vietnamese cooking, and it was they who introduced it to the Thais. Its fresh flavour is enjoyed in many salads, and in the delicious rice paper rolls that go by the name of *goi cuon*. Thai cooks like to add a handful of mint leaves just before serving some of their soups and highly spiced dishes. As it has such a dominant flavour, mint is seldom used with other herbs.

Preparation

Wash the leaves on the stem under cold water, shake off the excess moisture and pat dry using kitchen paper.

Storage

Wrap loosely in kitchen paper and keep in the salad compartment of the refrigerator, or stand the stems in a jug (pitcher) of cold water covered with a plastic bag in the refrigerator.

Below: Mint

BASIL

THAI: *BAI HORAPA* (SWEET BASIL), *BAI KRAPOW* (HOLY BASIL), *BAI MANGLAK* (HAIRY OR LEMON-SCENTED BASIL); INDONESIAN: *INDRING;* JAPANESE: *MEBOKI*

Basil is one of the oldest herbs known to man. It is an annual and is believed to have originated in India. Hindus hold it sacred and often plant it around their holy places.
In India, however, it is not used in cooking as much as it is in the rest of Asia. In Vietnam, Laos and Cambodia it is an important ingredient, but it is in Thailand that basil is most widely used, and it is the varieties of basil favoured by the Thais that you will find most frequently in Asian shops in the West. *Horapa* (sweet basil) comes closest to the Mediterranean varieties with which we are most familiar. It has shiny green leaves and the stems are sometimes purple. *Krapow,* commonly known as holy basil, is another sweet basil, but with narrower leaves that tend to be dull rather than shiny. The leaves have serrated red or purple edges. Thais also use a lemon-scented basil – sometimes called hairy basil – but this does not travel well and is seldom seen outside Thailand. If you cannot obtain Asian basil when cooking an Asian dish, any European variety can be used instead, but the flavour will not be the same, and you should use a little more than the amount recommended. Basil is best used fresh, but freeze-dried leaves are also available from larger supermarkets.

Aroma and flavour

Of the Asian basils, *horapa* has a faint aniseed flavour, while holy basil is more pungent. Hairy basil has a lemon scent and is slightly peppery.

Above: Sweet basil

Below: Thai basil

Culinary uses

Sweet basil leaves are added to curries or salads both as an ingredient and also as a garnish. They impart a fresh spicy flavour. Holy basil leaves only release their full flavour when cooked and are therefore frequently used in stir-fries.

Preparation

Strip the leaves from the stem and either tear them into pieces or add them whole to the other ingredients. Avoid chopping basil leaves.

Storage

Wrap bunches of basil loosely in kitchen paper and keep them in the salad compartment of the refrigerator. Alternatively, stand the stems in a jug (pitcher) of water covered with a plastic bag. Keep in the refrigerator and change the water daily.

Growing basil

If you have difficulty locating supplies of fresh basil for Thai or Vietnamese recipes, it might be worth growing your own from seed. Many garden centres and hardware stores sell the full range of Asian varieties, and they do well wherever the climate is relatively mild. Start them off in pots on a warm window sill, and move them to a sunny patio after the threat of frost has passed.

SHISO

JAPANESE: *SHISO* (GREEN), *AKA SHISO* (RED); KOREAN: *KKAENNIP*

Also known as *perilla* or the beefsteak plant, this annual herb is grown in China, Korea, Laos and Vietnam and is very well known in Japan, where it is also called *oba.* The leaves can be green or reddish-purple. When crushed, they release a pungent aroma, similar to that of mint. Japanese cooks use shiso in tempura and when making *umeboshi* (pickled plums). In the presence of an acid, the red-leafed variety dyes ginger red.

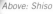

Above: Shiso

CORIANDER/CILANTRO

MANDARIN: *XIANGCAI*; CANTONESE: *YUAN SUI*;
MYANMAR: *NAN NAN BIN*; THAI: *PAK CHEE*

Also known as Chinese parsley – and
familiar to Americans as cilantro –
coriander is one of the oldest known
herbs in the world, and also one of
the most popular. Although a native
of southern Europe, fresh coriander
has become an indispensable
ingredient throughout Asia and
the Middle East, as well as
in Latin America.

Aroma and flavour

Coriander takes its name from
the Greek *koris,* meaning a bug. The
leaves of the plant are supposed to give
off a smell similar to that of a room
infested with bed bugs, yet the Chinese,
displaying a wicked sense of humour,
call coriander "fragrant leaves". When
dry-fried, the seeds smell rather like
burnt orange, while the ground seeds
impart a warm, spicy aroma to food.

Culinary uses

Asian cooks use every part of the plant:
the stems are used for flavouring; the
leaves in stir-fries, soups and noodle
dishes; and as a garnish, the seeds for

Above: Coriander –
Asian cooks use the
roots as well as the leaves
and stems.

Below: Ground coriander

spice pastes and
in curries. Ground
coriander is widely used, often in
combination with ground cumin.
In Thailand, the roots are
used, too. This can
present problems for
the Western cook,
because the thin roots
are usually removed
before the coriander
reaches the market.
One answer is to grow
your own, but if this is
impractical, use the bottom
portion of the stem as
a substitute.

Preparation and cooking techniques

Try not to chop fresh
coriander too finely,
or the beauty of the
serrated leaves will be
lost. Never overcook
the leaves or they will
become limp and
unpalatable; either
use them raw as a
garnish, or add them
to a dish at the
very last moment.
If a recipe
calls for ground
coriander, it is

Left: Coriander seeds

preferable to dry-fry and grind the
seeds yourself, as the aroma and
flavour will be more pronounced than
when ready-ground coriander is used.

Storage

Fresh coriander will not keep for more
than a couple of days unless stood in a
jug (pitcher) of cold water and covered
with a plastic bag, in which case it will
stay fresh for a little longer. Coriander
roots are seldom available, but if you do
locate a supply, the cleaned roots can
be frozen.

Dried coriander seeds keep well,
but the ready-ground powder rapidly
loses its aroma and flavour. Buy small
quantities so that you can replenish
your supplies regularly.

*Right:
Ground
and fresh
turmeric*

Preparation and cooking methods

Using a sharp knife, slice off the skin, then slice, grate or chop the flesh. It can be ground with other ingredients to make a curry paste. Some people like to wear gloves when preparing fresh turmeric as it can stain the skin. Ground dried turmeric is easy to use as it needs no preparation.

Storage

Fresh turmeric will keep for up to 2 weeks, if stored in a cool, dry place away from strong light. It can be stored in the refrigerator, but must be well wrapped to keep it moist. Like all ground spices, ground turmeric will lose its potency on keeping, so buy only small quantities and keep the powder in an airtight container in a cupboard away from strong light. The only time whole pieces of dried turmeric are likely to be called for is in the preparation of some pickles. Do not attempt to grind the whole dried spice to make powder; the rhizomes are too hard.

TURMERIC

Myanmar: *hsanwen*; Mandarin: *wong geung*; Cantonese: *yu chin*;
Japanese: *ukon*

Turmeric comes from the ginger family but does not have the characteristic "heat" associated with fresh root ginger. The plant, a rhizome, is indigenous to hot, humid, hilly areas of South-east Asia from Vietnam to Southern India. Frequently referred to as "Indian saffron", it shares with saffron the capacity to tint foods yellow, but is nowhere near as subtle as the much more expensive spice. The bright yellow colour, which can clearly be seen when the rhizome is sliced, is also used as a dye of silks and cottons, including the fabric used to make robes for Buddhist monks. When mixed to a paste, turmeric is sometimes smeared on the cheeks to protect the skin from the sun. The world's largest producer of turmeric is India, but Indonesia and China also grow significant quantities of this spice.

The bulk of the turmeric crop is used for domestic consumption or ground and sold as powder.

Aroma and flavour

Fresh turmeric is sometimes available from oriental stores. When cut it has a peppery aroma with a hint of wood in the background. It imparts a warm, slightly musky flavour and a rich colour to any food with which it is cooked. The dried spice has similar properties.

Culinary uses

Ground turmeric is an essential ingredient in curry powders, being responsible for the characteristic yellow colour. It is also used in the preparation of some blends of mustard powder and is the spice that gives piccalilli its lurid colour. That famous Anglo-Indian breakfast dish – kedgeree – contains turmeric, and it is also used in pilau rice, dhals and vegetable dishes. Turmeric has a natural affinity with fish, and is often used in Malayan recipes.

Preparing fresh turmeric

1 Using a sharp knife, scrape off the skin.

2 Grate the flesh using a standard box grater, or slice or chop, depending on the recipe.

*Above: Star-shaped
star anise*

CLOVES

MANDARIN: *TING HSIANG*; CANTONESE;
DING HEUNG; JAPANESE: *CHOJI*;
THAI: *KAAN PLOO*

Cloves are the unopened flower buds of a tree which is a member of the myrtle family. They originated in the Spice Islands in Indonesia and were taken to the Seychelles and Mauritius early in the 18th century. The biggest producer now is Zanzibar where the fresh pink buds are picked twice a year. They are then dried on palm leaf mats or over gentle heat when they turn the familiar reddish brown. The name clove is derived from the Latin *clavus*, meaning a nail.

Aroma and flavour

Cloves have an intense fragrance and an aromatic flavour that can be fiery. They are slightly astringent.

Culinary uses

In Asia, cloves are mainly used in savoury dishes, and their warm aromatic flavour complements rich meats. Thai cooks use cloves to cut the rich flavour of duck, and also use them with tomatoes, salty vegetables and in ham or pork dishes. Ground cloves are an essential ingredient in many spice mixtures, including the famous Chinese five-spice powder. They are also one of the ingredients in Worcestershire sauce.

Preparation

Cloves need no preparation. When purchasing, look for plump cloves.

Storage

Whole cloves have a long shelf life if kept in a cool place. Ground cloves should be bought in small quantities and stored in an airtight jar away from strong light, so that the spice retains its colour and flavour. To make a small amount of ground cloves, crush the central bud at the top of the clove and use immediately.

STAR ANISE

MANDARIN: *PAK KOK*; CANTONESE: *BOAT GOK*;
INDONESIAN: *BUNGA LAWANG*; THAI: *POY
KAK BUA*

Star anise is the unusual star-shaped fruit of an evergreen tree native to south-west China and Vietnam. The tree has yellow flowers that resemble narcissus. These give way to the star-like fruits, which are harvested before they ripen. The points of the star contain amber seeds. Both the seeds and the husk are used for the ground spice. In China, one point, the name given to one section of the star, is often chewed after a meal as a digestive.

Aroma and flavour

Star anise both smells and tastes like liquorice. The flavour can also be detected in the alcoholic drinks pastis and anisette.

Culinary uses

The aromatic flavour of star anise complements rich meats. Star anise is very popular in Chinese cuisine, especially with pork and duck, and it is used to flavour beef soups in Vietnam. It is also sometimes used in sweet dishes, such as fruit salads. Ground star anise is one of the main ingredients of five-spice powder.

Preparation and cooking methods

Star anise can be added whole, and looks so attractive that it is often left in a dish when serving, even though it no longer fulfils any culinary function. When a small quantity is required, the spice can be broken and just one or two points or segments added. It is possible to grind star anise at home, but it should be used sparingly as it has a quite powerful flavour.

Storage

As a whole spice star anise has a long shelf life. Buy the ground spice in small quantities from a shop with a high turnover of stock, and store in a cool, dry place, away from direct light, to retain the maximum aroma and flavour.

*Below: The best cloves are plump
and unbroken.*

Above: Cinnamon sticks and
ground cinnamon

CINNAMON

INDONESIAN: *KAYU MANIS PADANG;*
THAI: *OB CHUEY*

The best quality cinnamon is grown
in Sri Lanka but it also flourishes
elsewhere in Asia, particularly on
the coastal strip of South India and
Myanmar. The spice is actually the bark
of a bushy tree that is a member of
the laurel family. After three years, the
branches are cut off and a long incision
is made in the bark, so that this can be
lifted off. The operation is carried out
during the rainy season, when the
humidity speeds the peeling process.
The bark is then dried in the sun and
hand rolled to produce the familiar
quills or sticks. Ground cinnamon is
also produced.

Aroma and flavour

Cinnamon has a delightfully exotic
bouquet, sweet and fragrant, thanks to
an essential oil, oil of cinnamon, which
is used medicinally. The flavour is warm
and aromatic.

Culinary uses

Cinnamon has universal appeal as a
flavouring both in sweet and savoury
dishes and in a multitude of cakes and
breads. In Asia, the sticks are used in
spicy meat dishes, often with star anise,
with which cinnamon has an affinity.
Indonesian cooks use cinnamon in
their famous spiced beef and coconut
milk stew known as rendang.

Preparation

Add the whole or broken cinnamon
stick as directed in the recipe. The
sticks are very hard and it is difficult to
grind them at home, so it is preferable
to buy ready-ground cinnamon.

Storage

Cinnamon sticks have a long shelf life,
and will keep for a year or more in an
airtight container. Buy ground cinnamon
in small quantities from a shop with a
high turnover of stock and store it in an
airtight container away from both heat
and strong light.

Below: Ground cassia and cassia bark

CASSIA

CHINESE: *KUEI;* JAPANESE: *KEIHI;*
THAI: *OB CHOEY*

Cassia is sometimes known
as Chinese cinnamon. Like
cinnamon, it comes from
the bark of a tree which is
related to laurel, but whereas
cinnamon is native to Sri Lanka,
cassia comes from Myanmar, and
is also cultivated in China, Indo-China
and Indonesia. It is harvested in much
the same way as cinnamon, but the
bark is not as fine, so although it curls,
it will not form the fine quills we
associate with cinnamon.

Aroma and flavour

Cassia smells rather like cinnamon,
but is more pungent.

Culinary uses

Chinese cooks make much use of
cassia. It is one of the constituents of
Chinese five-spice powder and is also
an important ingredient in the elaborate
spiced stock known as *lu* which is used
throughout China for simmering foods.
When this stock is first made, it is very
strongly flavoured, and is generally used
for cooking beef, pot-roast style. The
stock is not served with the beef, but is
saved to be used again, perhaps with
poultry. It may well be boiled up
a third time, to simmer

fish or shellfish. In some homes, a pan of *lu* will be kept going for months. Cracked cassia quills and cassia buds, which look like cloves, are used in the East to give a warm aromatic flavour to pickles, curries and spiced meat dishes.

Preparation and cooking methods

Cassia is quite tough. Break the pieces as required with the end of a rolling pin or put them in a mortar and use a stout pestle to shatter them. Where ground cassia is required, it is best to buy it in that form.

Storage

As for cinnamon.

CUMIN

CHINESE: *KUMING;* JAPANESE: *KUMIN;* THAI: *YEERAA*

Cumin has been cultivated since earliest times. It is believed to have originated in the Eastern Mediterranean, but is now widely cultivated, especially in China, India, Indonesia and Japan. The plant is a member of the parsley family, but only the seeds (whole or ground) are used in cooking.

Above: Small green and large black cardamom pods

Aroma and flavour

Cumin has a sweet spicy aroma and the flavour is pungent and slightly bitter.

Culinary uses

Cumin is often partnered with whole or ground coriander seeds. Indian cooks are particularly partial to cumin, and it was they who introduced the spice to Singapore, Malaysia and Indonesia.

Preparation

To bring out their full flavour, the seeds are often dry-fried. They are then used whole or ground in a spice mill or in a mortar using a pestle.

Storage

Buy the whole spice in small quantities. Store in a cool place away from bright light. For best results dry-fry and grind the whole spice as

Above: Cumin seeds and ground cumin

and when required. You can buy ready ground cumin from supermarkets, but it loses its flavour rapidly.

CARDAMOM

MYANMAR: *PHALAZEE;* JAPANESE: *KARUDAMON;* THAI: *LUK KRAVAN*

A native of South India, cardamom is a tall herbaceous perennial belonging to the ginger family. It is largely grown for its pods, although Thai cooks sometimes use the leaves for flavouring. The pods are either added whole to spicy dishes, or opened so that the tiny dark seeds can be extracted. The most familiar pods are pale green, and there are also white pods, which are simply bleached green ones. Black cardamoms, which come from Vietnam and India, are large and coarse, and taste quite different. Cardamom pods are harvested by hand, and this makes them more costly than most other spices.

Aroma and flavour

Cardamoms are sweet, pungent and highly aromatic. They have a pleasantly warm flavour, with hints of lemon and eucalyptus. When chewed after a meal, the pods are said to aid digestion as well as sweeten the breath.

Culinary uses

Indian cooks use cardamom to flavour curries, pilaus and desserts, so it is not surprising that the spice is popular wherever there are Indian communities.

Preparation

The pods can be used whole or bruised and dry-fried to enhance the flavour. If just the seeds are required, discard the outer husks. For ground cardamom, grind the seeds in a mortar using a pestle.

Storage

Buy the whole pods and store in an airtight jar in a cool dry place. Grind seeds as required.

FENNEL SEEDS

MANDARIN: *WOOI HEUNG;* CANTONESE: *HUI XIANG;* THAI: *YIRA*

Although native to the Mediterranean, this member of the parsley family is widely grown in India and Japan. The ridged seeds are sage green in colour.

Aroma and flavour

Sweet, warm and aromatic, fennel seeds have a distinct anise flavour.

Culinary uses

Fennel seeds are a constituent in many spice mixtures, especially those that are intended to be used with fish or shellfish. Ground fennel is one of the constituents of Chinese five-spice powder.

Preparation

Dry-fry before grinding to release the full flavour of the spice.

Storage

Buy small quantities of seeds at a time and store in an airtight jar away from strong light.

Above: Fennel seeds

Chinese five spice powder

Close your eyes as you enter a Chinese supermarket or store and the distinctive aroma of Chinese five-spice power seems to dominate. This reddish brown spice mixture is classically composed of equal quantities of Sichuan peppercorns, cassia or cinnamon, cloves, fennel seeds and star anise. Blends vary, however, and ginger, galangal, black cardamom and liquorice can be included. Ginger gives the spice blend a sweeter flavour, and this version is used in desserts. Five-spice powder is very popular in China, and is particularly complementary when used with duck, pork, red cooked meats (cooked in soy sauce) and barbecued meats such as spare ribs. Make your own powder by grinding equal amounts of the five spices with a mortar and pestle, or buy the ready-ground powder in small amounts and store in an airtight jar away from strong light. A five spice paste is now available in small jars from many of the larger supermarkets.

Japanese seven-spice powder

Seven-spice powder, which is also known as *shichimi-togarashi,* seven-flavour seasoning or seven-taste powder, is a delicious condiment that the Japanese like to shake on to food at the table much as we would use salt and pepper. It is especially popular as a seasoning for soups and noodles and other dishes such as sukiyaki and tempura. *Shichimi* is made from a combination of the following ingredients: ground chilli, hemp seed, poppy seed, rape seed, *sansho* (the Japanese name for Sichuan pepper-corns), black and

Right: Chinese five-spice powder (top) and Japanese seven-spice powder (bottom) can be bought ready-ground from supermarkets and Asian stores.

white sesame seeds, and dried ground tangerine peel. In some mixes ground nori (seaweed) is added. It would be usual to buy this mixture ready prepared. Blends of this spice mixture vary, from mild to very sharp.

PEPPER

MANDARIN: *HU-CHIAO;* CANTONESE: *WOO JIU;*
INDONESIAN: *MERICA;* THAI: *PRIK THAI;*
VIETNAMESE: *HAT-TRIEU*

Often referred to as the king of spices, pepper has an ancient and illustrious past. Known and valued in India for over 2,000 years, it was introduced into Europe in the 4th century BC. Demand rapidly grew, but transporting the spice across Asia by the caravan routes was costly, and the monopoly meant that the prices remained astronomically high. Even in Roman times there was outrage that the spices were sold at one hundred times their original cost.

It was the demand for pepper that inspired the search for sailing routes to the East which changed the course of history. When the Portuguese explorer Vasco da Gama opened up the sea route to India in the 15th century, Lisbon became the spice capital of the world, but still the prices stayed high. Even today pepper is the most important spice on world markets, both in terms of value and volume.

Pepper is a perennial climbing vine indigenous to the Malabar coast of India where it is said that the best pepper is still produced. It grows best near the equator and is cultivated intensively in Sarawak and Thailand, as well as in tropical Africa and Brazil. In the Malayan state of Sarawak the vines are trained up long ironwood frames or round tree trunks. The vines have to be controlled

Green peppercorns

These are simply unripe berries. They are sold on the stem in some Thai supermarkets, and are a popular ingredient in that country. They can be used fresh, but are also dried, pickled or canned. Those that are bottled or canned need to be rinsed and drained, then added whole or crushed as the recipe dictates. Freeze-dried green peppercorns can be ground in a peppermill. Green peppercorns have a less complex flavour than white or black peppercorns but are still quite fiery.

Above: Fresh green peppercorns are sometimes sold on the stem in Thai supermarkets.

to prevent them from climbing too high, which would make harvesting difficult. The leaves are long, green and pointed, and white flowers blossom on the catkins or "spikes".

The plant starts fruiting three to five years after planting, and the harvest continues every three years thereafter for forty years, which is the life of the plant. When the berries are harvested they are still unripe and green. In Sarawak they are dried on mats in the sun, and are raked frequently until the skin shrivels and the berries darken to become the familiar black peppercorns. Another method is to immerse the berries in boiling water, drain them well, and then dry them in kilns. White peppercorns are husked ripe berries. The berries are picked when they are red or orange. They are soaked in running water for several days, and then they are trampled underfoot to loosen the husks. Finally the

pepper berries are transferred to rattan baskets, where they are washed and the husks and stalks removed by hand to leave the white peppercorns. These are then left to dry on mats in the sun for several weeks, or kiln-dried.

Aroma and flavour

Black peppercorns have an earthy aroma, which is particularly noticeable when they are crushed. The flavour is hot and pungent. White peppercorns are slightly milder.

Culinary uses

Pepper is the one spice which is used before, during and after cooking. Its value as a seasoning is legendary, for it not only has its own flavour, but has the ability to enhance the flavour of other ingredients in a dish.

Preparation

Use a peppermill and grind fresh black pepper as it is required. White peppercorns are less pungent and are used where flecks of black might spoil the appearance of a dish, such as a light-coloured sauce.

Storage

Buy whole peppercorns. Store in a cool place in an airtight container. They keep for a long time.

*Right:
Black and
white peppercorns*

SICHUAN PEPPER

MANDARIN: *FAA JIU*; CANTONESE: *HU CHIAO*;
JAPANESE: *SANSHO*

To call this "pepper" is misleading. This spice actually comes from the prickly ash tree, which is native to the Sichuan province in China, but also grows elsewhere in Asia. Unusually, it is the seed pods themselves, not the seeds they contain, that are used for the spice. The tiny reddish brown pods or husks are harvested when ripe, the bitter black seeds are removed and discarded, and the pods – Sichuan peppercorns – are either added whole to stewed dishes or dried and ground as a seasoning spice.

The prickly ash also grows in Japan, where the ripened pods are called *mizansho* or Japanese peppercorns. When ground, the spice is known as *konazansho* or *sansho*. The wood of the prickly ash is sometimes used to make mortar and pestle sets, which are much sought after by Japanese cooks who claim they impart a subtle flavour when used to grind ingredients.

Aroma and flavour

Not as pungent as true pepper, Sichuan peppercorns have a warm aroma with a hint of citrus. The full flavour is released when they are dry-fried.

Culinary uses

Sichuan peppercorns are immensely popular in Chinese cuisine. They are excellent in duck, pork and chicken dishes. The ground peppercorns are used in both Chinese five-spice powder and Japanese seven-spice powder.

Left: Sichuan peppercorns

Preparation

The dried seed pods should be picked over carefully to remove any debris. Dry-fry the seed pods to heighten their flavour, then use as directed in recipes.

Storage

Although it is possible to buy ground Sichuan pepper, it is better to buy the peppercorns whole and grind them after dry-frying. Keep them in an airtight jar.

Wasabi

Sometimes described as horseradish mustard, this has much in common with both, although it is related to neither. Wasabi is a Japanese seasoning, derived from a slow-growing plant that is found near mountain streams. The peeled root reveals vivid green flesh. This is very finely grated, preferably on sharkskin, and then dried or powdered. When mixed to a cream with soy sauce or water, it makes an extremely hot condiment, which is traditionally served with sushi and sashimi.

Above: A tube of ready-made apple-green wasabi paste

Right: Wasabi powder is mixed to a paste with a little water or soy sauce.

MUSTARD

MALAY: *BIJI SAVI*

Mustard is one of the oldest spices known to man and has been cultivated as a crop for thousands of years. Both white *(alba)* and black *(nigra)* mustard seeds are indigenous to the Mediterranean region, while brown mustard seeds *(juncea)* are native to India. The word mustard

Below: Brown, black and white mustard seeds

Dry-frying mustard seeds

Mustard seeds have almost no smell until they are heated, so before adding them to dishes, they should be dry-fried to heighten their aroma.

1 Heat a little sunflower oil in a deep, wide pan. Add the seeds and shake the pan over the heat, stirring occasionally, until they start to change colour.

2 Have a pan lid ready to prevent the mustard seeds from popping out of the pan.

comes from the Latin *mustum* or *must*, the newly pressed grape juice that Romans mixed with the ground seeds to make what was aptly described as *mustum ardens* (the burning paste).

In Asia, the mustard plant is valued as much for its dark green leaves, which are called mustard greens and are a popular vegetable, as for its seeds. Mustard powders and pastes are not as widely used as they are in Europe or America.

Aroma and flavour

Mustard seeds have no aroma in their raw state. When they are roasted, however, they develop a rich, nutty small. Mustard's famous hot taste comes from an enzyme in the seeds, which is only activated when they are crushed and mixed with warm water. Brown mustard seeds, which have largely replaced the black seeds, are not as intensely pungent. White mustard seeds, which are actually a pale honey colour, are slightly larger than the other two varieties and a little milder.

Culinary uses

Throughout Asia, mustard seeds are used for pickling and seasoning. The whole seeds are often used in vegetable and dhal dishes, especially in countries such as Malaysia.

Preparation and cooking techniques

Mustard seeds are frequently roasted or fried before being used to bring out their flavour. A southern Indian technique involves spooning the seeds into hot ghee or oil, with a few curry leaves for extra flavour. A lid is placed over the pan to contain the seeds, which soon begin to splutter and pop. The seeds and oil are then poured, still sizzling, on to hot vegetable dishes, soups, stews or dhal as a flavoursome topping. Mustard oil is occasionally used for frying the seeds.

Mustard powder is used as a condiment. When it is mixed with warm water, milk or beer, a chemical reaction begins which allows the mustard to achieve its maximum potency. It takes about 15 minutes for the full flavour to develop. Boiling water or vinegar would inhibit the action of the enzyme responsible for the process, so should not be used.

Storage

Mustard seeds keep well. Store them in an airtight jar in a cool place.

Left: Tamarind block

may suggest using vinegar or lemon juice instead, but the results will not compare with using the real thing.

Preparation

Compressed tamarind This comes in a solid block and looks rather like a packet of dried dates. To prepare it, tear off a piece that is roughly equivalent to 15ml/1 tbsp and soak it in 150ml/¼ pint/⅔ cup warm water for about 10 minutes. Swirl the tamarind around with your fingers so that the pulp is released from the seeds. Using a nylon sieve (strainer), strain the juice into a bowl. Discard the contents of the sieve

TAMARIND

CHINESE: *ASAM KOH;* INDONESIAN: *ASAM JAVA;* THAI: *MAK KHAM;* MYANMAR: *MA-GYI-THI*

The handsome tamarind tree, commonly called the "date of India", is believed to be a native of East Africa but is now cultivated in India, Southeast Asia and the West Indies. The brown fruit pods are 15–20cm/6–8in long. Inside, the seeds are surrounded by a sticky brown pulp. This does not look very prepossessing, but is one of the treasures of the East. It has a high tartaric acid content, and is widely used as a souring agent.

dried tamarind have been around for a while, but it is now also possible to buy jars of fresh tamarind and cartons of tamarind concentrate and paste. There is no substitute for tamarind. Some recipes

Aroma and flavour

Tamarind doesn't have much of an aroma, but the flavour is wonderful. It is tart and sour without being bitter, and fruity and refreshing.

Culinary uses

Tamarind is used in many curries, chutneys and dhals, and is an essential ingredient of Thai hot and sour soups. It is also one of the ingredients in Worcestershire sauce. Tamarind is available in a variety of forms. Blocks of compressed tamarind and slices of

Above, from top: Tamarind paste, tamarind pods and dried tamarind slices

Stir-fried prawns with tamarind

Tamarind is used in many Thai dishes to give them a characteristic sour, tangy flavour. Fresh tamarind pods from the tamarind tree can sometimes be bought, but preparing them for cooking is a laborious process. The Thais usually prefer to use compressed blocks of tamarind paste, which is simply soaked in warm water and then strained.

SERVES 4–6

50g/2oz compressed tamarind
150ml/¼ pint/⅔ cup boiling water
30ml/2 tbsp vegetable oil
30ml/2 tbsp chopped onion
30ml/2 tbsp palm sugar (jaggery)
30ml/2 tbsp chicken stock
15ml/1 tbsp Thai fish sauce
6 dried red chillies, fried
450g/1lb raw shelled
  prawns (shrimp)
15ml/1 tbsp fried chopped garlic
30ml/2 tbsp fried sliced shallots
chopped and shredded spring
  onions (scallions), to garnish

1 Put the tamarind in a bowl, pour over the boiling water and stir well to break up any lumps. Leave for 10 minutes. Meanwhile, heat the oil in a wok. Add the chopped onion and stir-fry until golden brown.

2 Strain the tamarind juice, pushing as much of the juice through as possible. Measure 90ml/6 tbsp of the juice. Add to the wok along with the sugar, chicken stock, fish sauce and dried chillies. Stir well until the sugar dissolves.

3 Bring to the boil over medium-high heat, then add the prawns, garlic and shallots, and stir-fry about 3–4 minutes, or until the prawns are only just cooked. Sprinkle over the spring onions and serve immediately.

and use the liquid as required. Any leftover liquid can be stored in the refrigerator and used for another recipe. **Tamarind slices** These look a little like dried apple slices. Place them in a small bowl, then pour over enough warm water to cover and leave to soak

for about 30 minutes to extract the flavour, squeeze the tamarind slices with your fingers, then strain the juice. **Tamarind concentrate or paste** Mix 15ml/1 tbsp with 60–90ml/4–6 tbsp warm water. Stir until dissolved, then use as required.

Storage

Compressed tamarind and tamarind slices will keep perfectly well in a cool dry place. Jars labelled fresh tamarind, or tamarind concentrate or paste must be kept in the refrigerator once opened, and used within one or two months.

CURRY POWDERS AND PASTES

CURRY POWDERS

The word curry evolved from the Tamil word *kari,* meaning any food cooked in a sauce. There is little doubt that curry powder, a ready-made blend of spices, was an early convenience food, prepared for merchants, sailors and military men who had served in the East and wished to bring these exotic flavours home. In India, the spices would have been prepared in the kitchen on a daily basis.

Over the decades and centuries these spice and curry mixtures have changed and developed, as have our tastes, so that today our supermarket shelves carry a wealth of different spice mixtures from all parts of the globe.

For enthusiastic cooks it is fun and a creative challenge to make up your own curry powder. Keep experimenting until you find the balance of spicing which suits you and your family. Of course, it is perfectly possible to mix ground spices, but it is more satisfying (and more satisfactory in terms of flavour) to start with whole spices where possible.

Left: Curry powder

Right: Curry spices

Dry-frying

Many whole spices benefit from being dry-fried before they are ground. This not only makes sure that no surface moisture remains, but also heightens and develops the flavour. Use a heavy pan, shaking it constantly so the spices do not scorch. Purists dry-fry spices separately, but they can be heated together as long as you watch them closely. All spices react differently to heat, so here are some guidelines:

Coriander seeds often provide the dominant flavour, especially in powders from Southern India and Singapore.

Shake the pan to keep the seeds on the move, and remove them from the heat when they give off a mild, sweet, orangey perfume.

Dried chillies can be roasted in a cool oven, but it is better to sear them in a heavy pan, where you can keep an eye on them. Place the pan over medium heat for 2–3 minutes, until the chillies soften and puff up. Do not let them burn, or the flavour will be ruined.

Cumin seeds should be dry-fried in a pan, and will be ready for grinding when the seeds have a nutty smell.

Black peppercorns need gentle dry-frying, just to heighten the flavour.

Fenugreek needs to be watched carefully as it will become bitter if it is dry-fried for too long. It is ready when it turns brownish yellow.

Curry leaves can be dry-fried over low to medium heat when fresh. Grind or pound them, using a mortar and pestle, to release their characteristic flavour, then mix them with the other spices. This works well if you are making a curry powder or paste that is to be used immediately, but if it is to be kept, make up the powder, then add the whole fresh or frozen leaves just before you are ready to use it. Remove the leaves before serving the curry. Avoid using dried curry leaves if possible, as they will have lost most of their flavour.

Simple curry powder

This Malayan Chinese spice mixture is good for poultry, especially chicken, and robust fish curries.

MAKES ABOUT 60ML/4 TBSP

2 dried red chillies
6 whole cloves
1 small cinnamon stick
5ml/1 tsp coriander seeds
5ml/1 tsp fennel seeds
10ml/2 tsp Sichuan peppercorns
2.5ml/$\frac{1}{2}$ tsp grated nutmeg
5ml/1 tsp ground star anise
5ml/1 tsp ground turmeric

COOK'S TIPS

• If you prefer a very hot and punchy spice mixture, then add some or all of the chilli seeds and dry-fry with the other spices.
• Ensure that you wash your hands, and the chopping board and other utensils very thoroughly after preparing chillies.
• If your skin is particularly sensitive, then you should wear rubber gloves while you are preparing the chillies.

1 Remove the seeds from the dried chillies using the point of a knife, and discard any stems.

2 Put the chillies, cloves, cinnamon, coriander, fennel seeds and Sichuan peppercorns in a heavy frying pan. Dry-fry the spices, tossing them frequently until they give off a rich, spicy aroma.

3 Grind the spices to a smooth powder in a mortar, using a pestle. Alternatively, use a spice grinder, or an electric coffee grinder that is reserved for blending spices.

4 Add the grated nutmeg, star anise and turmeric. Use at once or store in an airtight jar away from strong light.

CURRY PASTES

On market stalls throughout Southeast Asia are mounds of pounded wet spices: lemon grass, chilli, ginger, garlic, galangal, shallots and tamarind. After purchasing meat, chicken or fish all the cook has to do is to call on the spice seller. He or she will ask a few questions: "What sort of curry is it to be? Hot or mild? How many servings?" Having ascertained the answers and perhaps exchanged a few more pleasantries (the buying of spices is a serious yet sociable affair) the appropriate quantities of each spice will be scooped on to a banana leaf and folded into a neat cone, ready to be taken home.

We may not be able to buy our ingredients in such colourful surroundings, but supermarkets stock some very good ready-made pastes, or you can make your own. By experimenting, you will find the balance of flavours you like, and can then make up one or more of your favourite mixtures in bulk.

If you grind wet spices a lot, you may wish to invest in a traditional, large Asian mortar with a rough, pitted or ridged bowl, which helps to "hold" the ingredients while they are being pounded with the pestle.

Alternatively, for speed, you can use a food processor or blender instead of a mortar and pestle. Store any surplus curry paste in plastic tubs in the freezer.

Above: Thai curry pastes

Malay spice paste for chicken rendang

This is a fairly pungent spice paste. It can be made milder by leaving out some of the chillies.

MAKES ABOUT 350G/12OZ

  6 fresh red chillies, seeded
    and sliced
  12 shallots, roughly chopped
  4 garlic cloves
  2.5cm/1in piece fresh turmeric
    root, peeled and sliced or 5ml/
    1 tsp ground turmeric
  10 macadamia nuts
  2.5cm/1in cube shrimp paste,
    prepared
  3 lemon grass stalks

1 Place the chillies, shallots, garlic, turmeric, nuts and shrimp paste in a food processor.

2 Trim the root end from the lemon grass and slice the lower 5cm/2in of the stalk into thin slices using a sharp knife.

3 Add the lemon grass to the remaining ingredients in the food processor and process them to a fine paste, scraping down the side of the bowl once or twice during the processing.

COOK'S TIP
Use the curry paste at once or spoon into a glass jar, seal it tightly and store in the refrigerator for up to 3 or 4 days. Alternatively, transfer the paste to a plastic tub and store in the freezer.

Thai mussaman curry paste

This hot and spicy paste is used to make the Thai version of a Muslim curry, which is traditionally made with beef, but can also be made with other meats such as chicken or lamb.

MAKES ABOUT 170G/6OZ

  12 large dried red chillies
  1 lemon grass stalk
  60ml/4 tbsp chopped shallots
  5 garlic cloves, roughly chopped
  10ml/2 tsp chopped fresh galangal
  5ml/1 tsp cumin seeds
  15ml/1 tbsp coriander seeds
  2 cloves
  6 black peppercorns
  5ml/1 tsp shrimp paste, prepared
  5ml/1 tsp salt
  5ml/1 tsp sugar
  30ml/2 tbsp oil

1 Remove the seeds from the dried chillies and discard. Fill a heatproof bowl with hot water and soak the chillies for about 15 minutes.

2 Trim the root end from the lemon grass stalk and slice the lower 5cm/2in of the stalk into small pieces.

3 Place the chopped lemon grass in a dry wok and then add the chopped shallots, garlic and galangal and dry-fry for a moment or two.

4 Stir in the cumin seeds, coriander seeds, cloves and peppercorns and dry-fry over low heat for 5–6 minutes, stirring constantly. Spoon the mixture into a large mortar.

5 Drain the chillies and add them to the mortar. Grind finely, using the pestle, then add the prepared shrimp paste, salt, sugar and oil and pound again until the mixture forms a rough paste. Use as required, then spoon any leftover paste into a jar, seal tightly and store in the refrigerator for up to 4 months.

COOK'S TIPS
• Preparing a double or larger quantity of paste in a food processor makes the blending of the ingredients much easier and the paste will be smoother.
• For the best results, before you start to process the ingredients, slice them up in the following order: galangal, lemon grass, fresh ginger and turmeric, chillies, nuts, shrimp paste, garlic and shallots. Add some of the oil (or coconut cream if that is to be your frying medium) to the ingredients in the food processor if the mixture is a bit sluggish. If you do this, however, remember to use less oil or coconut cream when you fry the curry paste to eliminate the raw taste of the individual ingredients before adding the meat, poultry, fish or vegetables.
• Shrimp paste is made from fermented shrimps. It can be bought in Asian stores. Unless it is to be fried as part of a recipe, it is always lightly cooked before use. If you have a gas cooker, simply mould the shrimp paste on to the end of a metal skewer and rotate over a low to medium gas flame, or heat under the grill (broiler) of an electric cooker, until the outside begins to look crusty, but not burnt.

COOKING FATS AND OILS

CHINESE: *SHI YOU*

Animal fats and vegetable oils are regarded as essential ingredients the world over, but in Asia they play a particularly important role, largely because so much of the food is fried. Animal fat or lard was historically the medium for frying (and remains so in China), but vegetable oils are valued because they can be heated to much higher temperatures without smoking, something which is essential for quick stir-frying, in which a high degree of heat is absolutely essential. Similarly, most deep-fried food also requires a high temperature in order to achieve the desired crispness.

Oil can be extracted from sources as diverse as radishes and poppies. Rapeseed (canola) oil was a popular cooking medium in China until the Portuguese introduced peanuts in the 16th century.

It was not immediately appreciated that the new crop could be a source of oil, but by the 19th century peanut oil was firmly established throughout Asia, a position it continues to hold despite competition from corn oil. In Japan, sesame oil originally held sway, but Japanese cooks soon appreciated that cooking with a mixture of sesame oil and peanut oil gave better results, especially when cooking their beloved tempura (a deep-fried vegetable and seafood dish introduced by Portuguese missionaries), as the mixed oil could be heated to higher temperatures without smoking.

Coconut and palm oil are common in South-east Asia, although both are less popular than they once were, as they are high in saturated fats.

Aroma and flavour

Fats and oils all have their own distinct aroma and flavour; some are quite strong, others fairly mild. Both lamb and beef fat, for instance are more strongly flavoured than lard or chicken fat, while peanut oil and rapeseed oil have more taste than soya, cottonseed or sunflower oils.

Culinary uses

In the East, fats and oils are mainly used as a cooking medium, but are sometimes ingredients in their own right. In some Chinese dishes, for instance, pure lard is often stirred in shortly before serving, much as Western cooks would use cream.

Left: Sunflower oil and groundnut oil

Above: Palm oil

Preparation and cooking techniques

Although many Asian recipes depend for their success on fats and oils, it is not considered appropriate for the flavour of the fat to dominate. A technique frequently employed to neutralize the flavour of an oil is to season it. The method is quite simple. While the oil is being heated, small pieces of aromatic ingredients such as fresh root ginger, spring onion (scallion) and garlic are added. When these have flavoured the oil, they are then removed before other ingredients are added to the wok or pan. The technique prevents the finished dish from tasting "oily".

Storage

In normal conditions, fats and oils exposed to the air gradually become rancid due to oxidation. Cooking oil should be stored in a cool, dark place. Oil that has been heated several times in a deep-fryer may acquire an unpleasant flavour. Chinese cooks heat the oil with some fresh ginger after every use to neutralize any off flavours. You may find that you have to discard the oil after using it three or four times.

FLAVOURING OILS

CHINESE: *TIAOWEI YOU*

Several types of flavouring oil are used in Asian cooking for dips and dressings, the most common one being sesame oil, but chilli oil is also popular.

SESAME OIL

MANDARIN: *ZHIMA YOU;* CANTONESE: *MA YOU;* JAPANESE: *GAMA-ABURA*

The type of sesame oil used for flavouring is quite different from the sesame oil used for cooking in India and the Middle East. In both China and Japan, the preferred oil for flavouring is a rich flavoured oil made from processed sesame seeds, which have been roasted or toasted to bring out their flavour.

Right: Toasted sesame oil

Aroma and flavour

Sesame oil from roasted seeds has a wonderfully nutty aroma and taste. It is much stronger than either walnut oil or olive oil. Blended sesame oil has a milder flavour and is much paler in colour.

Culinary uses

Because processed sesame oil smokes easily when heated, it is not really suitable for frying. It is used for salads and dipping sauces, and is added to soups or stir-fries.

Cooking techniques

Heating helps to intensify the aroma of sesame oil, but it should never be heated for too long. It is usual to add a few drops to a soup or stir-fry shortly before serving.

Storage

Always store bottled sesame oil in a cool, dark place, because it will lose its strong aroma if exposed to heat and strong light. It becomes rancid much sooner than ordinary cooking oils, so buy in small quantities.

CHILLI OIL

CHINESE: *LA YOU;* JAPANESE: *YU*

Chilli oil is made by infusing chopped dried red chillies, red chopped onions, garlic and salt in hot vegetable oil for several hours. There is also an "XO chilli oil", which is flavoured with dried

Blended sesame oil (above) and chilli oil

scallops, and is much more expensive. Chilli oil is easy to make at home; simply put about 20 seeded and chopped dried chillies in a heatproof container. Heat 250ml/8fl oz/1 cup groundnut (peanut) or corn oil until it just reaches smoking point, then leave to cool for 5 minutes. Carefully pour the oil into the heatproof container and leave to stand for at least an hour or two. Strain the oil, then use as required.

Aroma and flavour

Chilli oil has a pleasant aroma with a fiery taste that is much stronger than the flavour of either chilli bean paste or chilli sauce.

Culinary uses

Chilli oil is always used as a dipping sauce, never for cooking. In some South-east Asian countries, it is used as a dressing, and it is drizzled on top of the Myanmar fish soup, Mohinga. In Thai cooking, it is added to stir-fried prawns (shrimp) just before serving.

Storage

Store bottles of chilli oil in a cool and dark place; the oil will keep for many months in the refrigerator.

VINEGARS

RICE VINEGAR

MANDARIN: *MICU*; CANTONESE: *HUCK TSO*; JAPANESE: *SU*

Vinegar fermented from rice, or distilled from rice grains is used extensively in Asian cooking. The former is dark amber in colour and is referred to in China as red or black vinegar; the latter is clear, so is called white vinegar. The raw ingredients used for making rice vinegar consist of glutinous rice, long grain rice, wheat, barley, and rice husks. It is fermented twice and is matured for up to 6–7 months. Japan has a brown rice vinegar – *gaen mae su* – which is dark and heady. This vinegar, which has been likened to balsamic vinegar, is robust yet wonderfully smooth.

Aroma and flavour

Red or black vinegar has a pleasant fragrant aroma with a mild, sweetish flavour. The distilled white vinegar is much stronger. It smells vinegary and tastes quite tangy and tart. Japanese brown rice vinegar has a distinctive sweet and sour flavour.

Using sushi vinegar

The rice that is used to make sushi is moistened and flavoured with a mixture of hot rice vinegar, sugar and salt. The technique is simple, but it is important to use Japanese rice and good quality vinegar. The cooked rice is spread out in a shallow dish and the hot vinegar mixture is added. The rice is turned with a spatula until the grains are coated, and the mixture is simultaneously fanned so that it cools quickly and develops an attractive sheen. The rice is then covered until it cools completely before being moulded.

Above: Rice vinegar

Culinary uses

There's an old Chinese saying which goes something like this: "On rising in the morning, first check that you have the seven daily necessities for the kitchen: fuel, rice, oil, salt, soy sauce, vinegar and tea." Vinegar has always played a vital role in Chinese cookery, and in some parts of the country, particularly in the north, it is added to almost every dish as a matter of course, although the amounts are sometimes so minute as to be barely detectable. Rice vinegar is an important ingredient in the world-renowned sweet and sour sauce, which originated in northern China, and also in the popular hot and sour sauce from Sichuan.

Throughout Asia, rice vinegar also features in Thai cucumber sauce and dipping sauces, such as the Vietnamese vinegar and garlic fish sauce. It is also widely used in preserving and pickling.

Thai cooks add rice vinegar to several dishes, including their famous hot and sour soup. In Japan, rice vinegar is famously used for sushi rice.

Cooking techniques

If rice vinegar is heated for too long, its fragrance will be lost, the food will taste extremely tart and rather unpleasant. In Asian cooking, therefore, vinegar is generally the last item to be stirred into a dish. It is also important not to use too much vinegar; in a good sweet and sour sauce the key ingredients should be in perfect balance, the sour having a slight edge on the sweet.

Storage

Bottled rice vinegar will keep for a very long time, provided it is not exposed to either heat or strong light.

OTHER VINEGARS

Coconut vinegar Made from coconut nectar or "toddy" tapped from the flower sheaths of mature coconut palms, this amber vinegar is highly regarded in the Philippines.
Pon vinegar This Japanese vinegar is made from the juice of citrus fruit that resemble limes.

Coconut vinegar (right) and pon vinegar

SAUCES AND PASTES

SOY SAUCE

MANDARIN: *JIANG YOU*; CANTONESE: *CHI YOU*;
JAPANESE: *SHOYU*; INDONESIAN: *KECAP*;
KETJAP; MALAY: *KICHUP*; *TAUYU*;
THAI: *SIEW*

Soy sauce is made from fermented soya beans, and is one of Asia's most important contributions to the global pantry. It is used all over the world, not merely as a condiment in place of salt, but as an ingredient in a host of home-made and manufactured foods.

Making soy sauce involves quite a lengthy process. The soya beans are initially cleaned, soaked until soft and then steamed before being mixed with a yeast culture and wheat flour. The mixture is then fermented for up to two years before being filtered and bottled. There is no short cut to making soy sauce of high quality, and while some modern products may cost less than others, they have inferior flavour and should be avoided.

Aroma and flavour

There are basically three types of Chinese soy sauce on the market. **Light soy sauce** is the initial extraction, like the first pressing of virgin olive oil. It has the most delicate flavour and is light brown in colour with a lovely "beany" fragrance. **Dark soy sauce** is left to mature further, and has caramel added to it, so it is slightly sweeter and has a much darker colour with a powerful aroma. Then there is the regular soy sauce, which is a blend of the two.

There are several different types of Japanese soy sauce, too: **Usukuchi soy sauce** is light in colour and tastes less salty than the Chinese light soy. **Tamari** is dark and thick with a strong flavour, and is even less salty than the light type. **Shoyu** is a full-flavoured sauce

*Above: Dark (top)
and light soy
sauces*

that is aged for up to two years. In between, there is the very popular **Kikkoman**, which is a brand name for the equivalent of the Chinese regular soy sauce – not too weak, nor too strong. It is ideal as a dipping sauce to be used at the table, rather than for cooking.

The Indonesian **kecap manis** is thick and black, with a powerful aroma, but a surprisingly sweet taste. The light variety, **kecap asin**, is quite thin and weak, and is sometimes described as "white soy". Indonesian cooks also use the medium-bodied **kecap sedang**, but this is less popular than kecap manis.

*Above: There is
a range of Japanese soy
sauces, from dark and thick
to lighter, less rich types.*

small amount of soy sauce. When soy sauce is used in a dressing for a salad or similar cold dish, the dressing should be added only just before the dish is served.

Storage

Naturally fermented soy sauce will not keep for ever; it starts to lose its aroma and flavour as soon as it is exposed to the air for any length of time. Sealed bottles can be stored for a year or two, but once the bottle has been opened, soy sauce will deteriorate fairly rapidly. Try to use it up as fast as you can, certainly before the expiry date on the label. Check the label, too, for advice on storage. Some bottles do not contain preservatives and must be kept in the refrigerator once opened.

Above: Kecap manis (top) and kecap asin are Indonesian soy sauces

Right: Tamari sauce

Culinary uses

As a rule, light soy sauce is used for seafood, white meats, vegetables and soups, while the darker sauce is ideal for red meats, stews, barbecues and gravy. If you are serving soy sauce as a dip, choose the regular variety, or use a blend of three parts light sauce with two parts dark. This proportion also applies to marinades.

Cooking techniques

When soy sauce is used for cooking, it should be stirred in towards the end of the cooking time to avoid dulling the colour of the food, and so that the natural flavour of the principal ingredient is not overwhelmed. This point applies to soups, stews, stir-fries and quick-braised dishes, but not to slow-braised dishes, where the ingredients are simmered for a long time in a sauce that includes only a

---

Chicken yakitori

There are several classic marinades and sauces that have soy sauce as the main ingredient. This Japanese dish uses soy sauce, which is combined with sake and sugar, and thickened with flour, as a marinade for chicken kebabs. If you like, you can make twice the quantity of sauce and reserve half to serve with the cooked kebabs.

SERVES 4

6 boneless chicken thighs, cut into chunks
bunch of spring onions (scallions), cut into short batons
Japanese seven-spice powder, to serve

For the yakitori sauce
150ml/¼ pint/⅔ cup soy sauce
90g/3½oz/½ cup caster (superfine) sugar
25ml/5 tsp sake
15ml/1 tbsp plain (all-purpose) flour

1 For the sauce, place the soy sauce, sugar, sake and flour in a pan and stir well. Bring to the boil, stirring, then reduce the heat and simmer for 10 minutes, until reduced by a third. Set aside.

2 Thread the chicken and spring onion pieces alternately on to 12 bamboo skewers. Grill (broil) for 5–10 minutes until the chicken is cooked through, brushing generously with the sauce once or twice during cooking.

3 Sprinkle the kebabs with Japanese seven-spice powder and serve immediately, with a little extra yakitori sauce, if you like.

FISH SAUCE

CHINESE: *YU LU*; THAI: *NAM PLA*;
VIETNAMESE: *NUOC MAM*

Fish sauce is an essential seasoning
for Thai and Vietnamese cooking, in
much the same way that soy sauce
is important to the Chinese and the
Japanese. In Vietnam it is often made
using shrimps, but in Thailand, the
sauce is more often made using salted,
fermented fish.

Aroma and flavour

All types of fish sauce have a pungent
flavour and aroma and are very salty.
Thai *nam pla* has a slightly stronger
flavour and aroma than the Vietnamese
or Chinese versions. The colour of fish
sauce can vary considerably; lighter-
coloured sauces are considered to be
better than darker versions.

Culinary uses

Fish sauce is used extensively
throughout Asia as a seasoning in all
kinds of savoury dishes. It is also used
to make a dipping sauce, when it is
blended with extra flavourings such as
finely chopped garlic and chillies, and
sugar and lime juice.

*Right: Fish
sauce*

Storage

Fish sauce
generally
comes in
either glass or
plastic bottles. Once opened it should
be kept in a cool, dark place where it
will keep for up to a year.

OYSTER SAUCE

MANDARIN: *HAOYOU*; CANTONESE: *HO YOW*

Oyster sauce is a Cantonese speciality.
This thick, brown, soy-based sauce is
flavoured with oyster juice, salt and
caramel, and is thickened with
cornflour. It is thicker
than soy sauce and
fish sauce, but
lighter in
colour.

*Above: Oyster
sauce*

Aroma and flavour

Oyster sauce has a pleasant, fragrant
aroma, and has a delicious and delicate
flavour that, surprisingly, doesn't taste
of fish at all.

Culinary uses

Oyster sauce is a highly versatile
flavouring and can be used in a wide
variety of dishes. It is especially good
with fairly bland foods, such as chicken
and tofu, but also works very well with
more strongly flavoured ingredients
such as beef and seafood. It can be
used as a garnish and is often sprinkled
over the top of cooked dishes such as
rice and noodles.

Cooking techniques

The bottled sauce is only used as a
cooking ingredient, and it is never
served as a dip or sauce at the table.
Oyster sauce is best added to dishes
towards the end of the cooking time.

Storage

There are a number of different brands
of this sauce, and the more expensive
versions are usually far superior, and
have a much richer flavour than cheaper
versions. Once opened, the bottle
should be stored in the refrigerator
where the sauce will keep for a very
long time, although it is best used
before the expiry date.

Above:
Dark hoisin
sauce

Above:
Light
hoisin sauce

HOISIN SAUCE

MANDARIN: *HAIXIAN JIANG;* CANTONESE: *HOY SIN JIONG;* VIETNAMESE: *TUONG-DEN*

Another Cantonese speciality, hoisin is also known as barbecue sauce. Its Chinese name literally means "sea-flavour", which is a reflection on just how delicious it is, rather than an indication of its ingredients. Hoisin sauce does not contain so much as a trace of seafood, unlike oyster sauce and fish sauce.

Aroma and flavour

The main components of this very popular sauce are fermented beans, sugar, vinegar, salt, chilli, garlic and sesame oil, but there is no standard formula, so the aroma and flavour of different brands can vary considerably. A good quality product should have a fragrant aroma with a rich, warm, sweet yet salty flavour.

Culinary uses

Hoisin sauce is quite versatile and makes a valuable contribution to the kitchen. Mainly intended as a marinade, it can be used at the table as a dipping sauce, but should not accompany Peking duck as is the practice in some restaurants.

Cooking techniques

When used as a marinade, hoisin can be spooned straight from the jar over spare ribs, chicken or similar foods.

Storage

Hoisin sauce usually comes in glass jars or cans. Once opened, jars should be stored in the refrigerator, where the sauce will keep for several months. Canned hoisin should be decanted into non-metallic containers before being stored in the refrigerator.

CHILLI SAUCE

MANDARIN: *LAJIAO JIANG;* CANTONESE: *LA JYEW JYEUNG;* THAI: *SOD PRIK*

The best known Asian chilli sauce comes from China, although the Vietnamese have a very hot version and there is also a thick, spicy chilli sauce made in Thailand.

Aroma and flavour

This Chinese bottled chilli sauce is quite hot and spicy, with a touch of fruitiness, as it is made from fresh red chillies, salt, vinegar and apples or plums. The Thai version includes both hot and sweet chillies, and adds ginger, spices and vinegar. There is also a thick Chinese sauce which is made exclusively from chillies and salt. This is usually sold in jars and is much hotter than the bottled sauce.

Culinary uses

The bottled sauce is used both for cooking and as a dip, but the thicker sauce is mainly used for cooking as an alternative to chilli bean paste.

Cooking techniques

Use chilli sauce sparingly. It can be quite fiery.

Storage

Once a jar or bottle of chilli sauce has been opened it should be stored in the refrigerator, where it will keep almost indefinitely. Use before the expiry date.

Below: Sweet chilli sauce (top) and chilli sauce

PLUM SAUCE

MANDARIN: *MEIZI JIANG*; CANTONESE: *SHWIN MEI JIONG*; VIETNAMESE: *CUONG NGOT*

Made from plum juice with sugar, salt, vinegar and a thickening agent, plum sauce is a sort of sweet-and-sour sauce. It is generally associated with Chinese food. Thai cooks are partial to plum sauce, but they tend to make their own, using preserved plums and sugar.

Aroma and flavour

There seems to be no standard recipe for the commercially made plum sauce. The various brands all seem to use slightly different seasonings and some even add garlic, ginger or chilli to give it extra tang. Taste before use, as some brands can be quite fiery.

Culinary uses

One of the common uses for plum sauce in the West is to serve it with Peking duck. It is also used as a dip for spring rolls and other dim sum.

Storage

Plum sauce is usually sold in glass jars. One opened, the jar should be kept in the refrigerator.

LEMON SAUCE

MANDARIN: *NINGMENG JIANG*; CANTONESE: *NING MUNG JIONG*

Lemon sauce is one of those condiments that was especially created for the Western market. It probably originated in Hong Kong, like black bean sauce. Thick, smooth and velvety, it has an immediate appeal for the Western palate.

Aroma and flavour

The sauce has a rather piquant citrus aroma with a spicy and tangy sweet flavour. It is another sauce from the sweet-and-sour stable, but with the difference that it is made from fresh lemon juice and rind. Salt and sugar are added, and starch is used for thickening. Most brands have artificial colouring added to give the sauce a bright colour.

Above, from top: Oyster, plum and hoisin sauces

Culinary uses

The use of lemon sauce in cooking seems to be limited to a single dish, lemon chicken, which is on the menu of most Cantonese restaurants. Other than that, it can be served with deep-fried food, particularly seafood.

Storage

Once opened, the bottle or jar should be stored in the refrigerator. The fresh flavour of the sauce may be dulled if it is kept for too long, so use it before the expiry date.

Above: Lemon sauce

BLACK BEAN SAUCE

MANDARIN: *CHIZI JIANG;* CANTONESE: *SI JIR JIONG*

A mixture of puréed salted black beans with soy sauce, sugar and spice, this popular sauce is especially manufactured for the convenience of Western cooks, since people in China and South-east Asia generally use only whole fermented beans, and make their own sauce by crushing the beans in the wok while cooking.

Aroma and flavour

Fermented black beans have a powerful "fragrance" and a strong flavour that does not always appeal to the untutored Western palate, but once introduced to its rather earthy taste, many people grow to like it immensely.

Culinary uses

Black bean sauce should not be used cold straight from the jar or bottle, but should always be heated first. It is usually blended with other strongly flavoured seasonings such as spring onions (scallions), garlic, ginger and chillies before being added to stews, stir-fries, and braised or steamed dishes. Ready-made black bean sauces seasoned either with garlic or chillies are available too. These should also be heated before use, to bring out the aroma and flavour.

Storage

Once opened, the jar should be stored in the refrigerator. It keeps extremely well.

YELLOW BEAN SAUCE

MANDARIN: *HUANG JIANG;* CANTONESE: *MO SHIH JIONG;* THAI: *TAO JIEW KAOW*

Also known as brown bean sauce or ground bean sauce, this Chinese favourite consists of crushed fermented soya beans which have been mixed with salt, wheat flour and sugar to make a paste which is not only useful on its own, but is also the basis of numerous more elaborate sauces. Hoisin sauce, chu hou sauce, Guilin chilli sauce, Sichuan hot sauce and Peking duck sauce all owe their ancestry to yellow bean sauce.

Aroma and flavour

Regular yellow bean sauce has a wonderfully "beany" aroma with a delectable flavour. It is not as salty as black bean sauce, and cooks in every region of China add

Left: Fermented yellow beans and yellow bean sauce

Above: Black bean sauce

Above: Fermented black beans, which Chinese cooks use to make their own black bean sauce.

their own spices and seasonings to make individual blends.

Culinary uses

Yellow bean sauce is very versatile in the kitchen. It adds an extra dimension to most meat, poultry, fish and even some vegetable dishes, whether in stir-fries, braised dishes or roasts. It is also the ideal basis for a marinade, usually with additional ingredients such as garlic, spring onions (scallions) and rice wine.

Storage

Once a can or jar of yellow bean sauce has been opened, the contents should be transferred to a lidded plastic tub and stored in the refrigerator. Like black bean sauce, it keeps very well.

CHILLI BEAN PASTE

MANDARIN: *DOUBAN JIANG;* CANTONESE: *TOBAN DJAN*

This is a Sichuan speciality. What makes it unique is the fact that the beans used are not soya beans, but a type of broad (fava) bean , hence the name *douban* or *toban* in Chinese. Outside China the sauce is sold under various names, including chilli bean sauce, hot bean sauce or just plain Sichuan sauce.

Aroma and flavour

There are several chilli bean pastes on the market, ranging from mild to hot, but all have a lovely "beany" aroma with a rich flavour. The genuine Pixian paste made in Sichuan is seldom seen in the West, which is a pity, for it is superior in quality to the majority of brands made in Hong Kong, Taiwan or Singapore.

Above: Chilli bean paste

Right: Red bean paste

Miso

This is the collective name for several types of soya bean paste, made from steamed soya beans fermented with various natural yeasts. Some of these starter moulds are based upon rice, others on wheat or barley, and yet more on soya beans themselves. The pastes come in different colours, textures and flavours, depending on the yeast used and the length of the fermentation process. Red or *mugi* miso (*below centre*), the most popular paste, is more strongly flavoured than the sweeter white *kome* miso (*below left*). A third type, *hacho* miso (*below right*), is dark with a strong flavour. Miso is the key ingredient in a soup served at almost every Japanese meal. When mixed with mayonnaise it makes the increasingly popular miso-mayo.

Culinary uses

Chilli bean paste and chilli sauce are not interchangeable; each has its own distinct flavour and consistency. Chilli bean paste is slightly thicker than chilli sauce and is an indispensable seasoning in Sichuan cooking. It is used to add flavour to stir-fries and braised dishes.

Cooking techniques

Chilli bean paste must be thoroughly heated before being used and should never be served cold at the table as a dipping sauce.

Storage

Once opened, the jar should be stored in the refrigerator. Chilli bean paste keeps well, but should be used before the expiry date on the jar.

RED BEAN PASTE

MANDARIN: *DOUSHA;* CANTONESE: *DOW SA*

Made from either red kidney beans or aduki beans, this is a thick, smooth paste, which is sweetened with rock sugar. The paste comes in small cans and is generally only available from speciality Asian stores.

Aroma and flavour

The paste has a pleasant, mild fragrance with a subtle flavour. Although it is sweetened, the sauce is never cloying, and oriental cooks often add extra sugar to intensify the flavour. Occasionally, other flavourings such as essence of sesame seeds or ground cassia are blended in.

Culinary uses

Red bean paste is mainly used in sweet dishes and is a popular filling for cakes and steamed buns. It is also spread on pancakes, which are then deep-fried.

Storage

Once the can has been opened, the contents should be transferred to a sealed plastic tub and stored in the refrigerator, where the paste will keep for several months. Make a note of the use-by date on the can.

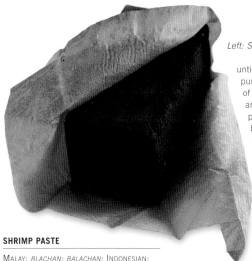

Left: Shrimp paste

until the aroma is very pungent. The colour of the paste can be anything from oyster pink to purplish brown, depending upon the type of shrimp and the precise process used. It is compressed and sold in block form or packed in tiny tubs or jars.

SHRIMP PASTE

MALAY: *BLACHAN; BALACHAN;* INDONESIAN: *TERASI; TRASSI;* THAI: *KAPI;* MYANMAR: *NGAPI*

Whether you call it *blachan, terasi, kapi* or *ngapi*, shrimp paste is an essential ingredient in scores of savoury dishes throughout South-east Asia. It is made from tiny shrimps which have been salted, dried, pounded and then left to ferment in the hot humid conditions

Sesame paste

The sesame paste used in Asian cooking is not the same as tahini, the ingredient that frequently crops up in recipes from the Middle East. Whereas tahini is made from raw sesame seeds, sesame paste is derived from seeds which have been dry-fried or roasted to bring out the rich nutty flavour. If an Asian recipe calls for sesame paste, don't be tempted to try tahini, therefore. Instead, use peanut butter with a little sesame oil stirred in to approximate the correct flavour.

Aroma and flavour

There's no disguising the origin of this paste. The moment you unwrap it or lift the lid, the smell of rotten fish is quite overwhelming. Do not let this put you off, however. The odour vanishes when the paste is cooked, and this is one of those ingredients that really does make a difference to the food, contributing depth, pungency and a recognizable South-east Asian signature.

Culinary uses

Shrimp paste is good source of protein and vitamin C. It is used to flavour rice dishes, is stirred into satay sauces and gives depth to salad dressings, dipping sauces, curries and braised dishes. It is the key ingredient in the famous *nam prik*, a dipping sauce whose other ingredients include garlic, chillies and fish sauce, and which appears as a condiment at almost every Thai meal. Myanmar cooks use it to intensify the flavour of *balachaung*, a spicy dried shrimp mixture forked into rice.

Preparation

Before using shrimp paste in a sambal, dressing or salad, it is necessary to heat it to temper the raw flavour (see right).

Storage

If you buy the paste in block form, store it in a screwtop jar in a cool place. It will keep for several months. Jars of paste should be kept in the refrigerator.

Preparing shrimp paste

Shrimp paste can be used straight from the packet if it is to be fried with other ingredients, but it needs to be heated to temper its raw taste before using in sambals, dressings and salads.

1 Cut off a small piece of shrimp paste and shape it into a 1cm/½in cube. Mould the paste on to the end of a metal skewer.

2 Holding the end of the skewer in an oven glove, rotate the paste over a low to medium gas flame, or under a grill (broiler) until the outside begins to look dry, but not burnt. This method works well, but gives off a very strong smell.

3 Alternatively, to avoid the strong smell, wrap the cube of paste in a piece of foil and dry-fry in a frying pan for about 5 minutes, turning it occasionally.

SAMBALS

In the West, sambals have come to mean the side dishes served with a curry, but this is several steps away from the original South-east Asian term, which was, and still is, applied to a number of hot, spicy relishes, sauces and similar accompaniments that are based on chillies. Sambals are particularly popular in Indonesia, and feature strongly in the famous *Rijstafel,* a veritable feast which includes dozens of different dishes, and which was developed in the days when Indonesia was still the Dutch East Indies. Thanks to the connection, *Rijstafel* is also well known and loved in the Netherlands, and bottled sambals are widely available in that country.

In Indonesia, a sambal can also be a main dish. *Sambal goreng,* for instance is a spicy chilli sauce, which may include a variety of foods such as tiny meat balls, cubes of fish, wedges of hard-boiled eggs or vegetables.

Culinary uses

In Malaysia, Singapore and Indonesia *sambal blachan* (chilli and shrimp paste sambal) is a favourite. Fresh red chillies are roughly chopped, then pounded with a little salt and prepared shrimp paste *(blachan).* A little lime or lemon juice is added to the mixture to loosen it slightly. *Sambal blachan* is extremely hot – especially when the seeds have been left in the chillies – so deserves to be served with a health warning! *Sambal oelek* is similar, but a little brown sugar is added to the chopped chillies to bring out the flavours. Sometimes labelled "chopped chilli", this product is now sold in jars in many supermarkets. One teaspoonful (5ml) is equivalent to 1 small chilli. After use, the jar should be closed tightly and kept in the fridge.

At a typical Thai meal there may be one or two sambals in addition to the much loved *nam prik,* a combination of dried prawns, shrimp paste, garlic, chillies, fish sauce, lemon juice and brown sugar. *Nam prik* complements raw, steamed, fried or boiled vegetables and is often simply stirred into a bowl of plain boiled or steamed Thai rice. Another popular sambal is made from fish sauce, lemon juice, shallots and chillies; a blend that enhances all kinds of fish and seafood dishes.

Sambal oelek

This chilli sambal will keep for about6 weeks in a sealed jar in the refrigerator, so it is worth making up a reasonable quantity if you frequently cook Indonesian-style dishes. Use a stainless-steel or plastic spoon to measure out the sauce as required. This sauce is fiercely hot, and it will irritate the skin, so should you get any on your fingers, immediately wash them well in soapy water.

MAKES ABOUT 350G/12OZ

450g/1lb fresh red chillies
10ml/2 tsp salt

1 Cut the chillies in half, scrape out the seeds using the point of a sharp knife and discard with the stalks. Plunge the chillies into a pan of boiling water and cook them for 5–8 minutes.

2 Drain the chillies, then place them in the bowl of a food processor or blender and process until finely chopped. The paste should be fairly coarse, so stop processing before it gets too smooth.

3 Spoon the paste into a glass jar, stir in the salt and cover with a piece of baking parchment or clear film (plastic wrap) before screwing on the lid.

4 Store the sambal in the refrigerator. Spoon it into small dishes as an accompaniment, or use it as suggested in recipes.

Left: Sambal oelek *(left),* sambal blachan *(front) and* nam prik *sauces are very hot chilli sauces.*

Below: Nuoc cham

In Vietnam the salt and pepper of the Western table is replaced by *nuoc cham*. This is a piquant sambal made from, chillies, garlic, sugar, lime juice or rice vinegar, and fish sauce and is the classic combination of hot, sweet, sour and salt flavours that is so typical of Vietnamese cooking.

Sambals and sauces are usually served in small bowls or saucers.

At a family meal pieces of cooked meat, fish or vegetables may be dipped into a communal bowl or a tiny spoonful of the sambal may be put on each diner's plate, but on special occasions small individual dishes are used. These little dishes are sold in many Asian stores and supermarkets.

Preparation

For the freshest flavours mix the sambal ingredients just before serving. Use a food processor or blender to blend the wet ingredients and a mortar and pestle to grind the dry ingredients.

Storage

Leftover sambals are best stored in a glass jar in the refrigerator. Before putting on the lid, cover the jar with a piece of baking parchment or clear film (plastic wrap) to protect the lid from corrosion.

Nuoc cham

This spicy Vietnamese sambal makes a delicious, if fiery, dipping sauce and is good served with crisp, fried spring rolls.

MAKES ABOUT 105ML/7 TBSP

2 fresh red chillies, seeded
2 garlic cloves, crushed
15ml/1 tbsp sugar
45ml/3 tbsp fish sauce
juice of 1 lime or ½ lemon

1 Place the chillies in a large mortar and pound to a paste using a pestle.

2 Transfer the chillies to a bowl and add the garlic, sugar and fish sauce. Stir in lime or lemon juice to taste.

COOK'S TIP

Be careful, when handling either fresh or dried chillies; they contain capsaicin, an oily substance which can cause intense irritation to sensitive skin, so wash your hands thoroughly after handling them, or wear rubber gloves. And do not touch or rub your eyes.

Sambal kecap

This Indonesian sauce or sambal can be served as a dip for satays instead of the usual peanut sauce, particularly with beef and chicken, and it is also very good with pieces of deep-fried chicken.

MAKES ABOUT 150ML/¼ PINT/⅔ CUP

1 fresh red chilli, seeded and
 finely chopped
2 garlic cloves, crushed
60ml/4 tbsp dark soy sauce
20ml/4 tsp lemon juice or 15ml/
 1 tbsp tamarind juice
30ml/2 tbsp hot water
30ml/2 tbsp deep-fried onion slices
 (optional)

1 Place the chopped chilli, crushed garlic, soy sauce, and lemon juice or tamarind juice in a small bowl with the hot water and mix together well.

2 Stir in the deep-fried onion slices, if using, and leave the sambal to stand at room temperature for about 30 minutes before serving.

Sambal blachan

Serve this hot and pungent sambal as an accompaniment to rice meals.

MAKES ABOUT 30ML/2 TBSP

2–4 fresh red chillies, seeded
salt
1cm/½in cube of shrimp paste
juice of ½ lemon or lime

1 Place the chillies in a mortar, add a little salt and pound them to a paste using a pestle.

2 Cut off a small piece of shrimp paste and shape it into a 1cm/½in cube. Mould the paste on to the end of a metal skewer.

3 Hold the end of the skewer, using a kitchen cloth or oven glove, and rotate the paste over a low gas flame, or under an electric grill (broiler) until the outside begins to look dry, but not burnt.

4 Add the shrimp paste to the chillies and pound to mix well. Add lemon or lime juice to taste.

PRESERVED AND PICKLED VEGETABLES

Preserved and pickled food plays an important part in the Asian diet. In the days before refrigeration and rapid transportation, fresh food had to be preserved for the lean months, and so that it could be conveyed to regions that were often a long way from the source of supply.

Preserved and pickled vegetables and, to a lesser extent, fruit are used all over Asia. Some of the more famous examples include *chow chow,* the Chinese sweet mixed pickles that are now an American favourite, and *kimchee,* the tart, garlicky pickle that is served at almost every Korean meal. In Japan, pickled vegetables are hugely popular, as are pickled plums, while Indonesian cooks relish *atjar kuning,* a yellow mixed pickle which is mildly hot.

There are several ways of preserving and pickling food. The most common way is to use salt as a preservative, then dry the food in the sun or by another source of heat. Another age-old method is to partially dry the food, then pickle it in brine or a soy-based solution.

Below: Pickled mustard greens

Below: A selection of Chinese pickles

SICHUAN PRESERVED VEGETABLE

MANDARIN: *ZHACAI;* CANTONESE: *JA CHOI*

This pickle, made from the stems of mustard cabbage, originated in Sichuan province, but is now made in other parts of China. The stems are dried in the sun, then pickled in brine. After being trimmed and cleaned, they are pressed to extract excess liquid (the Mandarin name *zhacai* means "pressed vegetable"), before being blended with chillies and spices, and stored in sealed urns to mature.

Aroma and flavour

Sichuan preserved vegetable has a pungent aroma that may not appeal to the uninitiated. It has a smooth and crunchy texture and tastes quite salty and peppery.

Culinary uses

Unlike most other types of preserved and pickled vegetables, Sichuan preserved vegetable is a very versatile ingredient. It is not merely served raw as a relish, but is also cooked with other foods in stir-fries, soups and steamed dishes.

Preparation and cooking techniques

Because of its strong hot and salty flavour, Sichuan preserved vegetable is often rinsed in water to remove some of the excess salt and chillies before it is finely sliced or shredded for use.

Storage

Sichuan preserved vegetable is normally sold in cans, although you may be able to buy the pickle loose in some Asian stores. Any unused pickle should be transferred to an airtight container and stored in the refrigerator, where it will keep almost indefinitely.

CHINESE PICKLES

There is a wide range of Chinese pickles available in the West. Some appear in packets, some in jars, and some in cans. A pickle may consist of a single ingredient such as ginger, garlic, spring onion bulbs, chillies, cabbage, cucumber, gourd, runner beans, bamboo shoots, carrots or mooli (daikon) or a mixture. Individual items are generally pickled in a dark soy solution, while mixed vegetables tend to be pickled in clear brine to which sugar, Sichuan peppercorns,

Below: Cucumbers are a popular pickled vegetable in many Asian countries. These are from Korea.

distilled spirit and fresh ginger have been added, with chillies and vinegar as optional ingredients. The cleaned vegetables are pickled in the solution in a sealed earthenware urn. This is left in a cool, dark place for at least a week in summer, or up to a month in winter. The longer the pickling process, the better the taste.

JAPANESE PICKLES

JAPANESE: *TSUKEMONO*

There are many varieties of the Japanese pickles known as *tsukemono*. The vegetables that are used are more or less the same as those used in China, but the method of pickling is somewhat different. To start with, instead of earthenware urns, only

Below: Chow chow – Chinese sweet mixed pickles

wooden barrels are used in Japan and, instead of being pickled in a brine solution, the vegetables are layered with salt. When the barrel is full, a lid is put on top, and this is weighted down with a large stone or similar weight. The combined effect of the salt and the compression forces the liquid out of the vegetables and they are pickled in their own juices.

Other methods include pickling in sake, miso or rice bran, and the most popular types of vegetable used are mooli (daikon), pak choi (bok choy), cucumber, aubergine (eggplant), horseradish and the bulbs of spring onions (scallions). Thinly sliced pink pickled ginger (*gari*) is served with sushi and sashimi.

Japanese pickles form an essential part of a meal. They are served as a relish to accompany the cooked food, as well as a dessert or a means of cleansing the palate at the end. They are either served singly or in groups of two or three, always beautifully arranged in small individual dishes.

Umeboshi These small pickled plums (below) are a particular Japanese delicacy. The plums are picked before they are ripe and are pickled in salt, with red shiso leaves to give them their distinctive colour. They have a sharp and salty taste and are often chopped and used as a filling for rice balls.

Pickled bamboo shoots A delicacy in Vietnam, this consists of sliced bamboo shoots in spiced vinegar. The shoots are quite sour and should be soaked in water to remove some of the bitterness. They are mainly used in soups and stocks, and are often served with duck.

Pickled garlic This is a favourite in Thailand. The small bulbs are pickled whole in a sweet and sour brine (below).

Pickled limes Whole limes preserved in brine or a mixture of soy sauce, sugar, salt and vinegar are another Thai speciality.

COCONUT MILK AND CREAM

Coconut milk is an essential ingredient in South-east Asian cooking. There is an old saying that "he who plants a coconut palm, plants food and drink, vessels and clothing, a habitation for himself and a heritage for his children". Once mature, the palms will go on producing coconuts for 75–100 years, which helps to explain why they are so highly prized.

The coconut was called the nut of India until the Portuguese, struck by its appearance, changed its name to "coco", meaning clown or monkey. Fresh coconuts are available at certain times of the year in Asian stores and supermarkets. The liquid you can hear sloshing about inside the nut when it is shaken is coconut juice, not coconut milk. As any traveller who has tasted it will attest, the juice makes a refreshing drink, especially when tapped from a fresh green coconut. It can also be made into palm wine, which can be pretty potent.

An average size coconut weighs about 675g/1½lb. If it is fresh, it will be full of liquid, so test by shaking well before buying. To open a coconut, hold

Below: A fresh coconut will break neatly into two pieces if you hit it in just the right place.

Below: Coconut milk

it in the palm of your left hand, with the "eyes" just above your thumb. The fault line runs between the eyes. Hold the coconut over a bowl to catch the juice, then carefully strike the line with the unsharpened side of a cleaver or a hammer. If you have done this correctly, the coconut will break neatly into two pieces. Taste a little of the white flesh to make sure that the coconut is fresh, as on rare occasions the flesh may have become rancid. Slip a thin knife between the outer husk and the flesh and prize out the pieces of fresh

coconut. The thin brown skin on these pieces can be removed with a potato peeler, if you like.

Coconut milk and cream are both made from the grated flesh of the coconut, and in the East, it is possible to buy bags of freshly grated coconut for just this purpose. Warm water is added and the coconut is squeezed repeatedly until the mixture is cloudy and has a wonderful coconut flavour. When strained, this is coconut milk. If the milk is left to stand, coconut cream will float to the surface in much the same way as regular cream does on whole milk.

Coconut milk is now available in cartons and cans, and even in countries with a plentiful supply of coconuts cooks often use these products for convenience and speed. The quality is excellent, and it is even possible to buy a version that is 88 per cent fat free.

Creamed coconut comes in 200g/7oz block. This is a very useful product, as small quantities can be cut off and added to dishes to supply a little richness just before serving. When a very small quantity of coconut milk is called for dissolve 50g/2oz creamed coconut in 100ml/3½fl oz/scant ½ cup hot water.

Above: Creamed coconut block

Coconut cream can be made in the same way, but the amount of creamed coconut should be increased to 75g/3oz. Ready-to-use coconut cream comes in cartons and is a magical ingredient where a rich coconut aroma and flavour are required. In many Thai curries the spices are initially fried in bubbling coconut cream instead of the more usual oil.

Culinary uses

Coconut is widely used in South-east Asian cooking. The milk is used as a cooking medium instead of stock in a variety of dishes, and it is also added at the end of cooking to enrich stews and curries. It can be cooked with rice, to make a savoury accompaniment, or as the basis for rice cakes, and also to make a delicious creamy rice pudding. In Thailand, coconut milk is often used to make aromatic soups.

Below: Coconut cream

Making coconut milk

Coconut milk can be made at home, from desiccated (dry unsweetened shredded) coconut. Although the procedure takes time, it has plenty of advantages. Desiccated coconut is readily available and is an item that many cooks routinely stock in their store cupboards. You can make as much or as little as you like – although the method is more practical for large quantities – and coconut milk made this way is less expensive than any of the alternatives.

1 Place 225g/8oz/2⅔ cups desiccated coconut into the bowl of a food processor and pour over 450ml/¾ pint/scant 2 cups boiling water. Process for 20–30 seconds and allow to cool a little. If making several batches transfer immediately to a large bowl and repeat.

2 Place a strainer lined with muslin (cheesecloth) over a large bowl in the sink. Ladle some of the softened coconut into the muslin.

3 Bring up the ends of the cloth and twist it over the strainer to extract as much of the liquid as possible. Discard the spent coconut. Use the coconut milk as directed in recipes.

COOK'S TIPS
• When making coconut milk, instead of discarding the spent coconut, it can be re-used to make a second batch of coconut milk. This will be of a poorer quality and should only be used to extend a good quality first quantity of coconut milk.
• Any unused coconut milk or cream can be transferred to a plastic tub and stored in the refrigerator for a day or two, or poured into a freezer container and frozen for use on another occasion.
• Before using newly made coconut milk, leave it to stand for 10 minutes or more, and the coconut cream will float to the top. Skim off the cream using a large spoon if needed, or leave it to enrich the milk.

Beer, Wine and Spirits

The art of making alcoholic beverages is an ancient one. Man has been making alcoholic drinks ever since the discovery that a grain and water mash would ferment if left to stand, producing a sour brew that would intoxicate.

Archaeological finds in northern China provide evidence that the Chinese were using separate drinking cups and bowls for different beverages as long ago as the 22nd century BC. Historians

Below: Leading Japanese beers include Sapporo and Asahi, both of which are widely available in the West.

agree that a considerable length of time must have elapsed from the beginning of the making and drinking of a primitive type of "wine" to the sophistication of using vessels in a variety of shapes for specific purposes, so the Chinese may well have been imbibing some form of alcoholic beverage at the dawn of their civilization more than 5,000 years ago. By the time of the Shang Dynasty (c. 1600–1100 BC), a dark wine

Above: Chinese beers include Five Star beer and the light Pilsener, Tsingtao.

was being brewed from millet, and was ceremonially served in elaborate bronze drinking vessels.

A new development in the art of brewing was achieved during the early part of the 12th century BC, where textual evidence records that a form of barm or leaven was used in wine-making. With this discovery, the Chinese were able to control both the flavour and alcoholic content of a variety of wines made from different fruits and grains. Wine continues to be an important drink, although its popularity has now been overtaken by beer.

BEER

MANDARIN: *PI JIU*; CANTONESE: *PI CHIEW*

Beer brewing was not introduced into China and Japan until towards the end of the 19th century, but it rapidly became an extremely popular drink. Today, beer is the favourite alcoholic beverage in Asia, and almost every country in the region has breweries producing beers for export as well as for domestic consumption.

The style of beer most favoured by Asian drinkers is a bottom-fermented brew in the style of Pilsener (Pils), a pale, golden-coloured lager with a characteristically well-hopped palate and 4.5–5 per cent alcohol by volume.

Chinese beers

Without doubt, the best known Chinese beer is **Tsingtao**, a light, dry Pilsener-type beer which is brewed from the sweet spring water of Laoshan, using

Chinese barley and hops. It has a refreshing and delicate taste, and enjoys a huge popularity abroad, not just with expatriate Chinese, but among Westerners as well.

In 1898, part of the Shandong Peninsula was ceded to Germany as a colony. Besides the winery in Yantai, the Germans also established a brewery at Tsingtao in 1903, which was called the

Below: Singaporean Tiger beer is popular all over the world.

Anglo-German Brewery Company. Because of the vicissitudes of history, it went through a number of different owners – Britain, Germany and Japan – until after World War II, when it was taken over by the People's Republic of China. Since then a number of breweries have been established all over China, but Tsingtao Brewery remains the largest and most productive brewer in the land.

Other brands that can occasionally be seen in the West are **Beijing Beer**, **Shanghai Beer**, **Snowflake** and **Yu Chuan** ("Jade Spring") **Beer**. These all are Pilsener-type lagers, each with their own individual flavour.

Japanese beers

The huge beer industry of Japan also owes its origins to foreign investment. In 1869, the American firm of Wiegrand and Copeland started an experimental brewery at Yokohama. Soon afterwards, the Japanese Government sent a researcher to Germany to acquire technical know-how, and subsequently the Copeland operation was passed to Japanese management, taking the name Kirin in 1888.

Today, the Kirin Brewery Company has became one of the biggest brewers in the world. It is part of Japan's Mitsubishi conglomerate, and its output even surpasses that of Heineken. Kirin has nine breweries in different parts of Japan, and **Kirin Beer** is exported to almost every country in the world. It used to enjoy 60 per cent of domestic sales, but has recently been pushed down to about 40 per cent, partly owing to the surge of its chief rival **Asahi Beer**, which has rapidly increased its export market in recent years. Other strong contenders for the crown of the

Left: Canned Thai beer

Japanese beer industry are **Sapporo Beer**, which also challenges Kirin's claim of being the oldest brewer; and the newcomer **Suntory Beer**, which only started brewing in 1963.

South-east Asian beers

The world-renowned **Tiger Beer** of Singapore came into being by accident. The breweries were established after Heineken failed to reach an agreement with the Dutch Colonial Government to set up their breweries in Java in 1929, so established the Malayan Breweries in Singapore and later in Kuala Lumpur instead. Tiger Beer is now brewed by Asia Pacific Breweries of Singapore, and has achieved worldwide sales figures envied by all its competitors.

From Thailand, the biggest selling lager is **Singha**, brewed by Boon Rawd Brewery. The name Singha is a reference to the elegant but fearsome lion-like creature of local mythology.

Perhaps not that many people are aware that the Philippines is the home of one of the world's major brewing groups – **San Miguel**. This group has three breweries in the Philippines, one in Hong Kong, and one in Papua New Guinea. Outside of Asia, San Miguel has three breweries in Spain, but ironically these are only offshoots of its headquarters in the Philippines.

Dutch colonial links are still evident in Indonesia, where **Heineken** eventually did establish an associate company in Java to produce a Pilsener-style beer. Elsewhere in Asia, popular beers include the Vietnamese **"33"**; **Taiwan Beer** from Taiwan; and **OB** and **Crown** from Korea, but these are seldom seen in the West.

WINE

MANDARIN: *JIU*; CANTONESE: *CHIEW*

In contrast to their sophisticated approach to food, the Chinese, as a whole, are remarkably indiscriminating when it comes to alcoholic beverages. Unless they are connoisseurs, the Chinese often fail to distinguish between table wine, in which the alcoholic content is low, and distilled spirits, in which it is high. In everyday usage, the Chinese character *jiu* or *chiew* means any alcoholic beverage.

Chinese wines

As can be expected in a country where rice is the staple food, rice wine leads the field. There are hundreds of different varieties of rice wine in China, but only a few of these are exported.

Chinese rice wine is generally known as **huang jiu** (yellow wine) in Chinese, because of its golden amber colour. The best known and best quality rice wine is **Shao Xing**, named after the district where it is made. Shao Xing, or Shao Hsing is situated south of Hangzhou in Zhejiang province, and its wine-making history dates back to 470 BC. The main grains used for making Shao Xing are glutinous rice, millet and ordinary rice, and the water comes from a large lake

Left: Sake

Below: Shao Xing

Above: Glutinous rice wine

which is fed by the fountains and streams that flow down the sandy mountains on one side, and the dense bamboo-forested hills on the other. The water is so clear and the surface so smooth that the lake is known locally as "the mirror".

There are several varieties of Shao Xing wines, ranging in colour from golden amber to dark brown, and in the percentage of alcohol by volume from 14–16 per cent. The aroma is always quite distinctive, smelling subtly fragrant and smoky. Shao Xing should be drunk warm, and always with food. It is also used in cooking, and is added to the food towards the end of the cooking time so that the aroma is retained. One of the most famous Shao Xing wines is **Hua Tiao**, meaning "carved flower". This is a reference to the pretty patterns carved on the urns in which the wine is stored in underground cellars to mature.

As in beer brewing and whisky distilling, what distinguishes Shao Xing rice wine from all its imitators is the water used, which just cannot be replicated elsewhere. So beware of Shao

Xing/Hsing wine made in Taiwan, which pales, literally, by comparison. Read the small print on the label; if it says "made in ROC (Republic of China)" it is a fake.

China also produces some quite good grape wines. Several of these are exported to the West. The names to look for are **Dynasty**, **Great Wall** and **Huadong**. The whites (Riesling and Chardonnay) seem to be more successful than the red Cabernet Sauvignon. China may well become an important wine region in the future.

Mirin

This is a sweet rice wine with a low alcohol content. It is widely used in cooking, and is usually added towards the end, so that the subtle flavour is retained. Mirin is now available in the West. If you cannot locate it, dry sherry can be used instead, but the results will not be the same.

Pears with Chinese white wine, star anise and ginger

Star anise and ginger complement these sweet, wine-poached pears.

SERVES 4

75g/3oz/6 tbsp caster (superfine) sugar
300ml/½ pint/1¼ cups white wine
thinly pared rind and juice of
  1 lemon
7.5cm/3in piece fresh root
  ginger, bruised
5 star anise
10 cloves
600ml/1 pint/2½ cups cold water
6 slightly unripe pears
25g/1oz preserved stem ginger, sliced
natural (plain) yogurt, to serve

1 Place the caster sugar, wine, lemon rind and juice, fresh root ginger, star anise, cloves and water into a large pan. Bring to the boil.

2 Meanwhile, peel the pears. Add them to the wine mixture and ensure that they are covered in liquid, then lower the heat. Cover and simmer for 15 minutes or until the pears are tender.

3 Lift out the pears with a slotted spoon and keep them warm. Boil the wine syrup until reduced by half, then pour over the pears. Cool, then chill. Slice the pears and arrange on serving plates. Remove the root ginger from the sauce and add the stem ginger, then spoon the sauce over the pears.

Japanese wines

It is widely known that **sake** is the national drink of Japan. There are many varieties of this rice-based brew, but only a few are exported to the West. Unlike Chinese rice wine, sake is almost colourless, and it tastes slightly sweeter. It usually has an alcohol content of about 15 per cent. Like Chinese rice wine, sake should be drunk with food. Most types of sake are served warm, with the exception of **Ginjo**, a fine, dry wine which is invariably served chilled.

The traditional way of serving sake is in a porcelain jug (pitcher), which is immersed in hot water until the wine is judged to be at the right temperature for serving. It is then poured into small cups. The host lifts a cup in both hands and passes it to his guest with a courteous bow. The cup must not be passed in one hand, as this shows disrespect. Having received the cup, also in both hands, the guest bows and downs the wine in one swift movement.

Good quality grape wines are also produced in Japan, but the output is quite small, owing to the scarcity of land available for growing vines and the extreme climate, all of which make wine-making difficult.

The three big names are **Suntory**, **Mercian** and **Mann's**. All these companies produce both white and red wines, but very little of the wine output is exported overseas.

SPIRITS

Chinese spirits

The Chinese name for distilled spirit – *bai jiu* – means "white wine" and stems from the fact that it is colourless, as opposed to the "yellow" rice wine. Asking for white wine in China can, therefore, lead to some interesting and potentially disastrous social occasions, as most Chinese spirits have an alcohol content of over 50 per cent.

Most Chinese spirits are distilled from a variety of grains, the commonest of these is sorghum, which is a cross between rice and millet. China has far more distilled spirits than wines, and

Below: Mou-Tai, which is served at state banquets, and Chu Yeh Ching

some of the spirits are blended with herbs for use as medicinal tonics.

Mou-Tai is undoubtedly China's top spirit, and it is used for toasts at state banquets and other celebrations. It may be an acquired taste, but it was awarded a medal at the 1915 International Trade Fair in Panama, second only to France's cognac, but ahead of Scotch whisky as the world's top three spirits. Mou-Tai, which means "thatched terrace", is the name of a village in Kweichow in south-west China. The world-renowned spirit is distilled from two grains, wheat and sorghum, with the water taken from the stream running through a nearby gorge. The climate is moist and warm, and the thin layer of mist that hovers permanently over the fast-running stream is supposed to give the spirit its distinctive features.

CHU YEH CHING
CHINESE LIQUEUR

Traditionally, good rice wines came from south China, while the best spirits were historically produced in the north. Although the distillery in Mou-Tai was established in 1529, the spirit was relatively indifferent until 1704, when a salt merchant from Shanxi in north China visited the area and was so enchanted by the beauty of the village that he decided to settle down there. Seeking new employment, he discovered the local spirit and set about improving it, employing the techniques of distilling the famous Fen Chiew from his native northern province. Mou-tai was the result.

Fen Chiew – the inspiration for Mou-Tai – is one of a small group of Chinese spirits that are available in the West. It comes from the "apricot blossoms village" of Shanxi province in north China, and is distilled from millet and sorghum with the water from a tributary of the Yellow River. Fen Chiew has a history of well over 1,500 years, and has afforded inspiration for many of China's greatest poets. This spirit also forms the basis for the famous **Chu Yeh Ching** ("bamboo leaf green"), a medicinal liqueur which is blended with no fewer than twelve different herbs, including bamboo leaves, which give it a lovely, pale green hue. The liqueur tastes quite refreshing despite being 47 per cent alcohol by volume.

Other popular Chinese spirits are **Wu Liang Ye** ("five-grain liqueur") from Sichuan; **Mei Kuei Lu** ("rose dew"); **Wu Chia Pi** ("five-layer skin"); and **Dong Chiew** ("mellow wine"). All of these are quite heady, as they are usually more than 50 per cent proof.

China also produces Western-style brandy, whisky, vodka, rum and gin, but all these drinks are mainly sold for home consumption.

Japanese spirits

Japan has its own spirit distilled from sake called **Shochu** ("burnt wine"). It is quite rough, and is usually diluted with warm water for drinking, even though its alcohol content is only about 25 per cent by volume. Japan produces a

Above: Suntory whisky

Above: Suntory malt whisky

Other Asian spirits

Taiwan produces many of the mainland Chinese drinks as well as the Japanese-inspired **Shokushu** rice spirit. In Korea, look out for **Ginseng Ju**, which comes with what appears to be a parsnip, but is actually a large ginseng root, in every bottle. In the East Indies, the island states in the South China Sea, the local **arrack** or **raki** is crudely distilled from either coconut palm juice or sugar cane molasses. A common practice is to add rice to the fermenting base juice to boost the alcohol content of the spirit. The result is a drink that bears a strong resemblance to rum, and is often sold as such to unwary tourists.

Below: Ginseng Ju

really good quality whisky, however. The first distillery was established in 1923, and in recent years Japanese whisky has attracted considerable attention on the international market. The model for Japan's whiskies is single malt Scotch, but there are equally successful spirits made in the idiom of blended Scotch. Some distilleries blend the home-grown product with imported Scotch malt whisky.

Suntory is the biggest and best-known brand name. Several different labels are marketed worldwide, including **The Whisky**, **Excellence**, **Royal**, **Special Reserve**, **Old**, **Kakubin**, **Gold Label**, **Gold 1000**, **White Label**, **Red Label**, **Torys Extra** and **Rawhide**, which has a bourbon flavour. Suntory's rivals in terms of whisky production are Nikka distilleries (**G & G**, **Super Nikka**, **Black Nikka** and **Hi Nikka**); Kirin Seagram (**Robert Brown** and **Dunbar**); and Sanraku Ocean (**White Label**). Several other distillers and blenders make Japanese whisky, but they only have a very small output. Perhaps the best known of these is **Godo Shusei**.

Suntory also makes good brandy. The leading brands are **Imperial**, **XO**, **VSOP**, **VSO** and **VO**. Liqueurs include **Midori**, a green, melon-flavoured liqueur; **Ocha**, a green tea liqueur with a delicate tea fragrance; and the **Creme de Kobai**, a pale pink liqueur made from Japanese plums.

RECIPES

You are invited to take a cook's tour through China, Malaysia

and Singapore, Thailand, Myanmar, Indonesia, Vietnam,

the Philippines, Japan and Korea. Each has its own distinct

cuisine, and all are exotic, exciting and delicious.

CHINA AND HONG KONG

Chinese food is home cooking to at least a quarter of the world's population, central to the majority

of people's way of life. "Have you eaten?" and "Have you taken rice?" are common greetings

throughout China. In such a vast country, there is a wealth of different styles of cooking, and

many cooks and restaurants in the West are now distinguishing between Cantonese, Sichuan

and Peking-style cooking, introducing us all to some of the world's finest food.

HOT <u>AND</u> SOUR SOUP

ONE OF CHINA'S MOST POPULAR SOUPS, THIS IS FAMED FOR ITS CLEVER BALANCE OF FLAVOURS. THE "HOT" COMES FROM PEPPER; THE "SOUR" FROM VINEGAR. SIMILAR SOUPS ARE FOUND THROUGHOUT ASIA, SOME RELYING ON CHILLIES AND LIME JUICE TO PROVIDE THE ESSENTIAL FLAVOUR CONTRAST.

SERVES 6

INGREDIENTS

4–6 Chinese dried mushrooms
2–3 small pieces of cloud ear (wood
    ear) mushrooms and a few golden
    needles (optional)
115g/4oz pork fillet (tenderloin),
    cut into fine strips
45ml/3 tbsp cornflour (cornstatch)
150ml/¼ pint/⅔ cup water
15–30ml/1–2 tbsp sunflower oil
1 small onion, finely chopped
1.5 litres/2½ pints/6¼ cups good
    quality beef or chicken stock, or
    2 x 300g/11oz cans consommé made
    up to the full quantity with water
150g/5oz drained fresh firm
    tofu, diced
60ml/4 tbsp rice vinegar
15ml/1 tbsp light soy sauce
1 egg, beaten
5 ml/1 tsp sesame oil
salt and ground white or black pepper
2–3 spring onions (scallions),
    shredded, to garnish

1 Place the dried mushrooms in a bowl, with the pieces of cloud ear and the golden needles, if using. Add sufficient warm water to cover and leave to soak for about 30 minutes. Drain the mushrooms, reserving the soaking water. Cut off and discard the mushroom stems and slice the caps finely. Trim away any tough stem from the cloud ears, then chop them finely. Using kitchen string, tie the golden needles into a bundle.

2 Lightly dust the strips of pork fillet with some of the cornflour; mix the remaining cornflour to a smooth paste with the measured water.

3 Heat the oil in a wok or frying pan and fry the onion until soft. Increase the heat and fry the pork until it changes colour. Add the stock or consommé, mushrooms, soaking water, and cloud ears and golden needles, if using. Bring to the boil, then simmer for 15 minutes.

4 Discard the golden needles, lower the heat and stir in the cornflour paste to thicken. Add the tofu, vinegar, soy sauce, and salt and pepper.

5 Bring the soup to just below boiling point, then drizzle in the beaten egg by letting it drop from a whisk (or to be authentic, the fingertips) so that it forms threads in the soup. Stir in the sesame oil and serve immediately, garnished with spring onion shreds.

DRUNKEN CHICKEN

AS THE CHICKEN IS MARINATED FOR SEVERAL DAYS, IT IS IMPORTANT TO USE A VERY FRESH BIRD FROM A REPUTABLE SUPPLIER. "DRUNKEN" FOODS ARE USUALLY SERVED COLD AS PART OF AN APPETIZER, OR CUT INTO NEAT PIECES AND SERVED AS A SNACK WITH COCKTAILS.

SERVES 4–6

INGREDIENTS

1 chicken, about 1.4kg/3lb
1cm/¹/₂in piece of fresh root ginger,
   peeled and thinly sliced
2 spring onions (scallions), trimmed
1.75 litres/3 pints/7¹/₂ cups water
   or to cover
15ml/1 tbsp salt
300ml/¹/₂ pint/1¹/₄ cups dry sherry
15–30ml/1–2 tbsp brandy (optional)
spring onions, shredded, and fresh
   herbs, to garnish

4 Arrange the chicken portions in a shallow dish. Rub salt into the chicken and cover with clear film (plastic wrap). Leave in a cool place for several hours or overnight in the refrigerator.

VARIATION
To serve as a cocktail snack, take the meat off the bones, cut it into bitesize pieces, then spear each piece on a cocktail stick (toothpick).

5 Later, lift off any fat from the stock. Mix the sherry and brandy, if using, in a jug, add the stock and pour over the chicken. Cover again and leave in the refrigerator to marinate for 2 or 3 days, turning occasionally.

6 When ready to serve, cut the chicken through the bone into chunky pieces and arrange on a serving platter garnished with spring onion shreds and herbs.

1 Rinse and dry the chicken inside and out. Place the ginger and spring onions in the body cavity. Put the chicken in a large pan or flameproof casserole and just cover with water. Bring to the boil, skim and cook for 15 minutes.

2 Turn off the heat, cover the pan or casserole tightly and leave the chicken in the cooking liquid for 3–4 hours, by which time it will be cooked. Drain well. Pour 300ml/¹/₂ pint/1¹/₄ cups of the stock into a jug (pitcher). Freeze the remaining stock for use in the future.

3 Remove the skin from the chicken, joint it neatly. Divide each leg into a drumstick and thigh. Make two more portions from the wings and some of the breast. Finally cut away the remainder of the breast pieces (still on the bone) and divide each breast portion into two even pieces.

PEKING DUCK WITH MANDARIN PANCAKES

As the Chinese discovered centuries ago, this is quite the best way to eat duck.
The preparation is time-consuming, but it can be done in easy stages.

SERVES 8

INGREDIENTS
   1 duck, about 2.25kg/5¼lb
   45ml/3 tbsp clear honey
   30ml/2 tbsp water
   5ml/1 tsp salt
   1 bunch spring onions (scallions),
      cut into strips
   ½ cucumber, seeded and cut
      into matchsticks

For the mandarin pancakes
   275g/10oz/2½ cups strong white
      bread flour
   5ml/1 tsp salt
   45ml/3 tbsp peanut or sesame oil
   250ml/8fl oz/1 cup boiling water

For the dipping sauces
   120ml/4fl oz/½ cup hoisin sauce
   120ml/4fl oz/½ cup plum sauce

1 Bring a large pan of water to the boil. Place the duck on a trivet in the sink and pour the boiling water over the duck to scald and firm up the skin. Carefully lift it out on the trivet and drain thoroughly. Tie kitchen string firmly around the legs of the bird and suspend it from a butcher's hook from a shelf in the kitchen or cellar, whichever is the coolest. Place a bowl underneath to catch the drips and leave overnight.

2 Next day, blend the honey, water and salt and brush half the mixture over the duck skin. Hang up again and leave for 2–3 hours. Repeat and leave to dry completely for a further 3–4 hours.

3 Make the pancakes. Sift the flour and salt into a bowl or food processor. Add 15ml/1 tbsp of the oil, then gradually add enough of the boiling water to form a soft but not sticky dough. Knead for 2–3 minutes by hand or for 30 seconds in the food processor. Allow to rest for 30 minutes.

4 Knead the dough, then divide it into 24 pieces and roll each piece to a 15cm/6in round. Brush the surface of half the rounds with oil, then sandwich the rounds together in pairs.

5 Brush the surface of two heavy frying pans sparingly with oil. Add one pancake pair to each pan and cook gently for 2–3 minutes until cooked but not coloured. Turn over and cook for 2–3 minutes more.

6 Slide the double pancakes out of the pan and pull them apart. Stack on a plate, placing a square of non-stick baking parchment between each while cooking the remainder. Cool, wrap tightly in foil and set aside.

7 Preheat the oven to 230°C/450°F/ Gas 8. When it reaches that temperature, put the duck on a rack in a roasting pan and place it in the oven. Immediately reduce the temperature to 180°C/350°F/ Gas 4 and roast the duck for 1¾ hours without basting. Check that the skin is crisp and, if necessary, increase the oven temperature to the maximum. Roast for 15 minutes more.

8 Meanwhile, place the spring onion strips in iced water to crisp up. Drain. Pat the cucumber pieces dry on kitchen paper. Reheat the prepared pancakes by steaming the foil parcel for 5–10 minutes in a bamboo steamer over a wok or pan of boiling water. Pour the dipping sauces into small dishes to share between the guests.

9 Carve the duck into 4cm/1½in pieces. At the table, each guest smears some of the prepared sauce on a pancake, tops it with a small amount of crisp duck skin and meat and adds cucumber and spring onion strips before enjoying the rolled-up pancake.

COOK'S TIP
Mandarin pancakes can be cooked ahead and frozen. Simply separate the cooked pancakes with squares of freezer paper and wrap them in a plastic bag. They can be heated from frozen as described in the recipe. If time is short, use ready-made pancakes, available from large supermarkets and oriental stores.

MONGOLIAN FIREPOT

THIS MODE OF COOKING WAS INTRODUCED TO CHINA BY THE MONGOL HORDES WHO INVADED IN THE 13TH CENTURY. IT CALLS FOR PLENTY OF PARTICIPATION ON THE PART OF THE GUESTS, WHO COOK THE ASSEMBLED INGREDIENTS AT THE TABLE, DIPPING THE MEATS IN A VARIETY OF DIFFERENT SAUCES.

SERVES 6–8

INGREDIENTS

900g/2lb boned leg of lamb,
  preferably bought thinly sliced
225g/8oz lamb's liver and/or kidneys
900ml/1¹/₂ pints/3³/₄ cups lamb
  stock (see Cook's Tip)
900ml/1¹/₂ pints/3³/₄ cups
  chicken stock
1cm/¹/₂in piece fresh root ginger,
  peeled and thinly sliced
45ml/3 tbsp rice wine or
  medium-dry sherry
¹/₂ head Chinese leaves (Chinese
  cabbage), rinsed and shredded
few young spinach leaves
250g/9oz fresh firm tofu, diced
  (optional)
115g/4oz cellophane noodles
salt and ground black pepper

For the dipping sauce
50ml/2fl oz/¹/₄ cup red wine vinegar
7.5ml/¹/₂ tbsp dark soy sauce
1cm/¹/₂in piece fresh root ginger,
  peeled and finely shredded
1 spring onion (scallion),
  finely shredded

To serve
steamed flower rolls
bowls of tomato sauce, sweet chilli
  sauce, mustard oil and sesame oil
dry-fried coriander seeds, crushed

COOK'S TIP
When buying the lamb, ask your butcher for the bones and make your own lamb stock. Rinse the bones and place them in a large pan with water to cover. Bring to the boil and skim the surface well. Add 1 peeled onion, 2 peeled carrots, 1cm/¹/₂in piece of peeled and bruised ginger, 5ml/1 tsp salt and ground black pepper to taste. Bring back to the boil, then simmer for about an hour until the stock is full of flavour. Strain, leave to cool, then skim and use.

1 When buying the lamb, ask your butcher to slice it thinly on a slicing machine, if possible. If you have had to buy the lamb in the piece, however, put it in the freezer for about an hour, so that it is easier to slice thinly.

2 Trim the liver and remove the skin and core from the kidneys, if using. Place them in the freezer too. If you managed to buy sliced lamb, keep it in the refrigerator until needed.

3 Mix both types of stock in a large pan. Add the sliced ginger and rice wine or sherry, with salt and pepper to taste. Heat to simmering point; simmer for 15 minutes.

4 Slice all the meats thinly and arrange them attractively on a large platter.

5 Place the shredded Chinese leaves, spinach leaves and the diced tofu on a separate platter. Soak the noodles in warm or hot water, following the instructions on the packet.

6 Make the dipping sauce by mixing all the ingredients in a small bowl. The other sauces and the crushed coriander seeds should be spooned into separate small dishes and placed on a serving tray. Have ready a basket of freshly steamed flower rolls.

7 Fill the moat of the hotpot with the simmering stock. Alternatively, fill a fondue pot and place it over a burner. Each guest selects a portion of meat from the platter and cooks it in the hot stock, using chopsticks or a fondue fork. The meat is then dipped in one of the sauces and coated with the coriander seeds before being eaten with a steamed flower roll.

8 When all or most of the meat has been eaten, top up the stock if necessary, then add the vegetables, tofu and drained noodles. Cook for a minute or two, until the noodles are tender and the vegetables retain a little crispness. Serve the soup in warmed bowls, with any remaining steamed flower rolls.

ICED FRUIT MOUNTAIN

THIS DRAMATIC DISPLAY OF FRUIT ARRANGED ON A "MOUNTAIN" OF ICE CUBES IS BOUND TO DELIGHT YOUR GUESTS. CUT THE PIECES OF FRUIT LARGER THAN FOR A FRUIT SALAD AND SUPPLY COCKTAIL STICKS FOR SPEARING.

SERVES 6–8

INGREDIENTS
1 star fruit (carambola)
4 kumquats
6 physalis
225g/8oz seedless black grapes
225g/8oz large strawberries
1 apple and/or 1 Asian pear
2 large oranges, peeled
8 fresh lychees, peeled (optional)
1 Charentais melon and/or
  1/2 watermelon
caster (superfine) sugar, for dipping
wedges of kaffir lime, to decorate

COOK'S TIP
The list of fruits is just a suggestion.
Use any colourful seasonal fruits.

1 Slice the star fruit and halve the kumquats. Leave the hulls on the strawberries. Cut the apple and/or Asian pear into wedges, and the oranges into segments. Use a melon baller for the melon or, alternatively, cut the melon into neat wedges. Chill all the fruit.

2 Prepare the ice cube "mountain". Choose a wide, shallow bowl that, when turned upside down, will fit neatly on a serving platter. Fill the bowl with crushed ice cubes. Put it in the freezer, with the serving platter. Leave in the freezer for at least 1 hour.

3 Remove the serving platter, ice cubes and bowl from the freezer. Invert the serving platter on top of the bowl of ice, then turn platter and bowl over. Lift off the bowl and arrange the pieces of fruit on the "mountain".

4 Decorate the mountain with the kaffir lime wedges, and serve immediately, handing round a bowl of sugar separately for guests with a sweet tooth.

CHINESE HONEYED APPLES

THESE SCRUMPTIOUS TREATS ARE BEST PREPARED FOR A SELECT NUMBER AS THEY REQUIRE THE COOK'S COMPLETE ATTENTION. THE HONEY COATING CRISPENS WHEN THE FRITTERS ARE DIPPED IN ICED WATER.

SERVES 4–5

INGREDIENTS
4 crisp eating apples
juice of 1/2 lemon
25g/1oz/1/4 cup cornflour (cornstarch)
sunflower oil, for deep-frying
toasted sesame seeds, for sprinkling

For the fritter batter
115g/4oz/1 cup plain
  (all-purpose) flour
generous pinch of salt
120–150ml/4–5fl oz/1/2–2/3 cup
  water
30ml/2 tbsp sunflower oil
2 egg whites

For the sauce
250ml/8fl oz/1 cup clear honey
120ml/4fl oz/1/2 cup sunflower oil
5ml/1 tsp white wine vinegar

1 Peel, core and cut the apples into eighths, brush each piece lightly with lemon juice then dust with cornflour. Make the sauce. Heat the honey and oil in a pan, stirring until blended. Remove from the heat and stir in the vinegar.

2 Sift the flour and salt into a bowl, then stir in the water and oil. Whisk the egg whites until stiff; fold into the batter.

3 Spear each piece of apple in turn on a skewer, dip in the batter and fry in hot oil until golden. Drain on kitchen paper, place in a dish and pour the sauce over.

4 Transfer the fritters to a lightly oiled serving dish. Sprinkle with sesame seeds. Serve immediately, offering bowls of iced water for dipping.

CRISPY SHANGHAI SPRING ROLLS

IT IS SAID THAT THESE FAMOUS SNACKS WERE TRADITIONALLY SERVED WITH TEA WHEN VISITORS CAME TO CALL AFTER THE CHINESE NEW YEAR. AS THIS WAS SPRINGTIME, THEY CAME TO BE KNOWN AS SPRING ROLLS. BUY FRESH OR FROZEN SPRING ROLL WRAPPERS FROM ASIAN SHOPS.

MAKES 12

INGREDIENTS
    12 spring roll wrappers, thawed
      if frozen
    30ml/2 tbsp plain (all-purpose) flour
      mixed to a paste with water
    sunflower oil, for deep-frying

For the filling
    6 Chinese dried mushrooms, soaked
      for 30 minutes in warm water
    150g/5oz fresh firm tofu
    30ml/2 tbsp sunflower oil
    225g/8oz finely minced (ground) pork
    225g/8oz peeled cooked prawns
      (shrimp), roughly chopped
    2.5ml/¹/₂ tsp cornflour (cornstarch),
      mixed to a paste with 15ml/1 tbsp
      light soy sauce
    75g/3oz each shredded bamboo shoot
      or grated carrot, sliced water
      chestnuts and beansprouts
    6 spring onions (scallions) or 1 young
      leek, finely chopped
    a little sesame oil

For the dipping sauce
    100ml/3¹/₂ fl oz/scant ¹/₂ cup light
      soy sauce
    15ml/1 tbsp chilli sauce or finely
      chopped fresh red chilli
    a little sesame oil
    rice vinegar, to taste

1 Make the filling. Drain the mushrooms. Cut off and discard the stems and slice the caps finely. Cut the tofu into slices of a similar size.

2 Heat the oil in a wok and stir-fry the pork for 2–3 minutes or until the colour changes. Add the prawns, cornflour paste and bamboo shoot or carrot. Stir in the water chestnuts.

COOK'S TIP
Thaw frozen spring roll wrappers at room temperature. Open the parcel and separate with a palette knife or metal spatula. Cover with a damp cloth until needed.

3 Increase the heat, add the beansprouts and spring onions or leek and toss for 1 minute. Stir in the mushrooms and tofu. Off the heat, season, then stir in the sesame oil. Cool quickly on a large platter.

4 Separate the spring roll wrappers (see Cook's Tip). Place a wrapper on the work surface with one corner nearest you. Spoon some of the filling near the centre of the wrapper and fold the nearest corner over the filling. Smear a little of the flour paste on the free sides, turn the sides to the middle and roll up. Repeat this procedure with the remaining wrappers and filling.

5 Deep-fry the spring rolls in batches in oil heated to 190°C/375°F until they are crisp and golden. Drain on kitchen paper and serve immediately with the dipping sauce, made by mixing all the ingredients in a bowl.

LION'S HEAD MEAT BALLS

THESE LARGER-THAN-USUAL PORK MEAT BALLS ARE FIRST FRIED, THEN SIMMERED IN STOCK. THEY ARE TRADITIONALLY SERVED WITH A FRINGE OF GREENS SUCH AS PAK-CHOI TO REPRESENT THE LION'S MANE.

SERVES 2–3

INGREDIENTS

450g/1lb lean pork, minced (ground)
  finely with a little fat
4–6 drained canned water chestnuts,
  finely chopped
5ml/1 tsp finely chopped fresh
  root ginger
1 small onion, finely chopped
30ml/2 tbsp dark soy sauce
beaten egg, to bind
30ml/2 tbsp cornflour (cornstarch),
  seasoned with salt and ground
  black pepper
30ml/2 tbsp groundnut (peanut) oil
300ml/½ pint/1¼ cups chicken stock
2.5ml/½ tsp sugar
115g/4oz pak choi (bok choy), stalks
  trimmed and the leaves rinsed
salt and ground black pepper

1 Mix the pork, water chestnuts, ginger and onion with 15ml/1 tbsp of the soy sauce in a bowl. Add salt and pepper to taste, stir in enough beaten egg to bind, then form into eight or nine balls. Toss a little of the cornflour into the bowl and make a paste with the remaining cornflour and water.

VARIATION
Crab meat or prawns (shrimp) can be used instead of some of the pork in this recipe. Alternatively, you could try substituting minced (ground) lamb or beef for the minced pork used here.

2 Heat the oil in a large frying pan and brown the meat balls all over. Using a slotted spoon, transfer the meat balls to a wok or deep frying pan.

3 Add the stock, sugar and the remaining soy sauce to the oil that is left in the pan. Heat gently, stirring to incorporate the sediment on the bottom of the pan. Pour over the meat balls, cover and simmer for 20–25 minutes.

4 Increase the heat and add the pak choi. Continue to cook for 2–3 minutes or until the leaves are just wilted.

5 Lift out the greens and arrange on a serving platter. Top with the meat balls and keep hot. Stir the cornflour paste into the sauce. Bring to the boil, stirring, until it thickens. Pour over the meat balls and serve immediately.

TEA EGGS

THESE MARBLED EGGS WITH THEIR MAZE OF FINE LINES, HAVE AN ANTIQUE PORCELAIN APPEARANCE.
TEA EGGS CAN BE SERVED AS A SNACK WITH CONGEE, A POPULAR CHINESE SOFT RICE DISH. THEY
ALSO MAKE PERFECT PICNIC FARE; SHELL THEM JUST BEFORE EATING SO THAT THEY STAY MOIST.

MAKES 6

INGREDIENTS
  6 eggs
  30ml/2 tbsp dark soy sauce
  5ml/1 tsp salt
  1/2 star anise
  2 tea bags

COOK'S TIPS
• The soy sauce and tea not only colours
the eggs but adds a subtle flavour as
well. Use dark soy sauce, which has a
stronger flavour.
• Make sure that the eggs simmer very
gently and watch them carefully so that
the soy sauce liquid doesn't evaporate
too much. Keep topping up the liquid
with recently boiled water from the kettle
so that the eggs are always covered.

1 Add the eggs to a pan of cold water.
Heat it to simmering point and hard boil
the eggs for 20 minutes.

2 Drain the eggs and pour enough
fresh cold water into the pan to cover.
Set the eggs aside. When they are cold,
gently roll the eggs to craze the shells
without breaking them.

3 Stir the soy sauce, salt and star anise
into the pan of water. Add the tea bags
and eggs. Bring to the boil, cover and
simmer for 1 1/2–2 hours. Top up the
water to keep the eggs covered.

4 Allow the eggs to cool in the liquid
overnight, then shell carefully. Quarter
and serve as part of a meal.

ANITA WONG'S DUCK

THE CHINESE ARE PASSIONATELY FOND OF DUCK AND REGARD IT AS ESSENTIAL AT CELEBRATORY
MEALS. TO THE CHINESE, DUCK DENOTES MARITAL HARMONY.

SERVES 4–6

INGREDIENTS
  1 duck with giblets, about
    2.25kg/5–5 1/4lb
  60ml/4 tbsp vegetable oil
  2 garlic cloves, chopped
  2.5cm/1in piece fresh root ginger,
    peeled and thinly sliced
  45ml/3 tbsp bean paste
  30ml/2 tbsp light soy sauce
  15ml/1 tbsp dark soy sauce
  15ml/1 tbsp sugar
  2.5ml/1/2 tsp Chinese five-spice
    powder
  3 star anise points
  450ml/3/4 pint/scant 2 cups duck
    stock (see Cook's Tip)
  salt
  shredded spring onions (scallions),
    to garnish

1 Make the stock (see Cook's Tip),
strain into a bowl and blot with kitchen
paper to remove excess fat. Measure
450ml/3/4 pint/scant 2 cups into a bowl.

2 Heat the oil in a large pan. Fry the
garlic without browning, then add the
duck. Turn frequently until the outside
is slightly brown. Transfer to a plate.

3 Add the ginger to the pan, then stir
in the bean paste. Cook for 1 minute,
then add both soy sauces, the sugar
and the five-spice powder. Return
the duck to the pan and fry until the
outside is coated. Add the star anise
and stock, and season to taste. Cover
tightly; simmer gently for 2–2 1/2 hours
or until tender. Skim off the excess fat.
Leave the duck in the sauce to cool.

4 Cut the duck into serving portions
and pour over the sauce. Garnish with
spring onion and serve cold.

COOK'S TIP
To make stock, put the duck giblets in a
pan. Add a small onion and a piece of
bruised fresh root ginger. Cover with
600ml/1 pint/2 1/2 cups water, bring to
the boil. Simmer, covered, for 20 minutes.

SICHUAN CHICKEN WITH KUNG PO SAUCE

THIS RECIPE, WHICH HAILS FROM THE SICHUAN REGION OF WESTERN CHINA, HAS BECOME ONE OF THE CLASSIC RECIPES IN THE CHINESE REPERTOIRE.

SERVES 3

INGREDIENTS
2 skinless chicken breast fillets,
   total weight about 350g/12oz
1 egg white
10ml/2 tsp cornflour (cornstarch)
2.5ml/½ tsp salt
30ml/2 tbsp yellow salted beans
15ml/1 tbsp hoisin sauce
5ml/1 tsp light brown sugar
15ml/1 tbsp rice wine or
   medium-dry sherry
15ml/1 tbsp wine vinegar
4 garlic cloves, crushed
150ml/¼ pint/⅔ cup chicken stock
45ml/3 tbsp groundnut (peanut) oil
   or sunflower oil
2–3 dried chillies, broken into
   small pieces
115g/4oz roasted cashew nuts
fresh coriander (cilantro), to garnish

1 Cut the chicken into neat pieces. Lightly whisk the egg white in a dish, whisk in the cornflour and salt, then add the chicken and stir until coated.

COOK'S TIP
Peanuts are the classic ingredient in this dish, but cashew nuts have an even better flavour and have become popular both in home cooking and in restaurants.

2 In a separate bowl, mash the beans with a spoon. Stir in the hoisin sauce, brown sugar, rice wine or sherry, vinegar, garlic and stock.

3 Heat a wok, add the oil and then fry the chicken, turning constantly, for about 2 minutes until tender. Drain over a bowl in order to collect excess oil.

4 Heat the reserved oil and fry the chilli pieces for 1 minute. Return the chicken to the wok and pour in the bean sauce mixture. Bring to the boil and stir in the cashew nuts. Spoon into a heated serving dish and garnish with coriander leaves.

SICHUAN NOODLES WITH SESAME SAUCE

THIS TASTY VEGETARIAN DISH RESEMBLES THAMIN LETHOK, A MYANMAR DISH, WHICH ALSO CONSISTS OF FLAVOURED NOODLES SERVED WITH SEPARATE VEGETABLES THAT ARE TOSSED AT THE TABLE. THIS ILLUSTRATES NEATLY HOW RECIPES MIGRATE FROM ONE COUNTRY TO ANOTHER.

SERVES 3–4

INGREDIENTS

450g/1lb fresh or 225g/8oz dried
  egg noodles
1/2 cucumber, sliced lengthways,
  seeded and diced
4–6 spring onions (scallions)
a bunch of radishes, about 115g/4oz
225g/8oz mooli (daikon), peeled
115g/4oz/2 cups beansprouts, rinsed
  then left in iced water and drained
60ml/4 tbsp groundnut (peanut) oil
  or sunflower oil
2 garlic cloves, crushed
45ml/3 tbsp toasted sesame paste
15ml/1 tbsp sesame oil
15ml/1 tbsp light soy sauce
5–10ml/1–2 tsp chilli sauce, to taste
15ml/1 tbsp rice vinegar
120ml/4fl oz/1/2 cup chicken stock
  or water
5ml/1 tsp sugar, or to taste
salt and ground black pepper
roasted peanuts or cashew nuts,
  to garnish

1 If using fresh noodles, cook them in boiling water for 1 minute then drain well. Rinse the noodles in fresh water and drain again. Cook dried noodles according to the instructions on the packet, draining and rinsing them as for fresh noodles.

2 Sprinkle the cucumber with salt, leave for 15 minutes, rinse well, then drain and pat dry on kitchen paper. Place in a large salad bowl.

3 Cut the spring onions into fine shreds. Cut the radishes in half and slice finely. Coarsely grate the mooli using a mandolin or a food processor. Add all the vegetables to the cucumber and toss gently.

4 Heat half the oil in a wok or frying pan and stir-fry the noodles for about 1 minute. Using a slotted spoon, transfer the noodles to a large serving bowl and keep warm.

5 Add the remaining oil to the wok. When it is hot, fry the garlic to flavour the oil. Remove from the heat and stir in the sesame paste, with the sesame oil, soy and chilli sauces, vinegar and stock or water. Add a little sugar and season to taste. Warm through over low heat. Do not overheat or the sauce will thicken too much. Pour the sauce over the noodles and toss well. Garnish with peanuts or cashew nuts and serve with the vegetables.

SICHUAN SPICED AUBERGINE

THIS STRAIGHTFORWARD YET VERSATILE VEGETARIAN DISH CAN BE SERVED HOT, WARM OR COLD, AS THE OCCASION DEMANDS. TOPPED WITH A SPRINKLING OF TOASTED SESAME SEEDS, IT IS EASY TO PREPARE AND TASTES ABSOLUTELY DELICIOUS.

SERVES 4–6

INGREDIENTS

2 aubergines (eggplants), total
  weight about 600g/1lb 6oz,
  cut into large chunks
15ml/1 tbsp salt
5ml/1 tsp chilli powder or to taste
75–90ml/5–6 tbsp sunflower oil
15ml/1 tbsp rice wine or
  medium-dry sherry
100ml/3½fl oz/scant ½ cup water
75ml/5 tbsp chilli bean sauce
  (see Cook's Tip)
salt and ground black pepper
a few toasted sesame seeds,
  to garnish

1 Place the aubergine chunks on a plate, sprinkle them with the salt and leave to stand for 15–20 minutes. Rinse well, drain and dry thoroughly on kitchen paper. Toss the aubergine cubes in the chilli powder.

2 Heat a wok and add the oil. When the oil is hot, add the aubergine chunks, with the rice wine or sherry. Stir constantly until the aubergine chunks start to turn a little brown. Stir in the water, cover the wok and steam for 2–3 minutes. Add the chilli bean sauce and cook for 2 minutes. Season to taste, then spoon on to a serving dish, scatter with sesame seeds and serve.

COOK'S TIP
If you can't get hold of chilli bean sauce, use 15–30ml/1–2 tbsp chilli paste mixed with 2 crushed garlic cloves, 15ml/1 tbsp each of dark soy sauce and rice vinegar, and 10ml/2 tsp light soy sauce.

KAN SHAO GREEN BEANS

A PARTICULAR STYLE OF COOKING FROM SICHUAN, KAN SHAO MEANS "DRY-COOKED" – IN OTHER WORDS USING NO STOCK OR WATER. THE SLIM GREEN BEANS AVAILABLE ALL THE YEAR ROUND FROM SUPERMARKETS ARE IDEAL FOR USE IN THIS QUICK AND TASTY RECIPE.

SERVES 6

INGREDIENTS

175ml/6fl oz/¾ cup sunflower oil
450/1lb fresh green beans, topped,
  tailed and cut in half
5 × 1cm/2 × ½in piece fresh
  root ginger, peeled and cut
  into matchsticks
5ml/1 tsp sugar
10ml/2 tsp light soy sauce
salt and ground black pepper

VARIATION
This simple recipe works just as well with other fresh green vegetables such as baby asparagus spears and okra.

1 Heat the oil in a wok. When the oil is just beginning to smoke, carefully add the beans and stir-fry them for 1–2 minutes until just tender.

2 Lift out the green beans on to a plate lined with kitchen paper. Using a ladle carefully remove all but 30ml/2 tbsp oil from the wok.

3 Reheat the remaining oil, add the ginger and stir-fry for a minute or two to flavour the oil.

4 Return the green beans to the wok, stir in the sugar, soy sauce and salt and pepper, and toss together quickly to ensure the beans are well coated. Serve the beans immediately.

BANG BANG CHICKEN

WHAT A DESCRIPTIVE NAME THIS SPECIAL DISH FROM SICHUAN HAS! USE TOASTED SESAME PASTE TO GIVE THE SAUCE AN AUTHENTIC FLAVOUR, ALTHOUGH CRUNCHY PEANUT BUTTER CAN BE USED INSTEAD. BANG BANG CHICKEN IS PERFECT FOR PARTIES AND IDEAL FOR A BUFFET.

SERVES 4

INGREDIENTS
3 skinless chicken breast fillets,
   total weight about 450g/1lb
1 garlic clove, crushed
2.5ml/1/2 tsp black peppercorns
1 small onion, halved
1 large cucumber, peeled, seeded
   and cut into thin strips
salt and ground black pepper

For the sauce
45ml/3 tbsp toasted sesame paste
15ml/1 tbsp light soy sauce
15ml/1 tbsp wine vinegar
2 spring onions (scallions),
   finely chopped
2 garlic cloves, crushed
5 × 1cm/2 × 1/2in piece fresh root
   ginger, cut into matchsticks
15ml/1 tbsp Sichuan peppercorns,
   dry-fried and crushed
5ml/1 tsp soft light brown sugar

For the chilli oil
60ml/4 tbsp groundnut (peanut) oil
5ml/1 tsp chilli powder

1 Place the chicken in a pan. Just cover with water, add the garlic, peppercorns and onion and bring to the boil. Skim the surface, stir in salt and pepper to taste, then cover the pan. Cook for 25 minutes or until the chicken is just tender. Drain, reserving the stock.

2 Make the sauce by mixing the toasted sesame paste with 45ml/3 tbsp of the chicken stock, saving the rest for soup. Add the soy sauce, vinegar, spring onions, garlic, ginger and crushed peppercorns to the sesame mixture. Stir in sugar to taste.

3 Make the chilli oil by gently heating the oil and chilli powder together until foaming. Simmer for 2 minutes, cool, then strain off the red-coloured oil and discard the sediment.

4 Spread out the cucumber batons on a platter. Cut the chicken breast fillets into pieces of about the same size as the cucumber strips and arrange them on top. Pour over the sauce, drizzle on the chilli oil and serve.

VARIATION
Crunchy peanut butter can be used instead of sesame paste, if preferred. Mix it with 30ml/2 tbsp sesame oil and proceed as in Step 2.

CRISPY WONTON SOUP

*THE FRESHLY COOKED CRISP WONTONS ARE SUPPOSED TO SIZZLE AND "SING" IN THE HOT SOUP
AS THEY ARE TAKEN TO THE TABLE.*

2 Place the wonton wrappers under a slightly dampened dish towel so that they do not dry out. Next, dampen the edges of a wonton wrapper. Place about 5ml/1 tsp of the filling in the centre of the wrapper. Gather it up like a purse and twist the top or roll up as you would a baby spring roll. Fill the remaining wontons in the same way.

3 Make the soup. Drain the cloud ears, trim away any rough stems, then slice thinly. Bring the stock to the boil, add the ginger and the spring onions and simmer for 3 minutes. Add the sliced cloud ears, shredded spring greens, bamboo shoots and soy sauce. Simmer for 10 minutes, then stir in the sesame oil. Season to taste with salt and pepper, cover and keep hot.

SERVES 6

INGREDIENTS
  2 cloud ear (wood ear) mushrooms,
    soaked for 30 minutes in warm water
  1.2 litres/2 pints/5 cups home-made
    chicken stock
  2.5cm/1in piece fresh root ginger,
    peeled and grated
  4 spring onions (scallions), chopped
  2 rich-green inner spring greens
    (collards) leaves, finely shredded
  50g/2oz drained canned bamboo
    shoots, sliced
  25ml/1½ tbsp dark soy sauce
  2.5ml/½ tsp sesame oil
  salt and ground black pepper

For the filled wontons
  5ml/1 tsp sesame oil
  ½ small onion, finely chopped
  10 drained canned water
    chestnuts, finely chopped
  115g/4oz finely minced (ground) pork
  24 wonton wrappers
  groundnut (peanut) oil, for deep-frying

1 Make the filled wontons. Heat the sesame oil in a small pan, add the onion, water chestnuts and pork and fry, stirring occasionally, until the meat is no longer pink. Transfer into a bowl, season to taste and leave to cool.

COOK'S TIP
The wontons can be filled up to two hours ahead. Place them in a single layer on a baking sheet dusted with cornflour (cornstarch) to prevent them from sticking and leave in a cool place.

4 Heat the oil in a wok to 190°C/375°F and fry the wontons, in batches if necessary, for 3–4 minutes or until they are crisp and golden brown all over. Ladle the soup into six warmed soup bowls and share the wontons among them. Serve immediately.

EGG FOO YUNG – CANTONESE STYLE

HEARTY AND FULL OF FLAVOUR, THIS CAN BE COOKED EITHER AS ONE LARGE OMELETTE OR AS INDIVIDUAL OMELETTES. EITHER WAY, IT IS A CLEVER WAY OF USING UP LEFTOVERS SUCH AS COOKED HAM, SEAFOOD, CHICKEN, PORK OR VEGETABLES. SERVE IT CUT INTO PIECES.

2 Beat the eggs in a bowl. Add the meat and vegetables and mix well.

3 Wipe the frying pan and heat the remaining oil. Pour in the egg mixture and tilt the pan so that it covers the base. When the omelette has set on the underside, sprinkle the top with salt, pepper and sugar.

SERVES 3–4

INGREDIENTS
  6 Chinese dried mushrooms soaked
    for 30 minutes in warm water
  50g/2oz/1 cup beansprouts
  6 drained canned water chestnuts,
    finely chopped
  50g/2oz baby spinach leaves, washed
  60ml/4 tbsp sunflower oil
  50g/2oz roast pork, cut into
    thin strips
  4 eggs
  2.5ml/½ tsp sugar
  5ml/1 tsp rice wine or
    medium-dry sherry
  salt and ground black pepper
  fresh coriander (cilantro) sprigs,
    to garnish

1 Drain the mushrooms, cut off and discard the stems; slice the caps finely and mix them with the remaining vegetables. Heat half the oil in a large heavy frying pan. Add the pork and the vegetables and toss the mixture over the heat for 1 minute.

4 Invert a plate over the pan, turn both over, and slide it back into the pan to cook on the other side. Drizzle with rice wine or sherry and serve immediately, garnished with sprigs of coriander.

CANTONESE FRIED NOODLES

CHOW MEIN IS HUGELY POPULAR WITH THE THRIFTY CHINESE WHO BELIEVE IN TURNING LEFTOVERS INTO TASTY DISHES. FOR THIS DELICIOUS DISH, BOILED NOODLES ARE FRIED TO FORM A CRISPY CRUST, WHICH IS TOPPED WITH A SAVOURY SAUCE CONTAINING WHATEVER TASTES GOOD AND NEEDS EATING UP.

SERVES 2–3

INGREDIENTS

225g/8oz lean beef steak or
  pork fillet (tenderloin)
225g/8oz can bamboo shoots, drained
1 leek, trimmed
25g/1oz Chinese dried mushrooms,
  soaked for 30 minutes in 120ml/
  4fl oz/½ cup warm water
150g/5oz Chinese leaves
  (Chinese cabbage)
450g/1lb cooked egg noodles, drained
90ml/6 tbsp vegetable oil
30ml/2 tbsp dark soy sauce
15ml/1 tbsp cornflour (cornstarch)
15ml/1 tbsp rice wine or
  medium-dry sherry
5ml/1 tsp sesame oil
5ml/1 tsp caster (superfine) sugar
salt and ground black pepper

1 Slice the beef or pork, bamboo shoots and leek into matchsticks. Drain the mushrooms, reserving 90ml/6 tbsp of the soaking water. Cut off and discard the stems, then slice the caps finely. Cut the Chinese leaves into 2.5cm/1in diamond-shaped pieces and sprinkle with salt. Pat the noodles dry with kitchen paper.

2 Heat a third of the oil in a large wok or frying pan and sauté the noodles. After turning them over once, press the noodles evenly against the bottom of the pan with a wooden spatula until they form a flat, even cake. Cook over medium heat for about 4 minutes or until the noodles at the bottom have become crisp.

3 Turn the noodle cake over with a metal spatula or fish slice or invert on to a large plate and slide back into the wok. Cook for 3 minutes more, then slide on to a heated plate. Keep warm.

4 Heat 30ml/2 tbsp of the remaining oil in the wok. Add the strips of leek, then the meat strips and stir-fry for 10–15 seconds. Sprinkle over half the soy sauce and then add the bamboo shoots and mushrooms, with salt and pepper to taste. Toss over the heat for 1 minute, then transfer this mixture to a plate and set aside.

5 Heat the remaining oil in the wok and sauté the Chinese leaves for 1 minute. Return the meat and vegetable mixture to the wok and sauté with the leaves for 30 seconds, stirring constantly.

6 Mix the cornflour with the reserved mushroom water. Stir into the wok with the rice wine or sherry, sesame oil, sugar and remaining soy sauce. Cook for 15 seconds to thicken. Divide the noodles among two to three serving dishes and pile the meat and vegetables on top.

STEAMED FISH WITH FIVE WILLOW SAUCE

A FISH KETTLE WILL COME IN USEFUL FOR THIS RECIPE. CARP IS TRADITIONALLY USED, BUT ANY CHUNKY FISH THAT CAN BE COOKED WHOLE SUCH AS SALMON OR SEA BREAM CAN BE GIVEN THIS TREATMENT. MAKE SURE YOU HAVE A SUITABLE LARGE PLATTER FOR SERVING THIS SPECTACULAR DISH.

SERVES 4

INGREDIENTS
 1–2 carp or similar whole fish, total
  weight about 1kg/2¼lb, cleaned
  and scaled
 2.5cm/1in piece fresh root ginger,
  peeled and thinly sliced
 4 spring onions (scallions), cut into
  thin strips
 2.5ml/½ tsp salt

For the five willow sauce
 375g/13oz jar chow chow (Chinese
  sweet mixed pickles)
 300ml/½ pint/1¼ cups water
 30ml/2 tbsp rice vinegar
 25ml/1½ tbsp sugar
 25ml/1½ tbsp cornflour (cornstarch)
 15ml/1 tbsp light soy sauce
 15ml/1 tbsp rice wine or
  medium-dry sherry
 1 small green (bell) pepper, seeded
  and diced
 1 carrot, peeled and cut into matchsticks
 1 tomato, peeled, seeded and diced

2 Fold up one or two pieces of foil to make a long wide strip. You will need one for each fish. Place the fish on the foil and then lift the fish on to the trivet. Lower the trivet into the fish kettle and tuck the ends of the foil over the fish.

3 Pour boiling water into the fish kettle to a depth of 2.5cm/1in. Bring to a full rolling boil, then lower the heat and cook the fish until the flesh flakes, topping up the kettle with boiling water as necessary. See Cook's Tip for cooking times.

5 In a small bowl, mix the cornflour to a paste with the remaining water. Stir in the soy sauce and rice wine or sherry.

6 Add the mixture to the sauce and bring to the boil, stirring until it thickens and becomes glossy. Add all the vegetables, the chopped pickles and the pickle liquid and cook over low heat for 2 minutes.

7 Using the foil strips as a support, carefully transfer the cooked fish to a platter, then ease the foil away. Spoon the warm sauce over the fish and serve.

4 Meanwhile, prepare the sauce. Transfer the chow chow into a strainer placed over a bowl and reserve the liquid. Cut each of the pickles in half. Pour 250ml/8fl oz/1 cup of the water into a pan and bring to the boil. Add the vinegar, and then the sugar, stirring until dissolved.

1 Rinse the fish inside and out. Dry with kitchen paper. Create a support for each fish by placing a broad strip of oiled foil on the work surface. Place the fish on the foil. Mix the ginger, spring onions and salt, then tuck the mixture into the body cavity.

COOK'S TIP
If using one large fish that is too long to fit in a fish kettle, cut it in half and cook it on a rack placed over a large roasting pan. Pour in a similar quantity of boiling water as for the fish kettle, cover with foil and cook on top of the stove. Allow about 20–25 minutes for a 1kg/2¼lb fish; 15–20 minutes for a 675g/1½lb fish. Reassemble the halved fish before coating it with the sauce.

DUCK BREASTS WITH PINEAPPLE AND GINGER

USE THE BONELESS DUCK BREAST FILLETS THAT ARE WIDELY AVAILABLE OR ALTERNATIVELY DO AS THE CHINESE AND USE A WHOLE BIRD, SAVING THE LEGS FOR ANOTHER MEAL AND USING THE CARCASS TO MAKE STOCK FOR SOUP. MUCH MORE IN LINE WITH CHINESE FRUGALITY.

SERVES 2–3

INGREDIENTS

2 boneless duck breast fillets
4 spring onions (scallions), chopped
15ml/1 tbsp light soy sauce
225g/8oz can pineapple rings
75ml/5 tbsp water
4 pieces drained Chinese preserved
   stem ginger in syrup, plus 45ml/
   3 tbsp syrup from the jar
30ml/2 tbsp cornflour (cornstarch)
   mixed to a paste with a little water
1/4 each red and green (bell) pepper,
   seeded and cut into thin strips
salt and ground black pepper
cooked thin egg noodles, baby
   spinach and green beans, blanched,
   to serve

1 Strip the skin from the duck breast fillets. Select a shallow bowl that will fit into your steamer and will accommodate the duck breasts side by side. Spread out the chopped spring onions in the bowl, arrange the duck breasts on top and cover with baking parchment. Set the steamer over boiling water and cook the duck breasts for about 1 hour or until tender. Remove the breasts from the steamer and leave to cool slightly.

2 Cut the breasts into thin slices. Place on a plate and moisten them with a little of the cooking juices from the steaming bowl. Strain the remaining juices into a small pan and set aside. Cover the duck slices with the baking parchment or foil and keep warm.

3 Drain the canned pineapple rings, reserving 75ml/5 tbsp of the juice. Add this to the reserved cooking juices in the pan, together with the measured water. Stir in the ginger syrup, then stir in the cornflour paste and cook, stirring until thickened. Season to taste.

4 Cut the pineapple and ginger into attractive shapes. Put the cooked noodles, baby spinach and green beans on a plate, add slices of duck and top with the pineapple, ginger and pepper strips. Pour over the sauce and serve.

SPICY SHREDDED BEEF

THE ESSENCE OF THIS RECIPE IS THAT THE BEEF IS CUT INTO VERY FINE STRIPS. THIS IS EASIER TO ACHIEVE IF THE PIECE OF BEEF IS PLACED IN THE FREEZER FOR 30 MINUTES UNTIL IT IS VERY FIRM BEFORE BEING SLICED WITH A SHARP KNIFE.

SERVES 2

INGREDIENTS
225g/8oz rump (round) or fillet
   (tenderloin) of beef
15ml/1 tbsp each light and dark
   soy sauce
15ml/1 tbsp rice wine or
   medium-dry sherry
5ml/1 tsp soft dark brown sugar
   or golden sugar
90ml/6 tbsp vegetable oil
1 large onion, thinly sliced
2.5cm/1in piece fresh root ginger,
   peeled and grated
1–2 carrots, cut into matchsticks
2–3 fresh or dried chillies, halved,
   seeded (optional) and chopped
salt and ground black pepper
fresh chives, to garnish

1 With a sharp knife, slice the beef very thinly, then cut each slice into fine strips or shreds.

2 Mix together the light and dark soy sauces with the rice wine or sherry and sugar in a bowl. Add the strips of beef and stir well to ensure they are evenly coated with the marinade.

3 Heat a wok and add half the oil. When it is hot, stir-fry the onion and ginger for 3–4 minutes, then transfer to a plate. Add the carrot, stir-fry for 3–4 minutes until slightly softened, then transfer to a plate and keep warm.

4 Heat the remaining oil in the wok, then quickly add the beef, with the marinade, followed by the chillies. Cook over high heat for 2 minutes, stirring all the time.

5 Return the fried onion and ginger to the wok and stir-fry for 1 minute more. Season with salt and pepper to taste, cover and cook for 30 seconds. Spoon the meat into two warmed bowls and add the strips of carrots. Garnish with fresh chives and serve.

COOK'S TIP
Remove and discard the seeds from the chillies before you chop them – unless, of course, you like really fiery food. In which case, you could add some or all of the seeds with the chopped chillies.

STEAMED FLOWER ROLLS

THESE ATTRACTIVE LITTLE ROLLS ARE TRADITIONALLY SERVED WITH MONGOLIAN FIREPOT.

MAKES 16

INGREDIENTS

   1 quantity basic dough (below) made
     using only 5ml/1 tsp sugar
   15ml/1 tbsp sesame seed oil
   chives, to garnish

1 Divide the risen and knocked back
(punched down) dough into two equal
portions. Roll each into a rectangle, 30 x
20cm/12 x 8in. Brush the surface of one
with sesame oil and lay the other on top.
Roll up and cut into 16 pieces.

2 Take each dough roll in turn and
press down firmly on the rolled side
with a chopstick. Place the rolls on the
work surface, coiled side uppermost.

3 Pinch the opposite ends of each
roll with the fingers of both hands, then
pull the ends underneath and seal.
The dough should separate into petals.
Place the buns on baking parchment in
a steamer and leave to double in size.
Steam over rapidly boiling water for
30–35 minutes. Serve hot, garnished
with chives.

COOK'S TIP

When lining the steamer, fold the paper
several times, then cut small holes like
a doily. This lets the steam circulate, yet
prevents the steamed flower rolls from
sticking to the steamer.

PORK-STUFFED STEAMED BUNS

THESE TREATS ARE JUST ONE EXAMPLE OF DIM SUM, *FEATHERLIGHT STEAMED BUNS WITH A RANGE
OF TASTY FILLINGS. THEY ARE NOW A POPULAR SNACK THE WORLD OVER.*

MAKES 16

INGREDIENTS

For the basic dough
   15ml/1 tbsp sugar
   300ml/½ pint/1¼ cups warm water
   25ml/1½ tbsp active dried yeast
   450g/1lb/4 cups strong white
     bread flour
   5ml/1 tsp salt
   15g/½oz/1 tbsp lard or white
     cooking fat
   chives, to garnish

For the filling
   30ml/2 tbsp oil
   1 garlic clove, crushed
   225g/8oz roast pork, very finely chopped
   2 spring onions (scallions), chopped
   10ml/2 tsp yellow bean sauce, crushed
   10ml/2 tsp sugar
   5ml/1 tsp cornflour (cornstarch)
     mixed to a paste with water

1 Make the dough. In a small bowl,
dissolve the sugar in half the water.
Sprinkle in the yeast. Stir well, then
leave for 10–15 minutes until frothy. Sift
the flour and salt into a bowl and rub
in the lard. Stir in the yeast mixture with
enough of the remaining water to make
a soft dough. Knead on a floured
surface for 10 minutes. Transfer to an
oiled bowl and cover. Leave in a warm
place for 1 hour until doubled in bulk.

2 Meanwhile, make the filling. Heat the
oil and fry the garlic until golden, then
add the pork, spring onions, bean
sauce and sugar. Stir in the cornflour
paste and cook, stirring, until slightly
thickened. Leave to cool.

3 Knock back (punch down) the dough.
Knead it for 2 minutes, then divide into
16 pieces. Roll out each piece on a floured
surface to a 7.5–10cm/3–4in round.

4 Place a spoonful of filling in the
centre of each, gather up the sides and
twist the top to seal. Secure with string.

5 Set the buns on baking parchment
in a large steamer and leave in a warm
place until they have doubled in size.
Steam over rapidly boiling water for
30–35 minutes. Serve hot, garnished
with chives.

CONGEE <u>WITH</u> CHINESE SAUSAGE

CONGEE — SOFT RICE — IS COMFORT FOOD. GENTLE ON THE STOMACH, IT IS FREQUENTLY EATEN FOR BREAKFAST OR SERVED TO INVALIDS. THROUGHOUT THE EAST, PEOPLE WILL FREQUENTLY HAVE JUST A CUP OF TEA ON RISING; LATER THEY WILL SETTLE DOWN TO A BOWL OF CONGEE OR ITS REGIONAL EQUIVALENT.

SERVES 2–3

INGREDIENTS
 115g/4oz/generous ½ cup
  long-grain rice
 25g/1oz/3 tbsp glutinous rice
 1.2 litres/2 pints/5 cups water
 about 2.5ml/½ tsp salt
 5ml/1 tsp sesame oil
 thin slice of fresh root ginger,
  peeled and bruised
 2 Chinese sausages
 1 egg, lightly beaten (optional)
 2.5ml/½ tsp light soy sauce
 roasted peanuts, chopped, and thin
  shreds of spring onion (scallion),
  to garnish

1 Wash both rices thoroughly. Drain and place in a large pan. Add the water, bring to the boil and immediately reduce to the lowest heat, using a heat diffuser if you have one.

2 Cook gently for 1¼–1½ hours, stirring from time to time. If the congee thickens too much, stir in a little boiling water. It should have the consistency of creamy pouring porridge.

3 About 15 minutes before serving, add salt to taste and the sesame oil, together with the piece of ginger.

4 Steam the Chinese sausages for about 10 minutes, then slice and stir into the congee. Cook for 5 minutes.

5 Just before serving, remove the ginger and stir in the lightly beaten egg, if using. Serve hot, garnished with the peanuts and spring onions and topped with a drizzle of soy sauce.

VARIATION
If you prefer, use roast duck instead of Chinese sausages. Cut the cooked duck into bitesize pieces and add once the rice is cooked. Congee is also popular with tea eggs.

SALT AND PEPPER PRAWNS

THESE SUCCULENT SHELLFISH BEG TO BE EATEN WITH THE FINGERS, SO PROVIDE FINGER BOWLS
OR HOT CLOTHS FOR YOUR GUESTS.

SERVES 3–4

INGREDIENTS
  15–18 large raw prawns (shrimp),
    in the shell, about 450g/1lb
  vegetable oil, for deep-frying
  3 shallots or 1 small onion,
    very finely chopped
  2 garlic cloves, crushed
  1cm/¹/₂in piece fresh root ginger,
    peeled and very finely grated
  1–2 fresh red chillies, seeded and
    finely sliced
  2.5ml/¹/₂ tsp sugar or to taste
  3–4 spring onions (scallions),
    shredded, to garnish

For the fried salt
  10ml/2 tsp salt
  5ml/1 tsp Sichuan peppercorns

2 Carefully remove the heads and legs
from the raw prawns and discard. Leave
the body shells and the tails in place.
Pat the prepared prawns dry with
sheets of kitchen paper.

3 Heat the oil for deep-frying to 190°C/
375°F. Fry the prawns for 1 minute,
then lift them out and drain thoroughly
on kitchen paper. Spoon 30ml/2 tbsp
of the hot oil into a large frying pan,
leaving the rest of the oil to one side
to cool.

4 Heat the oil in the frying pan. Add
the fried salt, with the shallots or onion,
garlic, ginger, chillies and sugar. Toss
together for 1 minute, then add the
prawns and toss them over the heat
for 1 minute more until they are coated
and the shells are impregnated with
the seasonings. Serve immediately,
garnished with the spring onions.

1 Make the fried salt by dry-frying the
salt and peppercorns in a heavy frying
pan over medium heat until the
peppercorns begin to release their
aroma. Cool the mixture, then transfer
into a mortar and crush with a pestle.

COOK'S TIP
"Fried salt" is also known as "Cantonese
salt" or simply "salt and pepper mix". It
is widely used as a table condiment or as
a dip for deep-fried or roasted food, but
can also be an ingredient, as here. Black
or white peppercorns can be substituted
for the Sichuan peppercorns. It really is
best made when required.

FRAGRANT HARBOUR FRIED RICE

FRAGRANT HARBOUR IS THE CHINESE NAME FOR HONG KONG, THE CROSSROADS FOR SO MANY STYLES OF COOKING. FRIED RICE IS EVER POPULAR AS YET ANOTHER WAY OF USING UP LITTLE BITS OF THIS AND THAT TO MAKE A VERITABLE FEAST. COOK THE RICE THE DAY BEFORE IF POSSIBLE.

SERVES 4

INGREDIENTS

225g/8oz/generous 1 cup long
   grain rice
about 90ml/6 tbsp vegetable oil
2 eggs, beaten
4 Chinese dried mushrooms, soaked
   for 30 minutes in warm water to cover
8 shallots or 2 small onions, sliced
115g/4oz cooked, peeled prawns
   (shrimp), thawed if frozen
3 garlic cloves, crushed
115g/4oz cooked pork, cut into
   thin strips
115g/4oz Chinese sausage
30ml/2 tbsp light soy sauce
115g/4oz/1 cup frozen peas, thawed
2 spring onions (scallions), shredded
1–2 fresh or dried red chillies,
   seeded (optional)
salt and ground black pepper
fresh coriander (cilantro) leaves,
   to garnish

1 Bring a large pan of lightly salted water to the boil. Add the rice and cook for 12–15 minutes until just tender. Drain and leave to go cold. Ideally use the next day.

2 Heat about 15ml/1 tbsp of the oil in a large frying pan over medium heat, pour in the beaten eggs and allow to set without stirring. Slide the omelette on to a plate, roll it up and cut into fine strips. Set aside.

3 Drain the mushrooms, cut off and discard the stems and slice the caps finely. Heat a wok, add 15ml/1 tbsp of the remaining oil and, when hot, stir-fry the shallots or onions until crisp and golden brown. Remove with a slotted spoon and set aside.

4 Add the prawns and garlic to the wok, with a little more oil if needed, and fry for 1 minute. Remove the prawns and garlic and set aside. Add 15ml/ 1 tbsp more oil to the wok.

5 Stir-fry the shredded pork and mushrooms for 2 minutes; lift out and reserve. Steam the Chinese sausage in a colander for 5 minutes or until it plumps up. Trim and slice at an angle.

6 Wipe the wok, reheat with the remaining oil and stir-fry the rice, adding more oil if needed so the grains are coated. Stir in the soy sauce, salt and pepper, plus half the cooked ingredients.

7 Add the peas and half the spring onions and toss over the heat until the peas are cooked. Pile the fried rice on a heated platter and arrange the remaining cooked ingredients on top, with the remaining spring onions. Add the chilli, if using, and the coriander leaves, to garnish.

COOK'S TIP
There are many theories on the best way to cook rice. This gives excellent results every time: Put 225g/8oz/generous 1 cup long grain rice in a strainer and rinse thoroughly in cold water. Place in a large bowl, add salt to taste and pour in just under 600ml/1 pint/2½ cups boiling water. Cover with microwave film, leaving a gap and cook in a 675 watt microwave on full power for 10 minutes. Leave to stand for 5 minutes more. Cool, then stir with a chopstick.

LETTUCE PARCELS

KNOWN AS SANG CHOY IN HONG KONG, THIS IS A POPULAR "ASSEMBLE-IT-YOURSELF" TREAT. THE FILLING — AN IMAGINATIVE BLEND OF TEXTURES AND FLAVOURS — IS SERVED WITH CRISP LETTUCE LEAVES, WHICH ARE USED AS WRAPPERS.

SERVES 6

INGREDIENTS
2 chicken breast fillets, total weight about 350g/12oz
4 Chinese dried mushrooms, soaked for 30 minutes in warm water to cover
30ml/2 tbsp vegetable oil
2 garlic cloves, crushed
6 drained canned water chestnuts, thinly sliced
30ml/2 tbsp light soy sauce
5ml/1 tsp Sichuan peppercorns, dry-fried and crushed
4 spring onions (scallions), finely chopped
5ml/1 tsp sesame oil
vegetable oil, for deep-frying
50g/2oz cellophane noodles
salt and ground black pepper
1 crisp lettuce and 60ml/4 tbsp hoisin sauce, to serve

1 Remove the skin from the chicken breast fillets, pat dry and set aside. Chop the chicken into thin strips. Drain the soaked mushrooms. Cut off and discard the mushroom stems; slice the caps finely and set aside.

2 Heat the oil in a wok or large frying pan. Add the garlic, then add the chicken and stir-fry until the pieces are cooked through and no longer pink.

3 Add the sliced mushrooms, water chestnuts, soy sauce and peppercorns. Toss for 2–3 minutes, then season, if needed. Stir in half of the spring onions, then the sesame oil. Remove from the heat and set aside.

4 Heat the oil for deep-frying to 190°C/375°F. Cut the chicken skin into strips, deep-fry until very crisp and drain on kitchen paper. Add the noodles to the hot oil, deep-fry until crisp. Transfer to a plate lined with kitchen paper.

5 Crush the noodles and put in a serving dish. Top with the chicken skin, chicken mixture and the remaining spring onions. Wash the lettuce leaves, pat dry and arrange on a large platter.

6 Toss the chicken and noodles to mix. Invite guests to take one or two lettuce leaves, spread the inside with hoisin sauce and add a spoonful of filling, turning in the sides of the leaves and rolling them into a parcel. The parcels are traditionally eaten in the hand.

MALAYSIA AND SINGAPORE

The food of Malaysia is a rich blend of three of the world's most exciting cuisines: Malay, Chinese and Indian. The result is the Malayan melange — a mixture of flavours, some cool, some fiery, but always in perfect harmony. Singapore promises sophistication as well as sumptuous flavours, and introduces Nonya cooking, which is famously hot and spicy.

LAKSA LEMAK

THIS SPICY SOUP IS NOT A DISH YOU CAN THROW TOGETHER IN 20 MINUTES, BUT IT IS MARVELLOUS PARTY FOOD. GUESTS SPOON NOODLES INTO WIDE SOUP BOWLS, ADD ACCOMPANIMENTS OF THEIR CHOICE, TOP UP WITH SOUP AND THEN TAKE A FEW PRAWN CRACKERS TO NIBBLE.

SERVES 6

INGREDIENTS

675g/1¹/₂lb small clams
2 × 400ml/14fl oz cans coconut milk
50g/2oz ikan bilis (dried anchovies)
900ml/1¹/₂ pints/3³/₄ cups water
115g/4oz shallots, finely chopped
4 garlic cloves, chopped
6 macadamia nuts or blanched
  almonds, chopped
3 lemon grass stalks, root trimmed
90ml/6 tbsp sunflower oil
1cm/¹/₂in cube shrimp paste
25g/1oz/¹/₄ cup mild curry powder
a few curry leaves
2–3 aubergines (eggplants), total
  weight about 675g/1¹/₄lb, trimmed
675g/1¹/₂lb raw peeled prawns (shrimp)
10ml/2 tsp sugar
1 head Chinese leaves (Chinese
  cabbage), thinly sliced
115g/4oz/2 cups beansprouts, rinsed
2 spring onions (scallions), chopped
50g/2oz crispy fried onions
115g/4oz fried tofu
675g/1¹/₂lb mixed noodles (laksa,
  mee and beehoon) or one type only
prawn crackers, to serve

1 Scrub the clams and then put in a large pan with 1cm/¹/₂in water. Bring to the boil, cover and steam for 3–4 minutes until all the clams have opened. Drain. Make up the coconut milk to 1.2 litres/2 pints/5 cups with water. Put the ikan bilis in a pan and add the water. Bring to the boil and simmer for 20 minutes.

2 Meanwhile, put the shallots, garlic and nuts into a mortar. Cut off the lower 5cm/2in of two of the lemon grass stalks, chop finely and add to the mortar. Pound the mixture to a paste.

3 Heat the oil in a large heavy pan, add the shallot paste and fry until the mixture gives off a rich aroma. Bruise the remaining lemon grass stalk and add to the pan. Toss over the heat to release its flavour. Mix the shrimp paste and curry powder to a paste with a little of the coconut milk, add to the pan and toss the mixture over the heat for about 1 minute, stirring all the time, and keeping the heat low. Stir in the remaining coconut milk. Add the curry leaves and leave the mixture to simmer while you prepare the accompaniments.

4 Strain the stock into a pan. Discard the ikan bilis, bring to the boil, then add the aubergines; cook for about 10 minutes or until tender and the skins can be peeled off easily. Lift out of the stock, peel and cut into thick strips.

5 Arrange the aubergines on a serving platter. Sprinkle the prawns with sugar, add to the stock and cook for 2–4 minutes until they turn pink. Remove and place next to the aubergines. Add the Chinese leaves, beansprouts, spring onions and crispy fried onions to the platter, along with the clams.

6 Gradually stir the remaining ikan bilis stock into the pan of soup and bring to the boil. Rinse the fried tofu in boiling water, cool slightly and squeeze to remove excess oil. Cut each piece in half and add to the soup. Lower the heat to a very gentle simmer.

7 Cook the noodles according to the instructions, drain and pile in a dish. Remove the curry leaves and lemon grass from the soup. Place the noodles, soup and the platter of seafood and vegetables on the table, along with a bowl of prawn crackers. Guests can then help themselves.

VARIATION
You could substitute mussels for clams if preferred. Scrub them thoroughly, removing any beards, and cook them in lightly salted water until they open. Like clams, discard any that remain closed.

COOK'S TIP
Dried shrimp or prawn paste, also called blachan, is sold in small blocks and is available from Asian supermarkets.

CHICKEN SATAY

*ONE OF THE CLASSIC FOODS OF THE EAST. THE PIECES OF MEAT SHOULD NOT BE MORE THAN A
DELICATE MOUTHFUL OTHERWISE THEY WILL NOT ABSORB THE MARINADE SATISFACTORILY.*

SERVES 4

INGREDIENTS
  4 skinless chicken breast fillets
  10ml/2 tsp soft light brown sugar

For the marinade
  5ml/1 tsp cumin seeds
  5ml/1 tsp fennel seeds
  7.5ml/1½ tsp coriander seeds
  6 shallots or small onions, chopped
  1 garlic clove, crushed
  1 lemon grass stalk, root trimmed
  3 macadamia nuts or 6 cashew nuts
  2.5ml/½ tsp ground turmeric

For the peanut sauce
  4 shallots or small onions, sliced
  2 garlic cloves, crushed
  1cm/½in cube shrimp paste
  6 cashew nuts or almonds
  2 lemon grass stalks, trimmed, lower
    5cm/2in sliced
  45ml/3 tbsp sunflower oil
  5–10ml/1–2 tsp chilli powder
  400ml/14fl oz can coconut milk
  60–75ml/4–5 tbsp tamarind water or
    30ml/2 tbsp tamarind concentrate
    mixed with 45ml/3 tbsp water
  15ml/1 tbsp soft light brown sugar
  175g/6oz/½ cup crunchy
    peanut butter

1 Cut the chicken into thin strips,
sprinkle with the sugar and set aside.

2 Make the marinade. Dry-fry the
spices, then grind them to a powder.
Put the shallots or onions in a mortar
or a food processor and add the garlic.
Roughly chop the lower 5cm/2in of the
lemon grass and add it to the mortar or
processor with the nuts, ground spices
and turmeric. Grind to a paste and
place in a bowl.

COOK'S TIP
Soaking the skewers for 30 minutes in
a large bowl of warm water before use
ensures that they won't scorch when
placed under the grill (broiler).

3 Add the chicken pieces and stir well
until coated. Cover loosely with clear
film (plastic wrap) and leave to marinate
for at least 4 hours.

4 Prepare the sauce. Pound or process
the shallots or onions with the garlic
and shrimp paste. Add the nuts and the
lower parts of the lemon grass stalks.
Process to a fine purée. Heat the oil in
a wok and fry the purée for 2–3 minutes.
Add the chilli powder and cook for
2 minutes more.

5 Stir in the coconut milk and bring
slowly to the boil. Reduce the heat and
stir in the tamarind water and brown
sugar. Add the peanut butter and cook
over a low heat, stirring gently, until
fairly thick. Keep warm. Prepare the
barbecue or preheat the grill (broiler).

6 Thread the chicken on to 16 bamboo
skewers. Barbecue or grill (broil) for
about 5 minutes or until golden and
tender, brushing with oil occasionally.
Serve with the hot peanut sauce.

CHICKEN RENDANG

THIS MAKES A MARVELLOUS DISH FOR A BUFFET. SERVE IT WITH PRAWN CRACKERS OR WITH BOILED RICE AND DEEP-FRIED ANCHOVIES, ACAR PICKLE OR SAMBAL NANAS.

SERVES 4

INGREDIENTS

1 chicken, about 1.4kg/3lb
5ml/1 tsp sugar
75g/3oz/1 cup desiccated (dry
  unsweetened shredded) coconut
4 small red or white onions,
  roughly chopped
2 garlic cloves, chopped
2.5cm/1in piece fresh root ginger,
  peeled and sliced
1–2 lemon grass stalks, root trimmed
2.5cm/1in piece fresh galangal,
  peeled and sliced
75ml/5 tbsp groundnut (peanut) oil
  or vegetable oil
10–15ml/2–3 tsp chilli powder
400ml/14fl oz can coconut milk
10ml/2 tsp salt
fresh chives and deep-fried
  anchovies, to garnish

1 Joint the chicken into eight pieces and remove the skin, sprinkle with the sugar and leave to stand for 1 hour.

2 Dry-fry the coconut in a wok or large frying pan over medium to low heat, turning all the time until it is crisp and golden. Transfer the fried coconut to a food processor and process to an oily paste. Transfer to a bowl and reserve.

3 Add the onions, garlic and ginger to the processor. Cut off the lower 5cm/2in of the lemon grass, chop and add to the processor with the galangal. Process to a fine paste.

4 Heat the oil in a wok or large pan and fry the onion mixture for a few minutes. Reduce the heat, stir in the chilli powder and cook for 2–3 minutes, stirring constantly. Spoon in 120ml/4fl oz/½ cup of the coconut milk and add salt to taste.

5 As soon as the mixture bubbles, add the chicken pieces, turning them until they are well coated with the spices. Pour in the coconut milk, stirring constantly to prevent curdling. Bruise the top of the lemon grass stalks and add to the wok or pan. Cover and cook gently for 40–45 minutes until the chicken is tender.

6 Just before serving stir in the coconut paste. Bring to just below boiling point, then simmer for 5 minutes. Transfer to a serving bowl and garnish with fresh chives and deep-fried anchovies.

FISH MOOLIE

THIS IS A VERY POPULAR SOUTH-EAST ASIAN FISH CURRY IN A COCONUT SAUCE, WHICH IS TRULY DELICIOUS. CHOOSE A FIRM-TEXTURED FISH SO THAT THE PIECES STAY INTACT DURING THE BRIEF COOKING PROCESS. HALIBUT AND COD WORK EQUALLY WELL.

5 Heat the oil in a wok. Add the onion mixture and cook for a few minutes without browning. Stir in the coconut milk and bring to the boil, stirring constantly to prevent curdling.

SERVES 4

INGREDIENTS

500g/1¼lb monkfish or other
firm-textured fish fillets, skinned
and cut into 2.5cm/1in cubes
2.5ml/½ tsp salt
50g/2oz/²⁄₃ cup desiccated (dry
unsweetened shredded) coconut
6 shallots or small onions, chopped
6 blanched almonds
2–3 garlic cloves, roughly chopped
2.5cm/1in piece fresh root ginger,
peeled and sliced
2 lemon grass stalks, trimmed
10ml/2 tsp ground turmeric
45ml/3 tbsp vegetable oil
2 × 400ml/14fl oz cans coconut milk
1–3 fresh chillies, seeded and sliced
salt and ground black pepper
fresh chives, to garnish
boiled rice, to serve

1 Spread out the pieces of fish in a shallow dish and sprinkle them with the salt. Dry-fry the coconut in a wok or large frying pan over medium to low heat, turning all the time until it is crisp and golden (see Cook's Tip).

2 Transfer the coconut to a food processor and process to an oily paste. Scrape into a bowl and reserve.

3 Add the shallots or onions, almonds, garlic and ginger to the food processor. Cut off the lower 5cm/2in of the lemon grass, chop them roughly and add to the processor. Process the mixture to a paste.

4 Add the turmeric to the mixture in the processor and process briefly to mix. Bruise the remaining lemon grass and set the stalks aside.

6 Add the cubes of fish, most of the sliced chilli and the bruised lemon grass stalks. Cook for 3–4 minutes. Stir in the coconut paste (moistened with some of the sauce if necessary) and cook for a further 2–3 minutes only. Take care to not overcook the fish. Taste and adjust the seasoning.

7 Remove the lemon grass. Transfer to a hot serving dish and sprinkle with the remaining slices of chilli. Garnish with chopped and whole chives and serve with boiled rice.

COOK'S TIP
Dry-frying is a feature of Malay cooking. When dry-frying do not be distracted. The coconut must be constantly on the move so that it becomes crisp and of a uniform golden colour.

STEAMBOAT

THIS DISH IS NAMED AFTER THE UTENSIL IN WHICH IT IS COOKED — A TYPE OF FONDUE WITH A FUNNEL AND A MOAT. THE MOAT IS FILLED WITH STOCK, TRADITIONALLY KEPT HOT WITH CHARCOAL. ELECTRIC STEAMBOATS OR ANY TRADITIONAL FONDUE POTS CAN BE USED INSTEAD.

SERVES 8

INGREDIENTS
    8 Chinese dried mushrooms, soaked
      for 30 minutes in warm water
      to cover
    1.5 litres/2½ pints/6¼ cups
      well-flavoured chicken stock,
      home-made if possible
    10ml/2 tsp rice wine or
      medium-dry sherry
    10ml/2 tsp sesame oil
    225g/8oz each lean pork and rump
      (round) steak, thinly sliced
    1 skinless chicken breast fillet,
      thickly sliced
    2 chicken livers, trimmed and sliced
    225g/8oz raw prawns (shrimp), peeled
    450g/1lb white fish fillets, skinned
      and cubed
    200g/7oz fish balls (from Asian
      food stores)
    115g/4oz fried tofu, each piece halved
    leafy green vegetables, such as
      lettuce, Chinese leaves (Chinese
      cabbage), spinach leaves and
      watercress, cut into 15cm/6in lengths
    225g/8oz Chinese rice vermicelli
    8 eggs
    selection of sauces, including soy
      sauce with sesame seeds; soy sauce
      with crushed ginger; chilli sauce;
      plum sauce and hot mustard
    ½ bunch spring onions
      (scallions), chopped
    salt and ground white pepper

1 Drain the mushrooms, reserving the soaking liquid. Cut off and discard the stems; slice the caps finely.

2 Pour the stock into a large pan, with the rice wine or sherry, sesame oil and reserved mushroom liquid. Bring the mixture to the boil, then season with salt and white pepper. Reduce the heat and simmer gently while you prepare the remaining ingredients.

3 Put the meat, fish, tofu, green vegetables and mushrooms in bowls on the table. Soak the vermicelli in hot water for about 5 minutes, drain and place in eight soup bowls on a small table. Crack an egg for each diner in a small bowl; place on a side table. Put the sauces in bowls beside each diner.

4 Add the chopped spring onions to the pan of stock, bring it to a full boil and fuel the steamboat. Pour the stock into the moat and seat your guests immediately. Each guest lowers a few chosen morsels into the boiling stock, using chopsticks or fondue forks, leaves them for a minute or two, then removes them with a small wire mesh ladle, a fondue fork or pair of chopsticks.

5 When all the meat, fish, tofu and vegetables have been cooked, the stock will be concentrated and wonderfully enriched. Add a little boiling water if necessary. Bring the soup bowls containing the soaked noodles to the table, pour in the hot soup and slide a whole egg into each, stirring until it cooks and forms threads.

SIZZLING STEAK

THIS WAS ORIGINALLY A SPECIALITY OF THE COLISEUM RESTAURANT IN THE BATU ROAD IN KUALA LUMPUR. THE STEAKS WERE BROUGHT TO THE TABLE ON INDIVIDUAL HOT METAL PLATTERS, EACH SET ON A THICK WOODEN BOARD. THIS RECIPE COMES CLOSE TO RECREATING THIS WONDERFUL DISH.

<u>SERVES 2</u>

INGREDIENTS

   2 rump (round) or sirloin steaks,
    total weight about 450g/1lb
   15–30ml/1–2 tbsp vegetable oil
   shredded spring onion (scallion),
    to garnish

For the marinade and sauce
   15ml/1 tbsp brandy
   15ml/1 tbsp rich brown sauce
   30ml/2 tbsp groundnut (peanut) oil
   a few drops of sesame oil
   2 garlic cloves, halved or crushed
   150ml/¼ pint/⅔ cup beef stock
   30ml/2 tbsp tomato ketchup
   15ml/1 tbsp oyster sauce
   15ml/1 tbsp Worcestershire sauce
   salt and sugar

1 Put the steaks side by side in a bowl. Mix the brandy, brown sauce, groundnut oil, sesame oil and garlic in a jug (pitcher) and pour this marinade over the steaks. Cover loosely with clear film (plastic wrap) and leave for 1 hour, turning once. Drain the meat well, reserving the marinade.

2 Heat the oil in a heavy, ridged frying pan and fry the steaks for 3–5 minutes on each side, depending on how well done you like them. Transfer to a plate and keep warm while preparing the sauce: this allows the meat to relax, making it more tender.

3 Pour the marinade into the frying pan, if liked, discarding any large pieces of garlic.

4 Stir in the beef stock, ketchup, oyster sauce and Worcestershire sauce, with salt and sugar to taste. Bring to the boil, boil rapidly to reduce by half, then taste again for seasoning.

5 Serve each cooked steak on a very hot plate, pouring the sauce over each portion just before serving. Garnish with the shredded spring onion.

COOK'S TIP
If you don't have a ridged frying pan, simply use a large, heavy frying pan to fry the steaks instead.

SOTONG SAMBAL

SQUID IS READILY AVAILABLE THESE DAYS, AND IT NOW COMES CLEANED, WHICH IS A DEFINITE BONUS.
WASH THOROUGHLY INSIDE THE POCKET TO MAKE SURE THAT ALL THE QUILL HAS BEEN REMOVED.

SERVES 2

INGREDIENTS
 8 small squid, each about 10cm/4in
  long, total weight about 350g/12oz
 lime juice (optional)
 salt
 boiled rice, to serve

For the stuffing
 175g/6oz white fish fillets, such as
  sole or plaice, skinned
 2.5cm/1in piece fresh root ginger,
  peeled and finely sliced
 2 spring onions (scallions),
  finely chopped
 50g/2oz cooked, peeled prawns
  (shrimp), roughly chopped

For the sambal sauce
 4 macadamia nuts or
  blanched almonds
 1cm/^{1}/$_2$in piece fresh galangal,
  peeled, or 5ml/1 tsp drained
  bottled galangal
 2 lemon grass stalks, root trimmed
 1cm/^{1}/$_2$in cube shrimp paste
 4 fresh red chillies, or to taste,
  seeded and roughly chopped
 175g/6oz small onions, roughly
  chopped
 60–90ml/4–6 tbsp vegetable oil
 400ml/14fl oz can coconut milk

1 Clean the squid, leaving them whole.
Set aside with the tentacles. Put the
white fish, ginger and spring onions in
a mortar. Add a little salt and pound
to a paste with a pestle. Use a food
processor, if preferred.

2 Transfer the fish mixture to a bowl
and stir in the prawns.

3 Divide the filling among the squid,
using a spoon or a piping (pastry) bag
fitted with a plain nozzle. Tuck the
tentacles into the stuffing and secure
the tops with a cocktail stick (toothpick).

4 Make the sauce. Put the macadamia
nuts or almonds and galangal in a food
processor. Cut off the lower 5cm/2in
from the lemon grass stalks, chop them
roughly and add them to the processor
with the shrimp paste, chillies and
onions. Process to a paste.

5 Heat the oil in a wok and fry the
mixture to bring out the full flavours.
Bruise the remaining lemon grass and
add it to the wok with the coconut milk.
Stir constantly until the sauce comes
to the boil, then lower the heat and
simmer the sauce for 5 minutes.

6 Arrange the squid in the sauce, and
cook for 15–20 minutes. Taste and
season with salt and lime juice, if you
like. Serve with boiled rice.

MALAYSIAN COCONUT ICE CREAM

THIS ICE CREAM IS DELECTABLE AND VERY EASY TO MAKE IN AN ICE-CREAM MAKER, ESPECIALLY IF YOU USE THE TYPE WITH A BOWL THAT IS PLACED IN THE FREEZER TO CHILL BEFORE THE ICE-CREAM MIXTURE IS ADDED. THE ICE CREAM IS THEN CHURNED BY A MOTORIZED LID WITH A PADDLE.

2 Pour the mixture into the frozen freezer bowl of an ice-cream maker (or follow the appliance instructions) and churn till the mixture has thickened. (This will take 30–40 minutes.)

3 Transfer the mixture to a lidded plastic tub, cover and freeze until the consistency is right for scooping. If you do not have an ice-cream maker, pour the mixture into a shallow container and freeze on the coldest setting.

4 When ice crystals form around the sides of the ice cream, beat the mixture, then return it to the freezer. Do this at least twice. The more you do it, the creamier the mixture will be.

5 Make the sauce. Mix the sugar, measured water and ginger in a pan. Stir over medium heat until the sugar has dissolved, then bring the liquid to the boil. Add the pandan leaf, if using, tying it into a knot so that it can easily be removed with the ginger before serving. Lower the heat and simmer for 3–4 minutes. Set aside till required.

6 Serve the ice cream in coconut shells or in a bowl. Sprinkle with the strips of coconut and serve with the gula melaka sauce which can be hot, warm or cold.

COOK'S TIP
Coconut milk takes longer to freeze than double (heavy) cream, so allow plenty of time for the process.

SERVES 6

INGREDIENTS
400ml/14fl oz can coconut milk
400ml/14fl oz can sweetened
   condensed milk
2.5ml/¹/₂ tsp salt

For the gula melaka sauce
   150g/5oz/³/₄ cup palm sugar (jaggery)
   or muscovado (molasses) sugar
   150ml/¹/₄ pint/²/₃ cup water
   1cm/¹/₂in slice fresh root
   ginger, bruised
   1 pandan leaf (if available)
   coconut shells (optional) and thinly
   pared strips of coconut, to serve

1 Chill the cans of coconut and condensed milk very thoroughly. In a bowl, mix the coconut milk with the condensed milk. Gently whisk together with the salt.

COCONUT CHIPS

COCONUT CHIPS ARE A WONDERFULLY TASTY NIBBLE TO SERVE WITH DRINKS. THE CHIPS CAN BE SLICED AHEAD OF TIME AND FROZEN (WITHOUT SALT), ON OPEN TRAYS. WHEN FROZEN, SIMPLY SHAKE INTO PLASTIC BOXES OR BAGS. YOU CAN THEN TAKE OUT AS FEW OR AS MANY AS YOU WISH FOR THE PARTY.

3 Having opened the coconut, use a broad-bladed knife to ease the flesh away from the hard outer shell. Taste a piece of the flesh just to make sure it is fresh. Peel away the brown skin with a potato peeler, if you like.

4 Slice the flesh into wafer-thin shavings, using a food processor, mandoline or sharp knife. Sprinkle these evenly all over one or two baking sheets and sprinkle with salt. Bake for about 25–30 minutes or until crisp, turning them from time to time. Cool and serve. Any leftovers can be stored in airtight containers.

COOK'S TIP
This is the kind of recipe where the slicing blade on a food processor comes into its own. It is worth preparing two or three coconuts at a time, and freezing surplus chips. The chips can be cooked from frozen, but will need to be spread out well on the baking sheets, before being salted. Allow a little longer for frozen chips to cook.

SERVES 8 AS A SNACK

INGREDIENTS
  1 fresh coconut
  salt

1 Preheat the oven to 160°C/325°F/ Gas 3. First drain the coconut juice, either by piercing one of the coconut eyes with a sharp instrument or by breaking it carefully.

2 Lay the coconut on a board and hit the centre sharply with a hammer. The shell should break cleanly in two.

POPIAH

POPIAH ARE THE STRAITS CHINESE OR NONYA VERSION OF THE SPRING ROLL. DO NOT BE PUT OFF BY THE NUMBER OF INGREDIENTS; IT TAKES A LITTLE TIME TO GET EVERYTHING TOGETHER BUT ONCE IT IS ALL ON THE TABLE THE COOK CAN RETIRE AS GUESTS ASSEMBLE THEIR OWN.

MAKES 20–24 PANCAKES

INGREDIENTS
40g/1¹/₂oz/¹/₃ cup cornflour
  (cornstarch)
215g/7¹/₂oz/generous 1³/₄ cups
  plain (all-purpose) flour
salt
450ml/³/₄ pint/scant 2 cups water
6 eggs, beaten
lard or white vegetable fat, for frying

For the cooked filling
30ml/2 tbsp vegetable oil
1 onion, finely chopped
2 garlic cloves, crushed
115g/4oz cooked pork, chopped
115g/4oz crab meat or cooked, peeled
  prawns (shrimp), thawed if frozen
115g/4oz drained canned bamboo
  shoot, thinly sliced
1 small yam bean, peeled and grated
  or 12 drained canned water
  chestnuts, finely chopped
15–30ml/1–2 tbsp yellow salted beans
15ml/1 tbsp light soy sauce
ground black pepper

For the fresh fillings
2 hard-boiled eggs, chopped
2 Chinese sausages, steamed
  and sliced
115g/4oz packet fried tofu, each
  piece halved
225g/8oz/4 cups beansprouts
115g/4oz crab meat or cooked,
  peeled prawns (shrimp)
¹/₂ cucumber, cut into matchsticks
small bunch of spring onions
  (scallions), finely chopped
20 lettuce leaves, rinsed and dried
fresh coriander (cilantro) sprigs,
  to garnish
selection of sauces, including bottled
  chopped chillies, bottled chopped
  garlic and hoisin sauce, to serve

COOK'S TIP
Yam beans are large tubers with a mild sweet texture similar to water chestnuts.

1 Sift the flours and salt into a bowl. Add the measured water and eggs and mix to a smooth batter.

2 Grease a heavy frying pan with lard or vegetable fat. Heat the pan, pouring off any excess lard or fat, then pour in just enough batter to cover the base.

3 As soon as it sets, flip and cook the other side. The pancakes should be quite thin. Repeat with the remaining batter to make 20–24 pancakes in all. Pile the cooked pancakes on top of each other, with a layer of baking parchment between each to prevent them sticking. Wrap in foil and keep warm in a low oven.

4 Make the cooked filling. Heat the oil in a wok and stir-fry the onion and garlic for 5 minutes until softened but not browned. Add the pork, crab meat or prawns, bamboo shoot and grated yam bean or water chestnuts. Stir-fry the mixture over medium heat for 2–3 minutes.

5 Add the salted yellow beans and soy sauce to the wok, with pepper to taste. Cover and cook gently for 15–20 minutes, adding a little water if the mixture starts to dry out. Spoon into a serving bowl and allow to cool.

6 Meanwhile, arrange the chopped hard-boiled eggs, sliced Chinese sausages, sliced tofu, beansprouts, crab meat or prawns, cucumber, spring onions and lettuce leaves in piles on a large platter or in separate bowls. Spoon the bottled chopped chillies, bottled chopped garlic and hoisin into small bowls.

7 Each person makes up his or her own popiah by spreading a very small amount of chopped chilli, garlic or hoisin sauce on a pancake, adding a lettuce leaf, a little of the cooked filling and a small selection of the fresh ingredients. The pancake wrapper should not be over-filled.

8 The ends can be tucked in and the pancake rolled up in typical spring roll fashion, then eaten in the hand. They also look attractive simply rolled with the filling showing. The popiah can be filled and rolled before guests arrive, in which case, garnish with sprigs of coriander. It is more fun though for everyone to fill and roll their own.

SAMOSAS

THESE TASTY SNACKS ARE ENJOYED THE WORLD OVER. THROUGHOUT THE EAST, THEY ARE SOLD BY STREET VENDORS, AND EATEN AT ANY TIME OF DAY. FILO PASTRY CAN BE USED IF PREFERRED.

MAKES ABOUT 20

INGREDIENTS

    1 packet 25cm/10in square spring
      roll wrappers, thawed if frozen
    30ml/2 tbsp plain (all-purpose) flour,
      mixed to a paste with water
    vegetable oil, for deep-frying
    coriander (cilantro) leaves, to garnish
    cucumber, carrot and celery, cut into
      matchsticks, to serve (optional)

For the filling

    25g/1oz/2 tbsp ghee or unsalted butter
    1 small onion, finely chopped
    1cm/½in piece fresh root ginger,
      peeled and chopped
    1 garlic clove, crushed
    2.5ml/½ tsp chilli powder
    1 large potato, about 225g/8oz,
      cooked until just tender and
      finely diced
    50g/2oz/½ cup cauliflower florets,
      lightly cooked, chopped into
      small pieces
    50g/2oz/½ cup frozen peas, thawed
    5–10ml/1–2 tsp garam masala
    15ml/1 tbsp chopped fresh coriander
      (cilantro), leaves and stems)
    squeeze of lemon juice
    salt

2 Cut the spring roll wrappers into three strips (or two for larger samosas). Brush the edges with a little of the flour paste. Place a small spoonful of filling about 2cm/¾in in from the edge of one strip. Fold one corner over the filling to make a triangle and continue this folding until the entire strip has been used and a triangular pastry has been formed. Seal any open edges with more flour and water paste, if necessary adding more water if the paste is very thick.

3 Heat the oil for deep-frying to 190°C/375°F and fry the samosas, a few at a time, until golden and crisp. Drain well on kitchen paper and serve hot garnished with coriander leaves and accompanied by cucumber, carrot and celery matchsticks, if you like.

COOK'S TIP
Prepare samosas in advance by frying until just cooked through and draining. Cook in hot oil for a few minutes to brown and drain again before serving.

1 Heat the ghee or butter in a large wok and fry the onion, ginger and garlic for 5 minutes until the onion has softened. Add the chilli powder, cook for 1 minute, then stir in the potato, cauliflower and peas. Sprinkle with garam masala and set aside to cool. Stir in the chopped coriander, lemon juice and salt.

CHA SHAO

THIS DISH IS OFTEN KNOWN AS BARBECUED PORK, AND IS VERY POPULAR IN SOUTHERN CHINA AND MALAYSIA AS WELL AS SINGAPORE. IF YOU LIKE, THE MARINADE CAN BE HEATED THOROUGHLY, THEN SERVED WITH THE MEAT AS A SAUCE.

SERVES 6

INGREDIENTS
900g/2lb pork fillet (tenderloin), trimmed
15ml/1 tbsp clear honey
45ml/3 tbsp rice wine or medium-dry sherry
spring onion (scallion) curls, to garnish

For the marinade
150ml/1/4 pint/2/3 cup dark soy sauce
90ml/6 tbsp rice wine or medium-dry sherry
150ml/1/4 pint/2/3 cup well-flavoured chicken stock
15ml/1 tbsp soft light brown sugar
1cm/1/2in piece fresh root ginger, peeled and finely sliced
40ml/2½ tbsp chopped onion

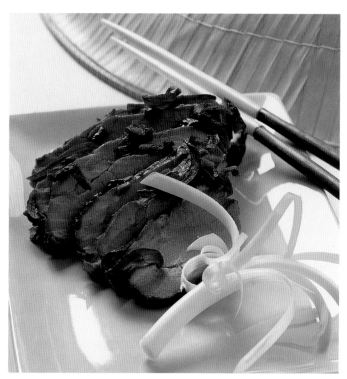

1 Mix all the marinade ingredients in a pan and stir over medium heat until the mixture boils. Lower the heat and simmer gently for 15 minutes, stirring from time to time. Leave to cool.

2 Put the pork fillets in a shallow dish that is large enough to hold them side by side. Pour over 250ml/8fl oz/1 cup of the marinade, cover and chill for at least 8 hours, turning the meat over several times.

COOK'S TIP
You will have extra marinade when making this dish. Chill or freeze this and use to baste other grilled dishes or meats such as spare ribs.

3 Preheat the oven to 200°C/400°F/ Gas 6. Drain the pork fillets, reserving the marinade in the dish. Place the meat on a rack over a roasting pan and pour water into the pan to a depth of 1cm/1/2in. Place the pan in the oven and roast for 20 minutes.

4 Stir the honey and rice wine or sherry into the marinade. Remove the meat from the oven and place in the marinade, turning to coat. Put back on the rack and roast for 20–30 minutes or until cooked. Serve hot or cold, in slices, garnished with spring onion curls.

CHILLI CRABS

EAT THESE CRABS SINGAPOREAN STYLE, WITH THE FINGERS. GIVE GUESTS CRAB CRACKERS FOR THE CLAWS AND HAVE SOME FINGER BOWLS OR HOT TOWELS TO HAND AS IT WILL BE MESSY!

SERVES 4

INGREDIENTS

2 cooked crabs, each about
    675g/1½lb
90ml/6 tbsp sunflower oil
2.5cm/1in piece fresh root ginger,
    peeled and chopped
2–3 garlic cloves, crushed
1–2 red chillies, seeded and pounded
    to a paste
175ml/6fl oz/¾ cup tomato ketchup
30ml/2 tbsp soft light brown sugar
15ml/1 tbsp light soy sauce
120ml/4fl oz/½ cup boiling water
salt
hot toast and cucumber chunks,
    to serve

COOK'S TIP
Ready-cooked whole crabs are available
from supermarkets and fish shops.

1 To prepare the crabs twist off the large claws, then turn the crab on its back with its mouth and eyes facing away from you. Using both of your thumbs, push the body, with the small legs attached, upwards from beneath the flap, separating the body from the main shell in the process. Discard the stomach sac and grey spongy lungs known as "dead men's fingers".

2 Using a teaspoon scrape the brown creamy meat from the large shell into a small bowl. Twist the legs from the body. Cut the body section in half. Pick out the white meat. If you like, pick out the meat from the legs, or leave for guests to remove at the table.

3 Heat the oil in a wok and gently fry the ginger, garlic and fresh chilli paste for 1–2 minutes without browning. Stir in the ketchup, sugar and soy sauce, with salt to taste and heat gently.

4 Stir in the crab meat together with the claws and crab legs, if these were reserved. Pour in the boiling water, stir well and cook over high heat until heated through. Pile the crab and crab claws mixture on serving plates with the chunks of cucumber and serve with pieces of toast.

NONYA PORK SATAY

WHEN CHINESE MERCHANTS CAME TO SINGAPORE AND PENANG AND TOOK MALAY WIVES, CULINARY TURMOIL ENSUED. THEIR BELOVED PORK WAS FORBIDDEN TO THEIR MUSLIM WIVES. NONYA, THE STYLE OF COOKING THAT EMERGED, IS A TESTAMENT TO COMPROMISE — MOSTLY BY THE WIVES.

MAKES 8–12

INGREDIENTS

450g/1lb pork fillet (tenderloin)
15ml/1 tbsp soft light brown sugar
1cm/½in cube shrimp paste
1–2 lemon grass stalks
30ml/2 tsp coriander seeds, dry-fried
6 macadamia nuts or blanched
    almonds, if preferred
2 onions, roughly chopped
3–6 fresh red chillies, seeded and
    roughly chopped
2.5ml/½ tsp ground turmeric
300ml/½ pint/1¼ cups canned
    coconut milk
30ml/2 tbsp groundnut (peanut) oil
    or sunflower oil
salt

1 Soak 8–12 bamboo skewers in water for at least 30 minutes to prevent them from scorching when they are placed under the grill (broiler).

2 Cut the pork into small chunks, then spread it out in a single layer in a shallow dish. Sprinkle with sugar to help release the juices. Fry the shrimp paste briefly in a foil parcel in a dry frying pan or warm it on a skewer held over the gas flame.

COOK'S TIP
Nonya Pork Satay can be served as part of a meal or as a snack, in which case serve with cubes of cucumber, which contrast well with the spicy meat.

3 Cut off the lower 5cm/2in of the lemon grass stalks and chop finely. Process the dry-fried coriander seeds to a powder in a food processor. Add the nuts and chopped lemon grass, process briefly, then add the onions, chillies, shrimp paste, turmeric and a little salt; process to a fine paste. Pour in the coconut milk and oil. Switch the machine on very briefly to mix. Pour the mixture over the pork and leave to marinate for 1–2 hours.

4 Preheat the grill or prepare the barbecue. Thread three or four pieces of marinated pork on each bamboo skewer and grill (broil) or barbecue for 8–10 minutes until tender, basting frequently with the remaining marinade. Serve immediately.

SAMBAL NANAS

SAMBALS ARE THE LITTLE SIDE DISHES SERVED AT ALMOST EVERY MALAY MEAL. IN POORER SOCIETIES, A MAIN MEAL MAY SIMPLY BE A BOWL OF RICE AND A SAMBAL MADE FROM POUNDED SHRIMP PASTE, CHILLIES AND LIME JUICE. THIS SAMBAL INCLUDES CUCUMBER AND PINEAPPLE.

SERVES 8–10 AS AN ACCOMPANIMENT

INGREDIENTS

1 small or ½ large fresh
    ripe pineapple
½ cucumber, halved lengthways
50g/2oz dried shrimps
1 large fresh red chilli, seeded
1cm/½in cube shrimp paste,
    prepared (see Cook's Tip)
juice of 1 large lemon or lime
light brown sugar, to taste (optional)

1 Cut off both ends of the pineapple. Stand it upright on a board, then slice off the skin from top to bottom, cutting out the spines. Slice the pineapple, removing the central core. Cut into thin slices and set aside.

2 Trim the ends from the cucumber and slice thinly. Sprinkle with salt and set aside. Place the dried shrimps in a food processor and chop fairly finely. Add the chilli, prepared shrimp paste and lemon or lime juice and process again to a paste.

3 Rinse the cucumber, drain and dry on kitchen paper. Mix with the pineapple and chill. Just before serving, spoon in the spice mixture with sugar to taste. Mix well and serve.

COOK'S TIP
The pungent shrimp paste, also called blachan, is popular in many South-east Asian countries, and is available in Asian supermarkets. Since it can taste a bit raw in a sambal, dry-fry it by wrapping in foil and heating in a frying pan over low heat for 5 minutes, turning from time to time. If the shrimp paste is to be fried with other spices, this preliminary cooking can be eliminated.

INDIAN MEE GORENG

*THIS IS A TRULY INTERNATIONAL DISH COMBINING INDIAN, CHINESE AND WESTERN INGREDIENTS.
IT IS A DELICIOUS TREAT FOR LUNCH OR SUPPER AND IN SINGAPORE AND MALAYSIA CAN BE BOUGHT
IN MANY STREETS FROM ONE OF THE MANY HAWKERS' STALLS.*

2 If using fried tofu, cut each cube in half, refresh it in a pan of boiling water, then drain well. Heat 30ml/2 tbsp of the oil in a large frying pan. If using plain tofu, cut into cubes and fry until brown, then lift it out with a slotted spoon and set aside.

3 Beat the eggs with the water and seasoning. Add to the oil in the frying pan and cook without stirring until set. Flip over, cook the other side, then slide it out of the pan, roll up and slice thinly.

SERVES 4–6

INGREDIENTS
    450g/1lb fresh yellow egg noodles
    60–90ml/4–6 tbsp vegetable oil
    115g/4oz fried tofu or 150g/5oz
      firm tofu
    2 eggs
    30ml/2 tbsp water
    1 onion, sliced
    1 garlic clove, crushed
    15ml/1 tbsp light soy sauce
    30–45ml/2–3 tbsp tomato ketchup
    15ml/1 tbsp chilli sauce (or to taste)
    1 large cooked potato, diced
    4 spring onions (scallions), shredded
    1–2 fresh green chillies, seeded
      and finely sliced (optional)

1 Bring a large pan of water to the boil, add the fresh egg noodles and cook for just 2 minutes. Drain the noodles and immediately rinse them under cold water to halt cooking. Drain again and set aside.

4 Heat the remaining oil in a wok and fry the onion and garlic for 2–3 minutes. Add the drained noodles, soy sauce, ketchup and chilli sauce. Toss well over medium heat for 2 minutes, then add the diced potato. Reserve a few spring onions for garnish and stir the rest into the noodles with the chilli, if using, and the tofu.

5 When hot, stir in the omelette. Serve on a hot platter garnished with the remaining spring onion.

THAILAND
AND MYANMAR

To eat a Thai meal is an exquisite experience. Curries are spicy but subtle; soups are

legendary and even the humble fish cake can be sensational if the product of an

accomplished cook. Myanmar has a more robust but equally interesting cuisine,

and is famous for one of the world's most delicious fish soups, Mohingha.

THAI SPRING ROLLS

CRUNCHY SPRING ROLLS ARE AS POPULAR IN THAILAND AS THEY ARE IN CHINA. THAIS FILL THEIR VERSION WITH A DELICIOUS GARLIC, PORK AND NOODLE MIXTURE.

MAKES ABOUT 24

INGREDIENTS
24 × 15cm/6in square spring
   roll wrappers
30ml/2 tbsp plain (all-purpose) flour
vegetable oil, for deep-frying
Thai sweet chilli dipping sauce,
   to serve (optional)

For the filling
4–6 Chinese dried mushrooms,
   soaked for 30 minutes in warm
   water to cover
50g/2oz cellophane noodles
30ml/2 tbsp vegetable oil
2 garlic cloves, chopped
2 fresh red chillies, seeded and chopped
225g/8oz minced (ground) pork
50g/2oz cooked, peeled prawns
   (shrimp), thawed if frozen
30ml/2 tbsp Thai fish sauce
5ml/1 tsp sugar
1 carrot, grated
50g/2oz drained canned bamboo
   shoots, chopped
50g/2oz/1 cup beansprouts
2 spring onions (scallions), chopped
15ml/1 tbsp chopped fresh
   coriander (cilantro)
ground black pepper

1 Make the filling. Drain the soaked mushrooms. Cut off the mushroom stems and discard; chop the caps finely.

2 Place the noodles in a large bowl, cover with boiling water and soak for 10 minutes. Drain the noodles and cut them into 5cm/2in lengths.

3 Heat the oil in a wok, add the garlic and chillies and stir-fry for 30 seconds. Transfer to a plate, add the pork and cook, stirring, until it has browned.

4 Add the noodles, mushrooms and prawns. Stir in the Thai fish sauce and sugar, then add pepper to taste.

5 Transfer the noodle mixture into a bowl and stir in the carrot, bamboo shoots, beansprouts, spring onions and chopped coriander together with the reserved chilli mixture.

6 Unwrap the spring roll wrappers. Cover them with a dampened dish towel while you are making the rolls, so that they do not dry out. Put the flour in a small bowl and stir in a little water to make a paste. Place a spoonful of filling in the centre of a spring roll wrapper.

7 Turn the bottom edge over to cover the filling, then fold in the left and right sides. Roll the wrapper up almost to the top then brush the top edge with the flour paste and seal. Fill the remaining wrappers in the same way.

8 Heat the oil in a wok or deep-fryer. Fry the spring rolls, a few at a time, until crisp and golden brown. Drain on kitchen paper and keep hot while cooking successive batches. Serve hot with Thai sweet chilli sauce, if you like.

COOK'S TIP
Fish sauce (nam pla) is made from anchovies, which are salted, then fermented in wooden barrels. The sauce accentuates the flavour of food, and does not necessarily impart a fishy flavour.

CRISP-FRIED CRAB CLAWS

CRAB CLAWS ARE READILY AVAILABLE IN THE FREEZER CABINET IN MANY ASIAN STORES AND SUPERMARKETS. THAW OUT THOROUGHLY AND DRY ON KITCHEN PAPER BEFORE DIPPING IN THE BATTER.

SERVES 4

INGREDIENTS
  50g/2oz/^{1}/$_3$ cup rice flour
  15ml/1 tbsp cornflour (cornstarch)
  2.5ml/^{1}/$_2$ tsp sugar
  1 egg
  60ml/4 tbsp cold water
  1 lemon grass stalk, root trimmed
  2 garlic cloves, finely chopped
  15ml/1 tbsp chopped fresh
    coriander (cilantro)
  1–2 fresh red chillies, seeded and
    finely chopped
  5ml/1 tsp Thai fish sauce
  vegetable oil, for frying
  12 half-shelled crab claws
  ground black pepper

For the chilli vinegar dip
  45ml/3 tbsp sugar
  120ml/4fl oz/^{1}/$_2$ cup water
  120ml/4fl oz/^{1}/$_2$ cup red wine vinegar
  15ml/1 tbsp Thai fish sauce
  2–4 fresh red chillies, seeded
    and chopped

1 Make the chilli dip. Mix the sugar and water in a pan, stirring until the sugar has dissolved. Bring to the boil, lower the heat and simmer for 5–7 minutes. Stir in the remaining ingredients and set aside.

2 Combine the rice flour, cornflour and sugar in a bowl. Beat the egg with the cold water, then stir the egg and water mixture into the flour mixture and mix well until it forms a light batter.

3 Cut off the lower 5cm/2in of the lemon grass stalk and chop it finely. Add the lemon grass to the batter, with the garlic, coriander, red chillies and Thai fish sauce. Stir in pepper to taste.

4 Heat the oil in a wok or deep-fryer. Pat the crab claws dry and dip into the batter. Drop the battered claws into the hot oil, a few at a time. Fry until golden brown. Drain on kitchen paper and keep hot. Pour the dip into a serving bowl and serve with the crab claws.

FISH CAKES WITH CUCUMBER RELISH

THESE WONDERFUL SMALL FISH CAKES ARE A VERY FAMILIAR AND POPULAR APPETIZER IN THAILAND AND INCREASINGLY THROUGHOUT SOUTH-EAST ASIA. THEY ARE USUALLY SERVED WITH THAI BEER.

MAKES ABOUT 12

INGREDIENTS
- 5 kaffir lime leaves
- 300g/11oz cod, cut into chunks
- 30ml/2 tbsp red curry paste
- 1 egg
- 30ml/2 tbsp Thai fish sauce
- 5ml/1 tsp sugar
- 30ml/2 tbsp cornflour (cornstarch)
- 15ml/1 tbsp chopped fresh coriander (cilantro)
- 50g/2oz green beans, finely sliced
- vegetable oil, for frying
- fresh coriander leaves, to garnish

For the cucumber relish
- 60ml/4 tbsp coconut or rice vinegar
- 50g/2oz/¼ cup sugar
- 1 head pickled garlic
- 15ml/1 tbsp fresh root ginger
- 1 cucumber, cut into matchsticks
- 4 shallots, finely sliced

1 Make the cucumber relish. Bring the vinegar and sugar to the boil in a small pan with 60ml/4 tbsp water, stirring until the sugar has dissolved. Remove from the heat and cool.

2 Separate the pickled garlic into cloves. Chop these finely along with the ginger and place in a bowl. Add the cucumber and shallots, pour over the vinegar mixture and mix lightly.

3 Reserve two kaffir lime leaves for garnish and thinly slice the remainder. Put the chunks of fish, curry paste and egg in a food processor and process to a smooth paste. Transfer the mixture to a bowl and stir in the fish sauce, sugar, cornflour, sliced kaffir lime leaves, coriander and green beans. Mix well, then shape the mixture into about twelve 5mm/¼in thick cakes, measuring about 5cm/2in in diameter.

4 Heat the oil in a wok or deep-frying pan. Fry the fish cakes, a few at a time, for about 4–5 minutes until cooked and evenly brown.

5 Lift out the fish cakes and drain them on kitchen paper. Keep each batch hot while frying successive batches. Garnish with the reserved kaffir leaves and serve with the cucumber relish.

GINGER, CHICKEN AND COCONUT SOUP

THIS AROMATIC SOUP IS RICH WITH COCONUT MILK AND INTENSELY FLAVOURED WITH GALANGAL,
LEMON GRASS AND KAFFIR LIME LEAVES.

SERVES 4–6

INGREDIENTS
    4 lemon grass stalks, roots trimmed
    2 × 400ml/14fl oz cans coconut milk
    475ml/16fl oz/2 cups chicken stock
    2.5cm/1in piece galangal, peeled
        and thinly sliced
    10 black peppercorns, crushed
    10 kaffir lime leaves, torn
    300g/11oz skinless chicken breast
        fillets, cut into thin strips
    115g/4oz/1 cup button
        (white) mushrooms
    50g/2oz/½ cup baby corn cobs,
        quartered lengthways
    60ml/4 tbsp lime juice
    45ml/3 tbsp Thai fish sauce
    chopped fresh red chillies, spring
        onions (scallions) and fresh
        coriander (cilantro) leaves, to garnish

1 Cut off the lower 5cm/2in from each lemon grass stalk and chop it finely. Bruise the remaining pieces of stalk. Bring the coconut milk and chicken stock to the boil in a large pan. Add all the lemon grass, the galangal, peppercorns and half the lime leaves, lower the heat and simmer gently for 10 minutes. Strain into a clean pan.

2 Return the soup to the heat, then add the chicken, mushrooms and corn. Simmer for 5–7 minutes or until the chicken is cooked.

3 Stir in the lime juice and Thai fish sauce, then add the remaining lime leaves. Serve hot, garnished with chillies, spring onions and coriander.

HOT-AND-SOUR PRAWN SOUP

THIS IS A CLASSIC THAI SEAFOOD SOUP – TOM YAM KUNG – AND IT IS PROBABLY THE MOST
POPULAR AND WELL-KNOWN SOUP FROM THAT COUNTRY.

SERVES 4–6

INGREDIENTS
    450g/1lb raw king prawns (jumbo
        shrimp), thawed if frozen
    1 litre/1¾ pints/4 cups chicken
        stock or water
    3 lemon grass stalks, root trimmed
    10 kaffir lime leaves, torn in half
    225g/8oz can straw mushrooms
    45ml/3 tbsp Thai fish sauce
    60ml/4 tbsp lime juice
    30ml/2 tbsp chopped spring
        onion (scallion)
    15ml/1 tbsp fresh coriander
        (cilantro) leaves
    4 fresh red chillies, seeded and sliced
    salt and ground black pepper

1 Shell the prawns, putting the shells in a colander. Devein the prawns and set them aside.

2 Rinse the shells under cold water, then put in a large pan with the stock or water. Bring to the boil.

3 Bruise the lemon grass stalks and add them to the stock with half the lime leaves. Simmer gently for 5–6 minutes, until the stock is fragrant.

4 Strain the stock, return it to the clean pan and reheat. Add the drained mushrooms and the prawns, then cook until the prawns turn pink.

5 Stir in the Thai fish sauce, lime juice, spring onion, coriander, chillies and the remaining lime leaves. Taste and adjust the seasoning. The soup should be sour, salty, spicy and hot.

STIR-FRIED CHICKEN WITH BASIL AND CHILLI

THIS QUICK AND EASY CHICKEN DISH IS AN EXCELLENT INTRODUCTION TO THAI CUISINE. THAI BASIL, WHICH IS SOMETIMES KNOWN AS HOLY BASIL, HAS A UNIQUE, PUNGENT FLAVOUR THAT IS BOTH SPICY AND SHARP. DEEP-FRYING THE LEAVES ADDS ANOTHER DIMENSION TO THIS DISH.

SERVES 4–6

INGREDIENTS

45ml/3 tbsp vegetable oil
4 garlic cloves, thinly sliced
2–4 fresh red chillies, seeded
   and finely chopped
450g/1lb skinless chicken breast
   fillets, cut into bitesize pieces
45ml/3 tbsp Thai fish sauce
10ml/2 tsp dark soy sauce
5ml/1 tsp sugar
10–12 Thai basil leaves
2 fresh red chillies, seeded and finely
   chopped and about 20 deep-fried
   Thai basil leaves, to garnish

1 Heat the oil in a wok or large frying pan. Add the garlic and chillies and stir-fry over medium heat for 1–2 minutes until the garlic is golden.

2 Add the pieces of chicken to the wok or pan and stir-fry until the chicken changes colour.

3 Stir in the Thai fish sauce, soy sauce and sugar. Continue to stir-fry the mixture for 3–4 minutes or until the chicken is fully cooked with the sauce.

4 Stir in the fresh Thai basil leaves. Spoon the entire mixture on to a warm serving platter, or individual serving dishes and garnish with the sliced chillies and deep-fried Thai basil.

COOK'S TIP
To deep-fry Thai basil leaves, first make sure that the leaves are completely dry or they will splutter when added to the oil. deep-fry the leaves briefly in hot oil until they are crisp and translucent – this will only take about 30–40 seconds. Lift out the leaves using a slotted spoon or wire basket and leave them to drain on kitchen paper.

GREEN PAPAYA SALAD

THIS SALAD APPEARS IN MANY GUISES IN SOUTH-EAST ASIA. AS GREEN PAPAYA IS NOT EASY TO GET HOLD OF, FINELY GRATED CARROTS, CUCUMBER OR GREEN APPLE CAN BE USED INSTEAD. ALTERNATIVELY, USE VERY THINLY SLICED WHITE CABBAGE.

2 Put the garlic, shallots, chillies and salt in a large mortar and grind to a paste with a pestle. Add the shredded papaya, a little at a time, pounding until it becomes slightly limp and soft.

3 Add the sliced beans and wedges of tomato to the mortar and crush them lightly with the pestle.

SERVES 4

INGREDIENTS

   1 green papaya
   4 garlic cloves, roughly chopped
   15ml/1 tbsp chopped shallots
   3–4 fresh red chillies, seeded
     and sliced
   2.5ml/½ tsp salt
   2–3 snake beans or 6 green beans,
     cut into 2cm/¾in lengths
   2 tomatoes, cut into thin wedges
   45ml/3 tbsp Thai fish sauce
   15ml/1 tbsp caster (superfine) sugar
   juice of 1 lime
   30ml/2 tbsp crushed roasted peanuts
   sliced fresh red chillies, to garnish

1 Cut the papaya in half lengthways. Scrape out the seeds with a spoon, then peel using a swivel vegetable peeler or a small sharp knife. Shred the flesh finely using a food processor or grater.

4 Season the mixture with the Thai fish sauce, sugar and lime juice. Transfer the salad to a serving dish and sprinkle with crushed peanuts and garnish with sliced red chillies.

LARP ᴼᶠ CHIANG MAI

CHIANG MAI IS A CITY IN THE NORTH-EAST OF THAILAND. THE CITY IS CULTURALLY VERY CLOSE TO
LAOS AND FAMOUS FOR ITS CHICKEN SALAD, WHICH WAS ORIGINALLY CALLED "LAAP" OR "LARP".
DUCK, BEEF OR PORK CAN BE USED INSTEAD OF CHICKEN.

SERVES 4–6

INGREDIENTS
    450g/1lb minced (ground) chicken
    1 lemon grass stalk, root trimmed
    3 kaffir lime leaves, finely chopped
    4 fresh red chillies, seeded
      and chopped
    60ml/4 tbsp lime juice
    30ml/2 tbsp Thai fish sauce
    15ml/1 tbsp roasted ground rice
      (see Cook's Tip)
    2 spring onions (scallions), chopped
    30ml/2 tbsp fresh coriander
      (cilantro) leaves
    thinly sliced kaffir lime leaves, mixed
      salad leaves and fresh mint sprigs,
      to garnish

1 Heat a large non-stick frying pan.
Add the minced chicken and moisten
with a little water. Stir constantly over
medium heat for 7–10 minutes until it
is cooked. Meanwhile, cut off the lower
5cm/2in of the lemon grass stalk and
chop finely.

2 Transfer the cooked chicken to a
bowl and add the chopped lemon grass,
lime leaves, chillies, lime juice, Thai
fish sauce, ground rice, spring onions
and coriander. Mix thoroughly.

3 Spoon the chicken mixture into a
salad bowl. Sprinkle sliced kaffir lime
leaves over the top and garnish with
salad leaves and sprigs of mint.

COOK'S TIP
Use glutinous rice for the roasted ground
rice. Put the rice in a frying pan and dry-
roast it until golden brown. Remove and
grind to a powder, using a mortar and
pestle or a food processor. When the rice
is cold, store it in a glass jar in a cool
and dry place.

THAI BEEF SALAD

A HEARTY MAIN MEAL SALAD, THIS COMBINES TENDER STRIPS OF STEAK WITH A WONDERFUL DRESSING
MADE USING CHILLI AND LIME.

SERVES 4

INGREDIENTS
    2 sirloin steaks, each about 225g/8oz
    1 lemon grass stalk, root trimmed
    1 red onion, finely sliced
    1/2 cucumber, cut into strips
    30ml/2 tbsp chopped spring
      onion (scallion)
    juice of 2 limes
    15–30ml/1–2 tbsp Thai fish sauce
    Chinese mustard cress or salad cress,
      to garnish

1 Pan-fry or grill (broil) the steaks for
6–8 minutes for medium-rare. Allow to
rest for 10–15 minutes. Meanwhile, cut
off the lower 5cm/2in from the lemon
grass stalk and chop it finely.

2 When the meat is cool, slice it thinly
and put the slices in a large bowl.

3 Add the sliced onion, cucumber,
lemon grass and chopped spring onion
to the meat slices.

4 Toss the salad and season with
the lime juice and Thai fish sauce.
Transfer to a serving bowl or plate and
serve at room temperature or chilled,
garnished with Chinese mustard cress
or salad cress.

COOK'S TIP
Look out for gui chai leaves in Thai stores.
These look like very thin spring onions
(scallions) and are often used as a
substitute for the more familiar vegetable.

STUFFED THAI OMELETTES

INDIVIDUAL OMELETTES CAN BE MADE OR MAKE TWO LARGE OMELETTE PARCELS TO SERVE FOUR.
THEY ARE REMARKABLY EASY TO MAKE AND MAKE A TASTY LUNCH OR LIGHT SUPPER.

2 Stir in the Thai fish sauce, sugar and tomatoes, with ground black pepper to taste. Simmer for 5–8 minutes, until the sauce thickens. Remove from the heat and stir in the chopped fresh coriander.

3 Make the omelettes. Whisk the eggs and fish sauce in a bowl. Heat a little of the oil in a 20cm/8in omelette pan. Add a quarter or half of the egg mixture, depending on whether you wish to make individual parcels or cut them in half. Tilt the pan to spread the egg into a thin, even sheet. As soon as it sets, spoon some of the filling over the centre of the omelette. Fold the top and bottom over, then the right and left sides to make a neat, square parcel.

4 Slide the omelette out on to a warm serving dish, folded side down, and keep hot while you make the remaining omelette(s). Serve garnished with sprigs of coriander.

SERVES 3–4

INGREDIENTS
  30ml/2 tbsp vegetable oil
  2 garlic cloves, finely chopped
  1 small onion, finely chopped
  225g/8oz minced (ground) pork
  30ml/2 tbsp Thai fish sauce
  5ml/1 tsp sugar
  2 tomatoes, peeled and chopped
  15ml/1 tbsp chopped fresh
    coriander (cilantro)
  fresh coriander sprigs, to garnish

For the omelettes
  6 eggs
  15ml/1 tbsp Thai fish sauce
  about 30ml/2 tbsp vegetable oil

1 Heat the oil in a wok or frying pan. Add the chopped garlic and onion and fry for 3–4 minutes until the onion is softened. Add the minced pork and stir-fry for 7–10 minutes, until broken up and lightly browned.

VARIATION
Replace half the pork with peeled tiger prawns (shrimp) or white crab meat.

BARBECUED CHICKEN

BARBECUED CHICKEN IS SERVED ALMOST EVERYWHERE IN THAILAND, FROM PORTABLE ROADSIDE STALLS TO SPORTS STADIUMS AND EVEN ON THE BEACH.

SERVES 4–6

INGREDIENTS
    1 chicken, about 1.5kg/3–3½lb,
      cut into 8–10 pieces
    lime wedges and red chillies, to garnish

For the marinade
    2 lemon grass stalks, root trimmed
    2.5cm/1in piece fresh root ginger,
      peeled and thinly sliced
    6 garlic cloves, roughly chopped
    4 shallots, roughly chopped
    ½ bunch coriander (cilantro) roots,
      chopped
    15ml/1 tbsp palm sugar (jaggery)
    120ml/4fl oz/½ cup coconut milk
    30ml/2 tbsp Thai fish sauce
    30ml/2 tbsp light soy sauce

1 First make the marinade. Cut off the lower 5cm/2in of both of the lemon grass stalks and chop them roughly. Put into a food processor along with all the other marinade ingredients and process until the mixture has reached a smooth consistency.

2 Place the chicken pieces in a dish, pour over the marinade and stir to mix well. Cover the dish and leave in a cool place to marinate for at least 4 hours or overnight.

3 Prepare the barbecue or preheat the oven to 200°C/400°F/Gas 6. If cooking in the oven, arrange the chicken pieces on a rack over a roasting pan.

4 Cook the chicken on a barbecue or bake in the oven for 20–30 minutes or until the pieces are cooked and golden brown. Turn the pieces and brush with the marinade once or twice during cooking. Transfer the chicken pieces to a serving platter and garnish with lime wedges and red chillies.

COOK'S TIP
Coconut milk is available fresh or in cans or cartons from most supermarkets, or use 50g/2oz creamed coconut, available in packets, and dissolve in warm water.

CRISPY FRIED RICE VERMICELLI

MEE KROB IS USUALLY SERVED AT CELEBRATION MEALS. IT IS A CRISP TANGLE OF FRIED RICE VERMICELLI, WHICH IS TOSSED IN A PIQUANT GARLIC, SWEET AND SOUR SAUCE.

SERVES 4–6

INGREDIENTS
    vegetable oil, for deep-frying
    175g/6oz rice vermicelli
    15ml/1 tbsp chopped garlic
    4–6 small dried red chillies
    30ml/2 tbsp chopped shallots
    15ml/1 tbsp dried shrimps, rinsed
    115g/4oz minced (ground) pork
    115g/4oz raw peeled prawns (shrimp),
        thawed if frozen, chopped
    30ml/2 tbsp brown bean sauce
    30ml/2 tbsp rice wine vinegar
    45ml/3 tbsp Thai fish sauce
    75g/3oz palm sugar (jaggery)
    30ml/2 tbsp tamarind juice or lime juice
    115g/4oz/2 cups beansprouts

For the garnish
    2 spring onions (scallions), shredded
    30ml/2 tbsp fresh coriander
        (cilantro) leaves
    2-egg omelette, rolled and sliced
    2 fresh red chillies, seeded and
        cut into thin strips

1 Heat the oil in a wok. Cut or break the rice vermicelli into small handfuls about 7.5cm/3in long. Deep-fry these for a few seconds in the hot oil until they puff up. Lift out with a slotted spoon and drain on kitchen paper.

VARIATION
Pickled garlic can also be used as one of the garnish ingredients. Thai garlic is smaller than European garlic; the heads are pickled whole, in sweet and sour brine.

2 Ladle off all but 30ml/2 tbsp of the oil, pouring it into a pan and setting aside to cool. Reheat the oil in the wok and fry the garlic, chillies, shallots and shrimps for about 1 minute.

3 Add the pork and stir-fry for 3–4 minutes, until no longer pink. Add the prawns and fry for 2 minutes. Spoon into a bowl and set aside.

4 Add the brown bean sauce, vinegar, Thai fish sauce and sugar. Heat gently, stirring in any sediment. Bring to a gentle boil, stir to dissolve the sugar and cook until thick and syrupy.

5 Add the tamarind or lime juice to the sauce and adjust the seasoning as necessary. The sauce should be sweet, sour and salty. Lower the heat, then return the pork and prawn mixture to the wok, add the beansprouts and stir them into the sauce.

6 Add the fried rice noodles to the wok and toss gently to coat them with the sauce without breaking them up too much. Transfer the mixture to a large, warm serving platter or individual serving dishes. Garnish with the shredded spring onions, coriander leaves, omelette strips and fresh red chillies and serve immediately.

COOK'S TIP
Always deep-fry rice vermicelli in small quantities, as it puffs up to two or three times its original volume. It cooks in seconds, so be ready to remove from the wok using a slotted spoon or wire basket as soon as it is puffy and before it takes on any colour.

RED CHICKEN CURRY WITH BAMBOO SHOOTS

BAMBOO SHOOTS HAVE A LOVELY CRUNCHY TEXTURE. IT IS QUITE ACCEPTABLE TO USE CANNED ONES, AS FRESH BAMBOO IS NOT READILY AVAILABLE IN THE WEST. BUY CANNED WHOLE BAMBOO SHOOTS, WHICH ARE CRISPER AND OF BETTER QUALITY THAN SLICED SHOOTS. RINSE BEFORE USING.

SERVES 4–6

INGREDIENTS
1 litre/1¾ pints/4 cups coconut milk
450g/1lb skinless chicken breast
   fillets, cut into bitesize pieces
30ml/2 tbsp Thai fish sauce
15ml/1 tbsp sugar
225g/8oz drained canned bamboo
   shoots, rinsed and sliced
5 kaffir lime leaves, torn
salt and ground black pepper
chopped fresh red chillies and kaffir
   lime leaves, to garnish

For the red curry paste
5ml/1 tsp coriander seeds
2.5ml/½ tsp cumin seeds
12–15 fresh red chillies, seeded
   and roughly chopped
4 shallots, thinly sliced
2 garlic cloves, chopped
15ml/1 tbsp chopped galangal
2 lemon grass stalks, chopped
3 kaffir lime leaves, chopped
4 fresh coriander (cilantro) roots
10 black peppercorns
good pinch of ground cinnamon
5ml/1 tsp ground turmeric
2.5ml/½ tsp shrimp paste
5ml/1 tsp salt
30ml/2 tbsp vegetable oil

2 Add the oil, a little at a time, mixing or processing well after each addition. Transfer to a jar and keep in the refrigerator until ready to use.

3 Pour half of the coconut milk into a large heavy pan. Bring the milk to the boil, stirring it constantly until it has separated.

1 Make the curry paste. Dry-fry the coriander and cumin seeds for 1–2 minutes, then put in a mortar or food processor with the remaining ingredients except the oil and pound or process to a paste.

4 Stir in 30ml/2 tbsp of the red curry paste and cook the mixture for 2–3 minutes, stirring constantly. Remaining red curry paste can be kept in the refrigerator for up to 3 months.

5 Add the chicken pieces, Thai fish sauce and sugar to the pan. Stir well, then cook for 5–6 minutes until the chicken changes colour and is cooked through, stirring constantly to prevent the mixture from sticking to the bottom of the pan.

6 Pour the remaining coconut milk into the pan, then add the sliced bamboo shoots and torn kaffir lime leaves. Bring back to the boil over medium heat, stirring constantly to prevent the mixture sticking, then taste and add salt and pepper if necessary.

7 To serve, spoon the curry into a warmed serving dish and garnish with chopped chillies and kaffir lime leaves.

VARIATION
Instead of, or as well as, bamboo shoots, use straw mushrooms. These are available in cans from Asian stores and supermarkets. Drain well and then stir into the curry at the end of the recipe.

COOK'S TIP
It is essential to use chicken breast fillets, rather than any other cut, for this curry, as it is cooked very quickly. Look out for diced chicken or strips of chicken (which are often labelled "stir-fry chicken") in the supermarket.

MUSSAMAN CURRY

THIS DISH IS TRADITIONALLY MADE WITH BEEF, BUT CHICKEN, LAMB OR TOFU CAN BE USED. IT HAS A RICH, SWEET AND SPICY FLAVOUR AND IS BEST SERVED WITH BOILED RICE. MUSSAMAN CURRY PASTE IS AVAILABLE FROM SPECIALIST STORES, OR YOU CAN MAKE YOUR OWN.

SERVES 4–6

INGREDIENTS
  600ml/1 pint/2½ cups canned
    coconut milk
  675g/1½ lb stewing beef, cut into
    2.5cm/1in chunks
  250ml/8fl oz/1 cup coconut cream
  45ml/3 tbsp Mussaman curry paste
    (see Cook's Tip)
  30ml/2 tbsp Thai fish sauce
  15ml/1 tbsp palm sugar (jaggery)
  60ml/4 tbsp tamarind juice
  6 green cardamom pods
  1 cinnamon stick
  1 large potato, about 225g/8oz,
    cut into even chunks
  1 onion, cut into wedges
  50g/2oz/½ cup roasted peanuts

1 Bring the coconut milk to a gentle boil in a large pan. Add the beef, lower the heat and simmer for about 40 minutes until tender.

2 Put the coconut cream into a pan and cook for 5–8 minutes, stirring, until it separates. Stir in the Mussaman curry paste and cook rapidly until fragrant. Add to the cooked beef, and mix well.

3 Stir in the Thai fish sauce, sugar, tamarind juice, cardamom pods, cinnamon, potato and onion. Simmer for 15–20 minutes or until the potato is cooked. Add the peanuts and mix well. Cook for 5 minutes and serve.

COOK'S TIP
To make Mussaman curry paste, soak 12 large, seeded dried chillies, in hot water for 15 minutes. Chop finely and pound or process with 60ml/4 tbsp shallots, 5 garlic cloves, 1 lemon grass stalk base and 30ml/2 tbsp chopped galangal. Put 5ml/1 tsp cumin seeds, 15ml/1 tbsp coriander seeds, 2 cloves and 6 black peppercorns in a pan; dry-fry over low heat for 1–2 minutes. Grind to a powder; add 5ml/1 tsp shrimp paste, 5ml/1 tsp salt, 5ml/1 tsp sugar and 30ml/2 tbsp vegetable oil. Stir in the shallot mixture to make a paste.

CURRIED PRAWNS IN COCONUT MILK

ANOTHER WONDERFULLY QUICK AND EASY DISH, THIS FEATURES PRAWNS IN A SPICY COCONUT GRAVY.

SERVES 4–6

INGREDIENTS

600ml/1 pint/2½ cups coconut milk
30ml/2 tbsp yellow curry paste
  (see Cook's Tip)
15ml/1 tbsp Thai fish sauce
2.5ml/½ tsp salt
5ml/1 tsp sugar
450g/1lb raw king prawns (jumbo
  shrimp) peeled, thawed if frozen
225g/8oz cherry tomatoes
fresh yellow and orange (bell)
  peppers, seeded and cut into thin
  strips, chives and juice of ½ lime,
  to garnish

VARIATION
Use cooked prawns (shrimp) for a quick
version of this dish. Add them after the
tomatoes for a minute or two.

1 Put half the coconut milk in a wok
or pan and bring to the boil. Add the
yellow curry paste, stir until it disperses,
then lower the heat and simmer for
about 10 minutes.

2 Add the Thai fish sauce, salt, sugar
and remaining coconut milk to the
sauce. Simmer for 5 minutes more.

3 Add the prawns and cherry tomatoes.
Simmer very gently for about 5 minutes
until the prawns are pink and tender.

4 Spoon into a serving dish, sprinkle
with lime juice and garnish with strips
of yellow peppers and chives.

COOK'S TIP
To make yellow curry paste, put into
a food processor or blender 6–8 fresh
yellow chillies, the chopped base of
1 lemon grass stalk, 4 chopped shallots,
4 chopped garlic cloves, 15ml/1 tbsp
chopped peeled fresh root ginger, 5ml/
1 tsp coriander seeds, 5ml/1 tsp mustard
powder, 5ml/1 tsp salt, 2.5ml/½ tsp
ground cinnamon, 15ml/1 tbsp light
brown sugar and 30ml/2 tbsp sunflower
oil. Process to a paste, scrape into a glass
jar, cover and keep in the refrigerator.

STEWED PUMPKIN IN COCONUT CREAM

STEWED FRUIT IS A POPULAR DESSERT IN THAILAND. PUMPKINS, BANANAS AND MELONS CAN ALL BE PREPARED IN THIS WAY, AND YOU CAN EVEN STEW CORN KERNELS OR PULSES SUCH AS MUNG BEANS AND BLACK BEANS IN COCONUT MILK.

SERVES 4–6

INGREDIENTS

  1kg/2¼lb kabocha pumpkin
  750ml/1¼ pints/3 cups
    coconut milk
  175g/6oz/¾ cup sugar
  pinch of salt
  toasted pumpkin seed kernels and
    fresh mint sprigs, to decorate

COOK'S TIP
To make the garnish, wash the pumpkin seeds to remove any fibres and pat them dry on kitchen paper. Roast them in a dry-frying pan or, alternatively, spread the seeds out on a baking sheet and grill (broil) until golden brown; toss them frequently.

1 Cut the pumpkin in half using a large, sharp knife, then cut away and discard the skin. Scoop out the seed cluster and reserve a few seeds. Using a sharp knife, cut the pumpkin flesh into pieces that are about 5cm/2in long and 2cm/¾in thick.

2 In a pan, bring the coconut milk, sugar and salt to the boil. Add the pumpkin and simmer for 10–15 minutes until it is tender. Serve warm, in individual dishes. Decorate each serving with a mint sprig and a few toasted pumpkin seed kernels.

MANGOES WITH STICKY RICE

EVERYONE'S FAVOURITE DESSERT: MANGOES, WITH THEIR DELICATE FRAGRANCE, SWEET AND SOUR FLAVOUR AND VELVETY FLESH, BLEND ESPECIALLY WELL WITH COCONUT STICKY RICE. YOU NEED TO START PREPARING THIS DISH THE DAY BEFORE YOU INTEND TO SERVE IT.

SERVES 4

INGREDIENTS

  115g/4oz/⅔ cup white
    glutinous rice
  175ml/6fl oz/¾ cup thick
    coconut milk
  45ml/3 tbsp sugar
  pinch of salt
  2 ripe mangoes, peeled and sliced
  strips of lime rind, to decorate

1 Rinse the glutinous rice thoroughly in several changes of cold water, then leave to soak overnight in a bowl of fresh cold water.

COOK'S TIP
Like cream, the thickest and richest part of coconut milk rises to the top. Spoon it off and pour over before serving.

2 Drain the rice and spread evenly in a steamer lined with muslin (cheesecloth). Cover and steam over simmering water for 20 minutes or until tender.

3 Reserve 45ml/3 tbsp of the top of the coconut milk. Bring the rest to the boil in a pan with the sugar and salt, stirring until the sugar dissolves. Pour into a bowl to cool.

4 Transfer the cooked rice into a bowl and pour over the cooled coconut milk mixture. Stir well, then leave to stand for about 10–15 minutes.

5 Spoon the rice on to individual serving plates. Arrange mango slices on one side and then drizzle with the reserved coconut milk. Decorate with strips of lime rind and serve.

MOHINGHA

MYANMAR HOUSEWIVES BUY THIS WELL-KNOWN AND DELICIOUS ONE-COURSE MEAL FROM HAWKERS, RECOGNIZED BY A BAMBOO POLE CARRIED ACROSS THEIR SHOULDERS. AT ONE END IS A CONTAINER WITH A CHARCOAL FIRE AND AT THE OTHER END IS EVERYTHING ELSE THEY NEED TO MAKE THE MEAL.

SERVES 8

INGREDIENTS
    675g/1½lb huss, cod or mackerel,
      cleaned but left on the bone
    3 lemon grass stalks
    2.5cm/1in piece fresh root
      ginger, peeled
    30ml/2 tbsp fish sauce
    3 onions, roughly chopped
    4 garlic cloves, roughly chopped
    2–3 fresh red chillies, seeded
      and chopped
    5ml/1 tsp ground turmeric
    75ml/5 tbsp groundnut (peanut) oil,
      for frying
    400ml/14fl oz can coconut milk
    25g/1oz/3 tbsp rice flour
    25g/1oz/3 tbsp gram flour
    pieces of banana trunk, or heart, if
      available, or 540g/1lb 5oz drained
      canned bamboo shoot, sliced
    salt and ground black pepper
    wedges of hard-boiled egg, thinly sliced
      red onions, finely chopped spring
      onions (scallions), a few deep-fried
      prawns (shrimp) and fried chillies
      (see Cook's Tip), to garnish
    450g/1lb dried or fresh rice noodles,
      cooked according to the instructions
      on the packet, to serve

1 Place the fish in a large pan and pour in cold water to cover. Bruise two lemon grass stalks and half the ginger and add to the pan. Bring to the boil, add the fish sauce and cook for 10 minutes. Lift out the fish and allow to cool while straining the stock into a large bowl. Discard any skin and bones from the fish and break the flesh into small pieces.

2 Cut off the lower 5cm/2in of the remaining lemon grass stalk and discard; roughly chop the remaining lemon grass. Put it in a food processor with the remaining ginger, the onions, garlic, chillies and turmeric. Process to a smooth paste. Heat the oil in a frying pan and fry the paste until it gives off a rich aroma. Remove from the heat and add the fish.

3 Stir the coconut milk into the reserved fish stock, then add enough water to make up to 2.5 litres/4 pints/ 10 cups and pour into a large pan. In a jug, mix the rice flour and gram flour to a thin cream with some of the stock. Stir this into the coconut and stock mixture and bring to the boil, stirring all the time.

4 Add the banana trunk or heart or bamboo shoots and cook for 10 minutes until just tender. Stir in the fish mixture and season. Cook until hot. Guests pour soup over the noodles and add hard-boiled egg, onions, spring onions, prawns and fried chillies as a garnish.

COOK'S TIP
To make fried chillies, dry roast 8–10 dried red chillies in a heavy frying pan, then pound them, fry in 30ml/2 tbsp peanut oil and stir in 25g/1oz dried shrimps (pounded).

THAMIN LETHOK

THIS IS THE MYANMAR WAY OF DEALING WITH LEFTOVERS, AND VERY SUCCESSFUL IT IS TOO. THE
NOODLES AND RICE ARE ARRANGED ON PLATTERS WITH SOME OR ALL OF THE ACCOMPANIMENTS.
EVERYTHING IS SERVED COLD, SO IT IS PERFECT FOR A SUMMER PARTY.

SERVES 6

INGREDIENTS
175g/6oz/scant 1 cup long grain rice
1–2 red chillies, seeded and
  roughly chopped
1 small onion, roughly chopped
15ml/1 tbsp vegetable oil
350g/12oz potatoes, diced
115g/4oz egg noodles, soaked for
  30 minutes in cold water to cover
115g/4oz rice noodles, soaked for
  10 minutes in cold water to cover
50g/2oz cellophane noodles (or
  increase either of the above)
225g/8oz spinach leaves
175g/6oz/3 cups beansprouts
25ml/1¹⁄₂ tbsp tamarind pulp or
  concentrate, soaked in 200ml/
  7fl oz/scant 1 cup warm water,
  or 6 lemon wedges
salt

For the accompaniments
1 very small onion, thinly sliced
3 spring onions (scallions),
  finely shredded
crisp fried onion
50g/2oz cellophane noodles,
  fried until crisp
25g/1oz/3 tbsp chickpeas,
  dry-roasted and pounded
3 dried chillies, dry-fried
  and pounded
fresh coriander (cilantro) leaves

1 Bring a large pan of water to the boil
and cook the rice for 12–15 minutes
until tender. Drain, transfer into a bowl
and set aside. In a mortar, pound the
chillies with the onion. Heat the oil in a
frying pan, add the mixture and fry for
2–3 minutes. Stir into the cooked rice.

2 Cook the potatoes in boiling salted
water for about 8–10 minutes until just
tender; drain and set aside. Drain the
noodles and cook them in separate
pans of salted, boiling water (see Cook's
Tip). Drain, refresh under cold water
and drain again.

3 Put the spinach into a large pan with
just the water that clings to the leaves
after washing. Cover the pan and cook
for 2 minutes until starting to wilt. Drain
well. Cook the beansprouts in the same
way. Leave both to get cold.

COOK'S TIP
Cook noodles following the instructions
on the packet: egg noodles need about
4 minutes and rice noodles are ready
when the water boils again.

4 Arrange the cold flavoured rice,
potato cubes, noodles, spinach and
beansprouts attractively on a large
serving platter. Set out the range of
accompaniments. Strain the tamarind
juice, if using, into a jug (pitcher) or
put the lemon wedges on a plate. Each
guest takes a little of whichever main
ingredients they fancy, adds some
accompaniments and drizzles over a
little tamarind juice or a squeeze of
lemon juice to taste.

INDONESIA

Over 13,000 islands make up this lush tropical archipelago. Numerous cultures
have flourished here, from the early Hindu and Buddhist empires to the rise of Islam.
In the following centuries, Portuguese and British merchants set up trading posts, but
the Dutch had the strongest impact, occupying the islands for 250 years. This culinary
heritage and the abundance of ingredients, such as rice, chillies, limes, tamarind
and spices, has led to the development of exciting dishes such as
Nasi Goreng, Gado-gado and Beef Rendang.

LAMB SATAY

THESE TASTY LAMB SKEWERS ARE TRADITIONALLY SERVED WITH DAINTY DIAMOND-SHAPED PIECES OF
COMPRESSED RICE, WHICH ARE SURPRISINGLY SIMPLE TO MAKE. OFFER THE REMAINING SAUCE FOR DIPPING.

MAKES 25–30 SKEWERS

INGREDIENTS
  1kg/2¼lb leg of lamb, boned
  3 garlic cloves, crushed
  15–30ml/1–2 tbsp chilli sambal
    or 5–10ml/1–2 tsp chilli powder
  90ml/6 tbsp dark soy sauce
  juice of 1 lemon
  salt and ground black pepper
  groundnut (peanut) or sunflower oil,
    for brushing

For the sauce
  6 garlic cloves, crushed
  15ml/1 tbsp chilli sambal or 2–3
    fresh chillies, seeded and ground
    to a paste
  90ml/6 tbsp dark soy sauce
  25ml/1½ tbsp lemon juice
  30ml/2 tbsp boiling water

To serve
  thinly sliced onion
  cucumber wedges (optional)
  compressed rice shapes (see
    Cook's Tip)

1 Cut the lamb into neat 1cm/½in cubes. Remove any pieces of gristle, but do not trim off any of the fat because this keeps the meat moist during cooking and enhances the flavour. Spread out the lamb cubes in a single layer in a shallow bowl.

2 Put the garlic, chilli sambal or chilli powder, soy sauce and lemon juice in a mortar. Add salt and pepper and grind to a paste. Alternatively, process the mixture using a food processor. Pour over the lamb and mix to coat. Cover and leave in a cool place for at least 1 hour. Soak wooden or bamboo skewers in water to prevent them from scorching during cooking.

3 Prepare the sauce. Put the garlic into a bowl. Add the chilli sambal or fresh chillies, soy sauce, lemon juice and boiling water. Stir well. Preheat the grill (broiler). Thread the meat on to the skewers. Brush the skewered meat with oil and grill (broil), turning often. Brush the satay with a little of the sauce and serve hot, with onion, cucumber wedges, if using, rice shapes and the sauce.

COOK'S TIP
Compressed rice shapes are easy to make. Cook two 115g/4oz packets of boil-in-the-bag rice in a large pan of salted, boiling water and simmer for 1¼ hours until the cooked rice fills each bag like a plump cushion. The bags must be covered with water throughout; use a saucer or plate to weigh them down. Let the bags cool completely before slitting them and removing the slabs of cooked rice. With a sharp, wetted knife, cut each rice slab horizontally in half, then into diamond shapes.

BALINESE VEGETABLE SOUP

THE BALINESE BASE THIS POPULAR SOUP ON BEANS, BUT ANY SEASONAL VEGETABLES CAN BE ADDED OR SUBSTITUTED. THE RECIPE ALSO INCLUDES SHRIMP PASTE, WHICH IS KNOWN LOCALLY AS TERASI.

2 Finely grind the chopped garlic, macadamia nuts or almonds, shrimp paste and the coriander seeds to a paste using a mortar and pestle or in a food processor.

3 Heat the oil in a wok, and fry the onion until transparent. Remove with a slotted spoon. Add the nut paste to the wok and fry it for 2 minutes without allowing it to brown.

SERVES 8

INGREDIENTS

225g/8oz green beans
1.2 litres/2 pints/5 cups lightly salted water
1 garlic clove, roughly chopped
2 macadamia nuts or 4 almonds, finely chopped
1cm/½in cube shrimp paste
10–15ml/2–3 tsp coriander seeds, dry-fried
30ml/2 tbsp vegetable oil
1 onion, finely sliced
400ml/14fl oz can coconut milk
2 bay leaves
225g/8oz/4 cups beansprouts
8 thin lemon wedges
30ml/2 tbsp lemon juice
salt and ground black pepper

1 Top and tail the beans, then cut them into small pieces. Bring the lightly salted water to the boil, add the beans to the pan and cook for 3–4 minutes. Drain, reserving the cooking water. Set the beans aside.

COOK'S TIP
Dry-fry the coriander seeds for about 2 minutes until the aroma is released.

4 Pour in the reserved vegetable water. Spoon off 45–60ml/3–4 tbsp of the cream from the top of the coconut milk and set it aside. Add the remaining coconut milk to the wok, bring to the boil and add the bay leaves. Cook, uncovered, for 15–20 minutes.

5 Just before serving, reserve a few beans, fried onions and beansprouts for garnish and stir the rest into the soup. Add the lemon wedges, reserved coconut cream, lemon juice and seasoning; stir well. Pour into individual soup bowls and serve, garnished with reserved beans, onion and beansprouts.

SPICY SQUID

THIS AROMATICALLY SPICED SQUID DISH, CUMI CUMI SMOOR, *IS SIMPLE YET DELICIOUS. GONE ARE THE DAYS WHEN CLEANING SQUID WAS SUCH A CHORE: TODAY THEY CAN BE BOUGHT READY-CLEANED FROM FISHMONGERS, MARKET STALLS AND THE FISH COUNTERS OF LARGE SUPERMARKETS.*

2 Heat a wok and add 15ml/1 tbsp of the oil. When hot, toss in the squid strips and stir-fry for 2–3 minutes, by which time the squid will have curled into attractive shapes or into firm rings. Lift out and set aside.

3 Wipe out the wok, add the remaining oil and heat it. Stir-fry the onion and garlic until soft and beginning to brown. Stir in the tomato, soy sauce, nutmeg, cloves, water and lemon or lime juice. Bring to the boil, lower the heat and add the squid with seasoning to taste.

4 Cook the mixture gently for a further 3–5 minutes stirring from time to time to prevent sticking. Take care not to overcook the squid.

SERVES 3–4

INGREDIENTS
675g/1½lb squid
45ml/3 tbsp groundnut (peanut) oil
1 onion, finely chopped
2 garlic cloves, crushed
1 beefsteak tomato, peeled and chopped
15ml/1 tbsp dark soy sauce
2.5ml/½ tsp grated nutmeg
6 cloves
150ml/¼ pint/⅔ cup water
juice of ½ lemon or lime
salt and ground black pepper
fresh coriander (cilantro) leaves and
  shredded spring onion (scallion),
  to garnish
boiled rice, to serve

1 Rinse and drain the squid, then slice lengthways along one side and open it out flat. Score the inside of the squid in a lattice pattern, using the blunt side of a sharp knife, then cut it crossways into long thin strips.

5 Divide the boiled rice among three to four serving plates and spoon the spicy squid on top. Garnish with coriander leaves and shredded spring onions and serve immediately.

Nasi Goreng

One of the most famous Indonesian dishes, this is a marvellous way to use up leftover rice, chicken and meats. It is important that the rice be quite cold and the grains separate before the other ingredients are added, so cook the rice the day before if possible.

SERVES 4–6

INGREDIENTS

2 eggs
30ml/2 tbsp water
105ml/7 tbsp oil
225g/8oz pork fillet (tenderloin) or fillet of beef, cut into neat strips
115g/4oz cooked, peeled prawns (shrimp), thawed if frozen
175–225g/6–8oz cooked chicken, finely chopped
2 fresh red chillies, halved and seeded
1cm/½in cube shrimp paste
2 garlic cloves, crushed
1 onion, roughly chopped
675g/1½lb/6 cups cold cooked long grain rice, preferably basmati (about 350g/12oz/1¾ cups raw rice)
30ml/2 tbsp dark soy sauce or 45–60ml/3–4 tbsp tomato ketchup
salt and ground black pepper
deep-fried onions, celery leaves and fresh coriander (cilantro) sprigs, to garnish

2 Put the shrimp paste in a food processor. Add the remaining chilli, the garlic and the onion. Process to a fine paste. Alternatively, pound the mixture in a mortar, using a pestle.

3 Heat the remaining oil in a wok and fry the paste, without browning, until it gives off a rich, spicy aroma. Add the pork or beef and toss over the heat to seal in the juices, then cook for 2 minutes more, stirring constantly.

4 Add the prawns and stir-fry for 2 minutes. Finally, stir in the chicken, cold rice, dark soy sauce or ketchup and seasoning to taste. Reheat the rice fully, stirring all the time to keep the rice light and fluffy and prevent it from sticking to the base of the pan.

5 Spoon into individual dishes and arrange the omelette strips and reserved chilli on top. Garnish with the deep-fried onions and coriander sprigs.

1 Put the eggs in a bowl and beat in the water, with salt and pepper to taste. Using a non-stick frying pan make two or three omelettes using as little oil as possible for greasing. Roll up each omelette and cut in strips when cold. Set aside. Place the strips of pork or beef in a bowl. Put the prawns and chopped chicken in separate bowls. Shred one of the chillies and reserve it.

SPICY MEAT BALLS

SERVE THESE SPICY LITTLE PATTIES — PERGEDEL DJAWA — WITH EGG NOODLES AND CHILLI SAMBAL.

SERVES 4–6

INGREDIENTS
  1cm/½in cube shrimp paste
  1 large onion, roughly chopped
  1–2 fresh red chillies, seeded
    and chopped
  2 garlic cloves, crushed
  15ml/1 tbsp coriander seeds
  5ml/1 tsp cumin seeds
  450g/1lb lean minced (ground) beef
  10ml/2 tsp dark soy sauce
  5ml/1 tsp soft dark brown sugar
  juice of 1½ lemons
  a little beaten egg
  vegetable oil, for shallow-frying
  salt and ground black pepper
  1 green and 2 fresh red chillies,
    to garnish
  chilli sambal, to serve

1 Wrap the shrimp paste in a piece of foil and warm in a frying pan for about 5 minutes, turning a few times. Unwrap and put in a food processor.

COOK'S TIP
When processing the shrimp paste, onion, chillies and garlic, do not process for too long, otherwise the onion will become too wet and spoil the consistency of the meat balls.

2 Add the onion, chillies and garlic to the food processor and process until finely chopped. Set aside. Dry-fry the coriander and cumin seeds in a hot frying pan for 1 minute, to release the aroma. Transfer the seeds into a mortar and grind with a pestle.

3 Put the meat in a large bowl. Stir in the onion mixture. Add the ground spices, soy sauce, brown sugar, lemon juice and beaten egg. Season to taste.

4 Shape the meat mixture into small, even balls, and chill these for 5–10 minutes to firm them up.

5 Heat the oil in a wok or large frying pan and fry the meat balls for about 4–5 minutes, turning often, until cooked through and browned. You may have to do this in batches.

6 Drain the meat balls on kitchen paper, and then pile them on to a warm serving platter or into a large serving bowl. Finely slice the green chilli and one of the red chillies and sprinkle over the meat balls. Garnish with the remaining red chilli, if you like. Serve with the Chilli Sambal (see below) handed round separately.

VARIATION
Minced (ground) beef is traditionally used for this dish, but pork, lamb – or even turkey – mince would also be good.

CHILLI SAMBAL

THIS FIERCE CONDIMENT IS BOTTLED AS SAMBAL OELEK, BUT IT IS EASY TO PREPARE AND WILL KEEP FOR SEVERAL WEEKS IN A WELL-SEALED JAR IN THE REFRIGERATOR. USE A STAINLESS-STEEL OR PLASTIC SPOON TO MEASURE; IF SAUCE DRIPS ON YOUR FINGERS, WASH WELL IN SOAPY WATER IMMEDIATELY.

MAKES 450G/1LB

INGREDIENTS
  450g/1lb fresh red chillies, seeded
  10ml/2 tsp salt

1 Bring a pan of water to the boil, add the seeded chillies and cook them for 5–8 minutes.

2 Drain the chillies and then grind them in a food processor, without making the paste too smooth.

3 Scrape into a screw-topped glass jar, stir in the salt and cover with a piece of baking parchment or clear film (plastic wrap). Screw on the lid and store in the refrigerator. Spoon into small dishes, to serve as an accompaniment, or to use in recipes as suggested.

SWEET AND SOUR SALAD

ACAR BENING MAKES A PERFECT ACCOMPANIMENT TO A VARIETY OF SPICY DISHES AND CURRIES, WITH ITS CLEAN TASTE AND BRIGHT, JEWEL-LIKE COLOURS, AND POMEGRANATE SEEDS, THOUGH NOT TRADITIONAL, MAKE A BEAUTIFUL GARNISH. THIS IS AN ESSENTIAL DISH FOR A BUFFET PARTY.

SERVES 8

INGREDIENTS
  1 small cucumber
  1 onion, thinly sliced
  1 small, ripe pineapple or 425g/
    15oz can pineapple rings
  1 green (bell) pepper, seeded
    and thinly sliced
  3 firm tomatoes, chopped
  30ml/2 tbsp golden sugar
  45–60ml/3–4 tbsp white wine vinegar
  120ml/4fl oz/1/2 cup water
  salt
  seeds of 1–2 pomegranates,
    to garnish

1 Halve the cucumber lengthways, remove the seeds, slice and spread on a plate with the onion. Sprinkle with salt. After 10 minutes, rinse and dry.

2 If using a fresh pineapple, peel and core it, removing all the eyes, then cut it into bitesize pieces. If using canned pineapple, drain the rings and cut them into small wedges. Place the pineapple in a bowl with the cucumber, onion, green pepper and tomatoes.

3 Heat the sugar, vinegar and measured water in a pan, stirring until the sugar has dissolved. Remove the pan from the heat and leave to cool. When cold, add a little salt to taste and pour over the fruit and vegetables. Cover and chill until required. Serve in small bowls, garnished with pomegranate seeds.

VARIATION
To make an Indonesian-style cucumber salad, salt a salad cucumber as described in the recipe. Make half the dressing and pour it over the cucumber. Add a few chopped spring onions (scallions). Cover and chill. Serve sprinkled with toasted sesame seeds.

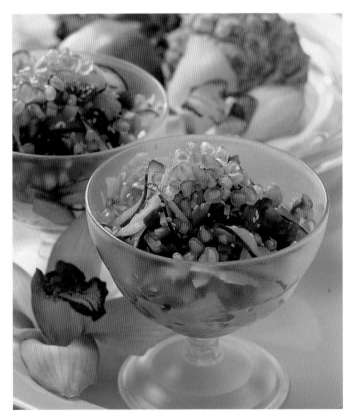

FRUIT AND RAW VEGETABLE GADO-GADO

A BANANA LEAF, WHICH CAN BE BOUGHT FROM ASIAN STORES, CAN BE USED INSTEAD OF THE MIXED SALAD LEAVES TO LINE THE PLATTER FOR A SPECIAL OCCASION.

SERVES 6

INGREDIENTS
  ½ cucumber
  2 pears (not too ripe) or 175g/6oz
    wedge of yam bean
  1–2 eating apples
  juice of ½ lemon
  mixed salad leaves
  6 small tomatoes, cut in wedges
  3 slices fresh pineapple, cored and
    cut in wedges
  3 eggs, hard-boiled and shelled
  175g/6oz egg noodles, cooked,
    cooled and chopped
  deep-fried onions, to garnish

For the peanut sauce
  2–4 fresh red chillies, seeded
    and ground, or 15ml/1 tbsp
    chilli sambal
  300ml/½ pint/1¼ cups
    coconut milk
  350g/12oz/1¼ cups crunchy
    peanut butter
  15ml/1 tbsp dark soy sauce or
    soft dark brown sugar
  5ml/1 tsp tamarind pulp, soaked
  in 45ml/3 tbsp warm water
  coarsely crushed peanuts
  salt

2 Simmer gently until the sauce thickens, then stir in the soy sauce or sugar. Strain in the tamarind juice, add salt to taste and stir well. Spoon into a bowl and sprinkle with a few coarsely crushed peanuts.

VARIATION
Quail's eggs can be used instead of normal eggs and look very attractive in this dish. Hard boil for 3 minutes and halve or leave whole.

3 To make the salad, core the cucumber and peel the pears or yam bean. Cut them into matchsticks. Finely shred the apples and sprinkle them with the lemon juice. Spread a bed of lettuce leaves on a flat platter, then pile the fruit and vegetables on top.

4 Add the sliced or quartered hard-boiled eggs, the chopped noodles and the deep-fried onions. Serve immediately, with the sauce.

1 Make the peanut sauce. Put the ground chillies or chilli sambal in a pan. Pour in the coconut milk, then stir in the peanut butter. Heat gently, stirring, until well blended.

BEEF RENDANG

IN INDONESIA, THIS SPICY DISH IS USUALLY SERVED WITH THE MEAT QUITE DRY; IF YOU PREFER MORE SAUCE, SIMPLY ADD MORE WATER WHEN STIRRING IN THE POTATOES.

SERVES 6–8

INGREDIENTS

2 onions or 5–6 shallots, chopped
4 garlic cloves, chopped
2.5cm/1in piece fresh galangal, peeled and sliced, or 15ml/1 tbsp galangal paste
2.5cm/1in piece fresh root ginger, peeled and sliced
4–6 fresh red chillies, seeded and roughly chopped
lower part only of 1 lemon grass stem, sliced
2.5cm/1in piece fresh turmeric, peeled and sliced, or 5ml/1 tsp ground turmeric
1kg/2¼lb prime beef in one piece
5ml/1 tsp coriander seeds, dry-fried
5ml/1 tsp cumin seeds, dry-fried
2 kaffir lime leaves, torn into pieces
2 x 400ml/14fl oz cans coconut milk
300ml/½ pint/1¼ cups water
30ml/2 tbsp dark soy sauce
5ml/1 tsp tamarind pulp, soaked in 60ml/4 tbsp warm water
8–10 small new potatoes, scrubbed
salt and ground black pepper
deep-fried onions (see below), sliced fresh red chillies and spring onions (scallions), to garnish

1 Put the onions or shallots in a food processor. Add the garlic, galangal, ginger, chillies, sliced lemon grass and fresh or ground turmeric. Process to a fine paste or grind in a mortar, using a pestle.

2 Cut the meat into cubes using a large sharp knife, then place the cubes in a bowl.

3 Grind the dry-fried coriander and cumin seeds, then add to the meat with the onion, chilli paste and kaffir lime leaves; stir well. Cover and leave in a cool place to marinate while you prepare the other ingredients.

COOK'S TIP
This dish is even better if you can cook it a day or two in advance of serving, which allows the flavours to mellow beautifully. Add the potatoes on reheating and simmer until tender.

4 Pour the coconut milk and water into a wok, then stir in the spiced meat and the soy sauce. Strain the tamarind water and add to the wok. Stir over medium heat until the liquid boils, then simmer gently, half-covered, for 1½ hours.

5 Add the potatoes and simmer for 20–25 minutes, or until meat and potatoes are tender. Add water if you like. Season and serve, garnished with deep-fried onions, chillies and spring onions.

DEEP-FRIED ONIONS

KNOWN AS BAWANG GORENG, THESE ARE A TRADITIONAL GARNISH AND ACCOMPANY MANY INDONESIAN DISHES. ASIAN STORES SELL THEM READY-PREPARED, BUT IT IS EASY TO MAKE THEM. THE SMALL RED ONIONS SOLD IN ASIAN SHOPS ARE EXCELLENT AS THEY CONTAIN LESS WATER.

MAKES 450G/1LB

INGREDIENTS
450g/1lb onions
vegetable oil, for deep-frying

1 Thinly slice the onions with a sharp knife or in a food processor. Spread the slices out in a single layer on kitchen paper and leave them to dry, in an airy place, for 30 minutes to 2 hours.

2 Heat the oil in a deep-fryer or wok to 190°C/375°F. Fry the onions in batches, until crisp and golden, turning all the time. Drain well on kitchen paper, cool and store in an airtight container, unless using immediately.

SAMBAL GORENG <u>WITH</u> PRAWNS

SAMBAL GORENG IS AN IMMENSELY USEFUL AND ADAPTABLE SAUCE. HERE IT IS COMBINED WITH PRAWNS AND GREEN PEPPER, BUT YOU COULD ADD FINE STRIPS OF CALF'S LIVER, CHICKEN LIVERS, TOMATOES, GREEN BEANS OR HARD-BOILED EGGS.

SERVES 4–6

INGREDIENTS
350g/12oz cooked, peeled
  prawns (shrimp)
1 green (bell) pepper, seeded and sliced
60ml/4 tbsp tamarind juice
pinch of sugar
45ml/3 tbsp coconut milk or cream
lime rind and red onion, to garnish
boiled rice, to serve

For the sambal goreng
2.5cm/1in cube shrimp paste
2 onions, roughly chopped
2 garlic cloves, roughly chopped
2.5cm/1in piece fresh galangal,
  peeled and sliced
10ml/2 tsp chilli sambal or 2 fresh
  red chillies, seeded and sliced
1.5ml/¼ tsp salt
30ml/2 tbsp vegetable oil
45ml/3 tbsp tomato purée (paste)
600ml/1 pint/2½ cups vegetable stock

1 Make the sambal goreng. Grind the shrimp paste with the onions and garlic using a mortar and pestle. Alternatively put in a food processor and process to a paste. Add the galangal, chilli sambal or sliced chillies and salt. Process or pound to a fine paste.

COOK'S TIP
Store the remaining sauce in the refrigerator for up to 3 days or freeze it for up to 3 months.

2 Heat the oil in a wok or frying pan and fry the paste for 1–2 minutes, without browning, until the mixture gives off a rich aroma. Stir in the tomato purée and the stock or water and cook for 10 minutes. Ladle half the sauce into a bowl and leave to cool. This leftover sauce can be used in another recipe (see Cook's Tip).

3 Add the prawns and green pepper to the remaining sauce. Cook over medium heat for 3–4 minutes, then stir in the tamarind juice, sugar and coconut milk or cream. Spoon into warmed serving bowls and garnish with strips of lime rind and sliced red onion. Serve immediately with boiled rice.

VARIATIONS
• To make tomato sambal goreng, add 450g/1lb peeled coarsely chopped tomatoes to the sauce mixture, before stirring in the stock or water.
• To make egg sambal goreng, add 3 or 4 chopped hard-boiled eggs, and 2 peeled chopped tomatoes to the sauce.

BAMIE GORENG

*THIS FRIED NOODLE DISH IS WONDERFULLY ACCOMMODATING. YOU CAN ADD OTHER VEGETABLES,
SUCH AS MUSHROOMS, TINY PIECES OF CHAYOTE, BROCCOLI, LEEKS OR BEANSPROUTS. USE WHATEVER
IS TO HAND, BEARING IN MIND THE NEED FOR A BALANCE OF COLOURS, FLAVOURS AND TEXTURES.*

SERVES 6–8

INGREDIENTS

450g/1lb dried egg noodles
2 eggs
25g/1oz/2 tbsp butter
90ml/6 tbsp vegetable oil
1 skinless chicken breast fillets, sliced
115g/4oz pork fillet, sliced
115g/4oz calf's liver, finely
  sliced (optional)
2 garlic cloves, crushed
115g/4oz cooked, peeled
  prawns (shrimp)
115g/4oz pak choi (bok choy)
2 celery sticks, finely sliced
4 spring onions (scallions), shredded
about 60ml/4 tbsp chicken stock
dark soy sauce and light soy sauce
salt and ground black pepper
deep-fried onions and shredded
  spring onions, to garnish (optional)

1 Bring a pan of lightly salted water to
the boil, add the noodles and cook them
for 3–4 minutes. Drain, rinse under cold
water and drain again. Set aside.

2 Put the eggs in a bowl, beat and add
salt and pepper to taste. Heat the butter
with 5ml/1 tsp oil in a small pan, add
the eggs and stir over low heat until
scrambled but still quite moist. Set aside.

3 Heat the remaining oil in a wok and
fry the chicken, pork and liver (if using)
with the garlic for 2–3 minutes, until
the meat has changed colour. Add the
prawns, pak choi, sliced celery and
shredded spring onions and toss to mix.

4 Add the noodles and toss over the
heat until the prawns and noodles are
heated through and the greens are
lightly cooked. Add enough stock just to
moisten and season with dark and light
soy sauce to taste. Finally, add the
scrambled eggs and toss to mix. Spoon
on to a warmed serving platter or into
individual dishes and serve immediately,
garnished with onions.

COOK'S TIP

Pak choi (bok choy) is similar to Swiss
chard and is available from Asian stores
and large supermarkets.

BANANA FRITTERS

KNOWN AS PISANG GORENG, *THESE DELICIOUS DEEP-FRIED BANANAS SHOULD BE COOKED AT THE LAST MINUTE, SO THAT THE BATTER IS CRISP AND THE BANANA INSIDE IS SOFT AND WARM.*

SERVES 8

INGREDIENTS
115g/4oz/1 cup self-raising
  (self-rising) flour
40g/1¹/₂ oz/¹/₄ cup rice flour
2.5ml/¹/₂ tsp salt
200ml/7fl oz/scant 1 cup water
finely grated lime rind (optional)
8 baby bananas
vegetable oil, for deep-frying
strips of lime rind, to garnish
caster (superfine) sugar and lime
  wedges, to serve

COOK'S TIP
Tiny bananas are available from some Asian stores and many larger supermarkets, alternatively use small bananas and cut in half lengthways and then in half again.

1 Sift together the self-raising flour, rice flour and salt into a bowl. Add just enough water to make a smooth, coating batter. Mix well, then add the lime rind, if using.

VARIATION
Instead of lime, add finely grated orange rind to the batter.

2 Heat the oil in a deep-fryer or wok to 190°C/375°F. Meanwhile, peel the bananas. Dip them into the batter two or three times until well coated, then deep-fry until crisp and golden. Drain on kitchen paper. Serve hot, dredged with the caster sugar and garnished with strips of lime. Offer the lime wedges for squeezing over the bananas.

BLACK GLUTINOUS RICE PUDDING

THIS VERY UNUSUAL RICE PUDDING, KNOWN AS BUBOR PULOT HITAM, *IS FLAVOURED WITH BRUISED FRESH ROOT GINGER AND IS QUITE DELICIOUS SERVED WITH COCONUT MILK OR CREAM. WHEN COOKED, BLACK RICE STILL RETAINS ITS HUSK AND HAS A LOVELY NUTTY TEXTURE.*

SERVES 6

INGREDIENTS
115g/4oz/²/₃ cup black glutinous rice
475ml/16fl oz/2 cups water
1cm/¹/₂in piece fresh root ginger,
  peeled and bruised
50g/2oz/¹/₃ cup soft dark brown sugar
50g/2oz/¹/₄ cup caster (superfine) sugar
300ml/¹/₂ pint/1¹/₄ cups coconut
  milk or coconut cream, to serve

COOK'S TIP
Canned coconut milk is available, but it is easy to make at home. Blend 225g/8oz/2²/₃ cups desiccated (dry unsweetened shredded) coconut with 450ml/³/₄ pint/1³/₄ cups boiling water in a food processor, then cool slightly. Transfer into a strainer lined with muslin (cheesecloth) and twist the muslin to extract the liquid.

1 Put the black glutinous rice in a strainer and rinse it well under plenty of cold running water. Drain the rice and put it in a large pan, along with the water. Bring the water to the boil and stir it as it heats, in order to prevent the rice from settling on the base of the pan. Cover the pan and cook over very low heat for about 30 minutes.

2 Add the ginger and both types of sugar to the pan. Cook for 15 minutes more, adding a little more water if necessary, until the rice is cooked and porridge-like.

3 Remove the ginger and pour into individual bowls. Serve warm, topped with coconut milk or coconut cream.

VIETNAM AND THE PHILIPPINES

Vietnam borders China, Laos and Cambodia, so it is not surprising that its cuisine has much in common with its neighbours. In the north nearest China, stir-fries and mild curries are popular; further south there is a French influence. Pâtés, herb salads, rare beef and casseroles feature alongside dishes served with the pungent fish sauce, nuoc mam. In the Philippines, many dishes owe much to their Spanish origins.

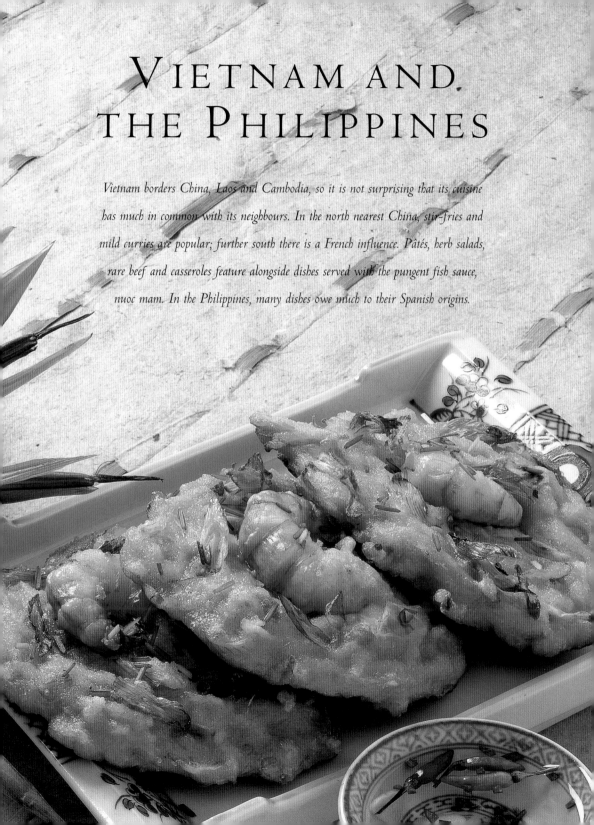

VIETNAMESE RICE PAPER ROLLS

RICE PAPER WRAPPERS COME IN SMALL AND LARGE ROUNDS AND CAN BE BOUGHT FROM ASIAN SUPERMARKETS. THEY SOFTEN WHEN BRUSHED WITH WARM WATER, BUT THEY ARE VERY BRITTLE SO MUST BE HANDLED WITH CARE. CASUALTIES CAN BE USED FOR PATCHING OTHER PAPERS.

SERVES 8

INGREDIENTS
2 litres/3½ pints/8 cups water
1 small onion, sliced
a few fresh coriander (cilantro) stems
30ml/2 tbsp fish sauce
225g/8oz piece belly pork, boned
  and rind removed
50g/2oz fine rice vermicelli
225g/8oz/4 cups beansprouts, rinsed
  and drained
8 crisp lettuce leaves, halved
fresh mint and coriander
  (cilantro) leaves
175g/6oz cooked, peeled prawns
  (shrimp), thawed if frozen
16 large rice papers
ground black pepper

For the black bean sauce
15–30ml/1–2 tbsp groundnut
  (peanut) oil
2 garlic cloves, crushed
1 fresh red chilli, seeded and sliced
60–75ml/4–5 tbsp canned black
  salted beans
30ml/2 tbsp fish sauce
5ml/1 tsp rice vinegar
10–15ml/2–3 tsp soft light brown sugar
15ml/1 tbsp crunchy peanut butter
15ml/1 tbsp sesame seeds, dry-fried
5ml/1 tsp sesame oil
90ml/6 tbsp fish, pork or chicken stock

1 Mix the water, onion slices, coriander stems and fish sauce in a large pan. Bring to the boil. Add the pork and boil for 20–30 minutes, turning it from time to time until tender. Lift the pork from the pan, leave to cool, then slice it into thin strips. (Strain the stock and reserve it for making soup.)

2 Make the sauce. Heat the groundnut oil in a frying pan and fry the garlic and chilli for 1 minute. Stir in all the remaining ingredients, mix well, then transfer to a food processor and process briefly. Pour into a serving bowl and leave to cool.

3 Soak the rice vermicelli in warm water until softened. Drain well, then chop into neat lengths. Bring a pan of water to the boil and add the vermicelli. As soon as the water boils again, after about 1 minute, drain the noodles, rinse them under cold water, then drain them again. Put them in a serving bowl. Put the beansprouts in a separate dish, and arrange the lettuce and herb leaves on a platter. Put the prawns in a bowl.

4 When almost ready to serve place the rice papers two at a time on a dish towel and brush both sides with warm water to soften them.

5 Transfer two rice papers very carefully to each of eight individual serving plates. Each guest places a piece of lettuce on a rice paper wrapper at the end closest to them, topping it with some of the noodles and beansprouts, a few mint or coriander leaves and some strips of pork.

6 Roll up one turn and then place a few prawns on the open part of the wrapper. Continue rolling to make a neat parcel. The roll can be cut in half, if preferred, then it is dipped in the black bean sauce before being eaten. The second wrapper is filled and eaten in the same way.

CHA GIO AND NUOC CHAM

CHINESE SPRING ROLL WRAPPERS ARE USED HERE INSTEAD OF THE RICE PAPERS TRADITIONALLY USED IN VIETNAM. CHA GIO IS AN IMMENSELY POPULAR SNACK – THE VEGETABLE CONTENT OF THE FILLING CAN BE VARIED AS LONG AS THE FLAVOURS ARE COMPLEMENTARY.

MAKES 15

INGREDIENTS
 25g/1oz cellophane noodles soaked
  for 10 minutes in hot water to cover
 6–8 dried cloud ear (wood ear)
  mushrooms, soaked for 30 minutes
  in warm water to cover
 225g/8oz minced (ground) pork
 225g/8oz fresh or canned crab meat
 4 spring onions (scallions), chopped
 5ml/1 tsp fish sauce
 flour and water paste, to seal
 250g/9oz packet spring roll wrappers
 vegetable oil, for deep-frying
 salt and ground black pepper

For the *nuoc cham* sauce
 2 fresh red chillies, seeded and
  pounded to a paste
 2 garlic cloves, crushed
 15ml/1 tbsp sugar
 45ml/3 tbsp fish sauce
 juice of 1 lime or ¹/2 lemon

1 Make the *nuoc cham* sauce by mixing the chillies, garlic, sugar and fish sauce in a bowl and stirring in lime or lemon juice to taste. Drain the noodles and cut into 2.5cm/1in lengths. Drain the cloud ears, trim away any rough stems and slice the cloud ears finely.

COOK'S TIP
Serve the rolls Vietnamese-style by wrapping each roll in a lettuce leaf together with a few sprigs of fresh mint and coriander and a stick of cucumber.

2 Mix the noodles and the wood ears with the pork and set aside. Remove any cartilage from the crab meat and add to the pork mixture with the spring onions and fish sauce. Season to taste, mixing well.

3 Place a spring roll wrapper in front of you, diamond-fashion. Spoon some mixture just below the centre, fold over the nearest point and roll once.

4 Fold in the sides to enclose, then brush the edges with flour paste and roll up to seal. Repeat with the remaining wrappers and filling.

5 Heat the oil in a wok or deep-fryer to 190°C/375°F. Deep-fry the rolls in batches for 8–10 minutes or until they are cooked through. Drain them well on kitchen paper and serve hot. To eat, dip the rolls in the *nuoc cham* sauce.

CHICKEN, VEGETABLE AND CHILLI SALAD

GOI TOM, A TYPICAL VIETNAMESE SALAD, IS FULL OF SURPRISING TEXTURES AND FLAVOURS.
SERVE AS A LIGHT LUNCH DISH OR FOR SUPPER WITH CRUSTY FRENCH BREAD.

SERVES 4

INGREDIENTS
   225g/8oz Chinese leaves
     (Chinese cabbage)
   2 carrots, cut in matchsticks
   1/2 cucumber, cut in matchsticks
   2 fresh red chillies, seeded and cut
     into thin strips
   1 small onion, sliced into fine rings
   4 pickled gherkins, sliced, plus
     45ml/3 tbsp of the liquid
   50g/2oz/1/2 cup peanuts,
     lightly ground
   225g/8oz cooked chicken,
     finely sliced
   1 garlic clove, crushed
   5ml/1 tsp sugar
   30ml/2 tbs cider or white wine vinegar
   salt

1 Finely slice the Chinese leaves and set aside with the carrot matchsticks. Spread out the cucumber matchsticks on a board and sprinkle with salt. Set aside for 15 minutes.

COOK'S TIP
Add a little more cider or white wine vinegar to the dressing if a sharper taste is preferred.

2 Mix together the chillies and onion rings and then add the sliced gherkins and peanuts. Transfer the cucumber into a colander, rinse well and pat dry.

3 Put all the vegetables into a salad bowl and add the chilli mixture and chicken. Mix the gherkin liquid with the garlic, sugar and vinegar. Pour over the salad, toss lightly and serve.

ASPARAGUS AND CRAB SOUP

ASPARAGUS OWES ITS POPULARITY TO THE FRENCH INFLUENCE ON VIETNAMESE COOKING. IT IS OFTEN
COMBINED WITH CRAB AND MADE INTO A DELICIOUS SOUP, CAHN CUA.

SERVES 4–6

INGREDIENTS
   350g/12oz asparagus spears,
     trimmed and halved
   900ml/1 1/2 pints/3 3/4 cups chicken
     stock, preferably home-made
   30–45ml/2–3 tbsp sunflower oil
   6 shallots, chopped
   115g/4oz crab meat, fresh or
     canned, chopped
   15ml/1 tbsp cornflour (cornstarch),
     mixed to a paste with water
   30ml/2 tbsp fish sauce
   1 egg, lightly beaten
   chopped chives, plus extra chives
     to garnish
   salt and ground black pepper

1 Cook the asparagus spears in the chicken stock for 5–6 minutes until tender. Drain, reserving the stock.

2 Heat the oil in a large wok or frying pan and stir-fry the chopped shallots for 2 minutes, without allowing them to brown. Add the asparagus spears, chopped crab meat and chicken stock.

3 Bring the mixture to the boil and cook for 3 minutes, then remove the wok or pan from the heat and spoon some of the liquid into the cornflour mixture. Return this to the wok or pan and stir until the soup begins to thicken slightly.

4 Stir in the fish sauce, with salt and pepper to taste, then pour the beaten egg into the soup, stirring briskly so that the egg forms threads. Finally, stir the chopped chives into the soup and serve it immediately, garnished with chives.

COOK'S TIP
If fresh asparagus isn't available, use 350g/12oz canned asparagus. Drain and halve the spears.

FILIPINO PRAWN FRITTERS

*U*KOY *ARE A FAVOURITE SNACK OR APPETIZER. UNUSUALLY, THEY ARE FIRST SHALLOW-FRIED, THEN*
DEEP-FRIED. THEY ARE BEST EATEN FRESH FROM THE PAN, FIRST DIPPED IN THE PIQUANT SAUCE.

4 Peel and grate the sweet potato using the large holes on a grater, and add it to the batter, then stir in the crushed garlic and the drained beansprouts.

5 Pour the oil for shallow-frying into a large frying pan. It should be about 5mm/¼in deep. Pour more oil into a wok for deep-frying. Heat the oil in the frying pan. Taking a generous spoonful of the batter, drop it carefully into the frying pan so that it forms a fritter, about the size of a large drop scone.

6 Make more fritters in the same way. As soon as the fritters have set, top each one with a single prawn and a few chopped spring onions. Continue to cook over medium heat for 1 minute, then remove with a fish slice or metal spatula.

7 Heat the oil in the wok to 190°C/375°F and deep-fry the prawn fritters in batches until they are crisp and golden brown. Drain the fritters on absorbent kitchen paper and then arrange on a serving plate or platter. Offer a bowl of the sauce for dipping.

SERVES 2–4

INGREDIENTS
  16 raw prawns (shrimp) in the shell
  225g/8oz/2 cups plain
    (all-purpose) flour
  5ml/1 tsp baking powder
  2.5ml/½ tsp salt
  1 egg, beaten
  1 small sweet potato
  1 garlic clove, crushed
  115g/4oz/2 cups beansprouts, soaked
    in cold water and well drained
  vegetable oil, for shallow and
    deep-frying
  4 spring onions (scallions), chopped

For the dipping sauce
  1 garlic clove, sliced
  45ml/3 tbsp rice or wine vinegar
  15–30ml/1–2 tbsp water
  6–8 small red chillies
  salt, to taste

1 Mix together all the ingredients for the dipping sauce and divide between two small bowls.

2 Put the whole prawns in a pan with water to cover. Bring to the boil, then simmer for 4–5 minutes or until the prawns are pink and tender. Lift the prawns from the pan with a slotted spoon. Discard the heads and the body shell, but leave the tails on. Strain and reserve the cooking liquid. Allow to cool.

3 Sift the flour, baking powder and salt into a bowl. Add the beaten egg and about 300ml/½ pint/1¼ cups of the prawn stock to make a batter that has the consistency of double (heavy) cream.

VARIATION
Use cooked tiger prawns (shrimp) if you prefer. In this case, make the batter using fish stock or chicken stock.

ESCABECHE

THIS PICKLED FISH DISH IS EATEN WHEREVER THERE ARE — OR HAVE BEEN — SPANISH SETTLERS.
HERE IT HAS BEEN MODIFIED IN ORDER TO REFLECT THE CHINESE INFLUENCE ON FILIPINO CUISINE.

SERVES 6

INGREDIENTS

675–900g/1¹/₂–2lb white fish fillets,
  such as sole, plaice or flounder
45–60ml/3–4 tbsp seasoned flour
vegetable oil, for shallow-frying

For the sauce
2.5cm/1in piece fresh root ginger,
  peeled and thinly sliced
2–3 garlic cloves, crushed
1 onion, cut into thin rings
30ml/2 tbsp vegetable oil
¹/₂ large green (bell) pepper, seeded
  and cut in small neat squares
¹/₂ large red pepper, seeded and cut
  in small neat squares
1 carrot, cut into matchsticks
25ml/1¹/₂ tbsp cornflour (cornstarch)
450ml/³/₄ pint/scant 2 cups water
45–60ml/3–4 tbsp herb or
  cider vinegar
15ml/1 tbsp soft light brown sugar
5–10ml/1–2 tsp fish sauce
salt and ground black pepper
1 small chilli, seeded and sliced
  and spring onions (scallions), finely
  shredded, to garnish (optional)
boiled rice, to serve

1 Wipe the fish fillets and leave them whole, or cut into serving portions, if you like. Pat dry on kitchen paper then dust lightly with seasoned flour.

2 Heat oil for shallow-frying in a frying pan and fry the fish in batches until golden and almost cooked. Transfer to an ovenproof dish and keep warm.

3 Make the sauce in a wok or large frying pan. Fry the ginger, garlic and onion in the oil for 5 minutes or until the onion is softened but not browned.

4 Add the pepper squares and carrot strips and stir-fry for 1 minute.

5 Put the cornflour in a small bowl and add a little of the water to make a paste. Stir in the remaining water, the vinegar and the sugar. Pour the cornflour mixture over the vegetables in the wok and stir until the sauce boils and thickens a little. Season with fish sauce and salt and pepper if needed.

6 Add the fish to the sauce and reheat briefly without stirring. Transfer to a warmed serving platter and garnish with chilli and spring onions, if you like. Serve with boiled rice.

COOK'S TIP
Red snapper or small sea bass could be used for this recipe, in which case ask your fishmonger to cut them into fillets.

ADOBO OF CHICKEN AND PORK

FOUR INGREDIENTS ARE ESSENTIAL IN AN ADOBO, ONE OF THE BEST-LOVED RECIPES IN THE FILIPINO REPERTOIRE. THEY ARE VINEGAR, GARLIC, PEPPERCORNS AND BAY LEAVES.

SERVES 4

INGREDIENTS

1 chicken, about 1.4kg/3lb, or
  4 chicken quarters
350g/12oz pork leg steaks, with fat
10ml/2 tsp sugar
60ml/4 tbsp sunflower oil
75ml/5 tbsp wine or cider vinegar
4 plump garlic cloves, crushed
2.5ml/½ tsp black peppercorns,
  crushed lightly
15ml/1 tbsp light soy sauce
4 bay leaves
2.5ml/½ tsp annatto seeds, soaked
  in 30ml /2 tbsp boiling water,
  or 2.5ml/½ tsp ground turmeric
salt

For the plantain chips
  1–2 large plantains and/or
  1 sweet potato
  vegetable oil, for deep-frying

1 Wipe the chicken and cut into eight even pieces, or halve the chicken quarters, if using. Cut the pork into neat pieces. Spread out all the meat on a board, sprinkle lightly with sugar and set aside.

2 Heat the oil in a wok or large frying pan and fry the chicken and pork pieces, in batches if necessary, until they are golden on both sides.

3 Add the vinegar, garlic, peppercorns, soy sauce and bay leaves and stir well.

4 Strain the annatto seed liquid and stir it into the pan or stir in the turmeric. Add salt to taste. Bring to the boil, cover, lower the heat and simmer for 30–35 minutes. Remove the lid and simmer for 10 minutes more.

5 Meanwhile, prepare the plantain chips. Heat the oil in a deep-fryer to 195°C/390°F. Peel the plantains or sweet potato (or both), if you like, and slice them into rounds or chips. Deep-fry them, in batches if necessary, until cooked but not brown. Drain on kitchen paper. When ready to serve, reheat the oil and fry the plantains or sweet potato until crisp – it will only take a few seconds. Drain. Spoon the adobo into a serving dish and serve with the chips.

COOK'S TIP
Sprinkling the chicken lightly with sugar turns the skin beautifully brown when fried, but do not have the oil too hot to begin with or they will over-brown.

SINIGANG

MANY FILIPINOS WOULD CONSIDER THIS SOURED SOUP-LIKE STEW TO BE THEIR NATIONAL DISH.
IT IS ALWAYS SERVED WITH NOODLES OR RICE, AND FISH — PRAWNS OR THIN SLIVERS OF FISH
FILLET — IS OFTEN ADDED FOR GOOD MEASURE.

3 Pour the prepared fish stock into a large pan and add the diced mooli. Cook the mooli for 5 minutes, then add the beans and continue to cook for 3–5 minutes more.

SERVES 4–6

INGREDIENTS
15ml/1 tbsp tamarind pulp
150ml/1/4 pint/2/3 cup warm water
2 tomatoes
115g/4oz spinach or Chinese
  kangkong leaves
115g/4oz peeled cooked large prawns
  (shrimp), thawed if frozen
1.2 litres/2 pints/5 cups prepared
  fish stock (see Cook's Tip)
1/2 mooli (daikon), peeled and diced
115g/4oz green beans, cut into
  1cm/1/2in lengths
225g/8oz piece of cod or haddock
  fillet, skinned and cut into strips
fish sauce, to taste
squeeze of lemon juice, to taste
salt and ground black pepper
boiled rice or noodles, to serve

1 Put the tamarind pulp in a bowl and pour over the warm water. Set aside while you peel and chop the tomatoes, discarding the seeds. Strip the spinach or kangkong leaves from the stems and tear into small pieces.

2 Remove the heads and shells from the prawns, leaving the tails intact.

4 Add the fish strips, tomato and spinach. Strain in the tamarind juice and cook for 2 minutes. Stir in the prawns and cook for 1–2 minutes to heat. Season with salt and pepper and add a little fish sauce and lemon juice to taste. Transfer to individual serving bowls and serve immediately, with rice or noodles.

COOK'S TIP
A good fish stock is essential for Sinigang. Ask your fishmonger for about 675g/11/2lb fish bones. Wash them, then place in a large pan with 2 litres/ 31/2 pints/8 cups water. Add half a peeled onion, a piece of bruised peeled ginger, and a little salt and pepper. Bring to the boil, skim, then simmer for 20 minutes. Cool slightly, then strain. Freeze unused fish stock.

PUCHERO

A Filipino pot-au-feu with Spanish connections. Sometimes it is served as two courses, first soup, then meat and vegetables with rice, but it can happily be served as is, on rice in a wide soup bowl. Either way it is very satisfying and a siesta afterwards is recommended.

SERVES 6–8

INGREDIENTS

225g/8oz/generous 1 cup chickpeas, soaked overnight in water to cover
1.4kg/3lb chicken, cut into 8 pieces
350g/12oz belly of pork, rinded, or pork fillet (tenderloin), cubed
2 chorizo sausages, thickly sliced
2 onions, chopped
2.5 litres/4 pints/10 cups water
60ml/4 tbsp vegetable oil
2 garlic cloves, crushed
3 large tomatoes, peeled, seeded and chopped
15ml/1 tbsp tomato purée (paste)
1–2 sweet potatoes, cut into 1cm/$\frac{1}{2}$in cubes
2 plantains, sliced (optional)
salt and ground black pepper
chives or chopped spring onions (scallions), to garnish
$\frac{1}{2}$ head Chinese leaves (Chinese cabbage), shredded, and boiled rice, to serve

For the aubergine sauce
1 large aubergine (eggplant)
3 garlic cloves, crushed
60–90ml/4–6 tbsp wine or cider vinegar

1 Drain the chickpeas and put them in a large pan. Cover with water, bring to the boil and boil rapidly for 10 minutes. Reduce the heat and simmer for 30 minutes until the chickpeas are half tender. Drain.

2 Put the chicken pieces, pork, sausage and half of the onions in a large pan. Add the chickpeas and pour in the water. Bring to the boil and lower the heat, cover and simmer for 1 hour or until the meat is just tender when tested with a skewer.

3 Meanwhile, make the aubergine sauce. Preheat the oven to 200°C/400°F/Gas 6. Prick the aubergine in several places, then place it on a baking sheet and bake for 30 minutes or until very soft.

4 Cool slightly, then peel away the aubergine skin and scrape the flesh into a bowl. Mash the flesh with the crushed garlic, season to taste and add enough vinegar to sharpen the sauce, which should be quite piquant. Set aside.

5 Heat the oil in a frying pan and fry the remaining onion and garlic for 5 minutes, until soft but not brown. Stir in the tomatoes and tomato purée and cook for 2 minutes, then add this mixture to a large pan with the diced sweet potato. Add the plantains, if using. Cook over low heat for about 20 minutes until the sweet potato is thoroughly cooked. Add the Chinese leaves for the last minute or two.

6 Spoon the thick meat soup into a soup tureen, and put the vegetables in a separate serving bowl. Garnish both with whole or chopped chives or spring onions and serve with boiled rice and the aubergine sauce.

ENSAIMADAS

THESE SWEET BREAD ROLLS ARE A POPULAR SNACK IN THE PHILIPPINES AND COME WITH VARIOUS FILLINGS, SEVERAL OF THEM SAVOURY. THIS VERSION INCLUDES CHEESE.

MAKES 10–12

INGREDIENTS
- 30ml/2 tbsp caster (superfine) sugar, plus extra for sprinkling
- 150ml/¼ pint/⅔ cup warm water
- 15ml/1 tbsp active dried yeast
- 450g/1lb/4 cups strong white bread flour
- 5ml/1 tsp salt
- 115g/4oz/½ cup butter, softened, plus 30ml/2 tbsp melted butter for the filling
- 4 egg yolks
- 90–120ml/6–8 tbsp warm milk
- 115g/4oz/1 cup grated Cheddar cheese (or similar hard cheese)

1 Dissolve 5ml/1 tsp of the sugar in the warm water, then sprinkle in the dried yeast. Stir, then set aside for 10 minutes or until frothy. Sift the flour and salt into a large bowl.

2 Cream the softened butter with the remaining sugar in a large bowl. When it is fluffy, beat in the egg yolks and a little of the sifted flour. Gradually stir in the remaining flour with the yeast mixture and enough milk to form a soft but not sticky dough. Transfer to an oiled plastic bag. Close the bag loosely, leaving plenty of room for the dough to rise. Leave in a warm place for about 1 hour, until the dough doubles in bulk.

3 On a floured surface, knock back (punch down) the dough, then roll it out into a large rectangle. Brush the surface with half the melted butter, sprinkle with the cheese, then roll up from a long side like a Swiss roll (jelly roll).

4 Knead the dough thoroughly to distribute the cheese, then divide the dough into 10–12 pieces.

5 Roll each piece of dough into a thin rope, about 38cm/15in long. On greased baking sheets, coil each rope into a loose spiral, spacing them well apart. Tuck the loose ends under to seal. Leave to rise, in a warm place, for about 45 minutes or until doubled in size. Meanwhile, preheat the oven to 220°C/425°F/Gas 7.

6 Bake the ensaimadas in the oven for 15–20 minutes, until golden and cooked through. Remove from the oven, then immediately brush with the remaining melted butter and sprinkle with caster sugar. Serve warm.

CHURROS

THESE IRRESISTIBLE FRITTERS, SERVED AT EVERY OPPORTUNITY WITH HOT CHOCOLATE OR COFFEE, CAME TO THE PHILIPPINES WITH THE SPANISH WHO WERE KEEN TO KEEP MEMORIES OF HOME ALIVE.

MAKES ABOUT 24

INGREDIENTS
450ml/15fl oz/scant 2 cups water
15ml/1 tbsp olive oil
15ml/1 tbsp sugar, plus extra
 for sprinkling
2.5ml/1/2 tsp salt
150g/5oz/11/4 cups plain
 (all-purpose) flour
1 large egg
sunflower oil, for deep-frying
caster (superfine) sugar,
 for sprinkling

COOK'S TIP
If you don't have a piping (pastry) bag, you could fry teaspoons of mixture in the same way. Don't try to fry too many churros at a time as they swell a little during cooking.

1 Mix the water, oil, sugar and salt in a large pan and bring to the boil. Remove from the heat, and then sift in the flour. Beat well with a wooden spoon until smooth.

2 Beat in the egg to make a smooth, glossy mixture with a piping consistency. Spoon into a piping (pastry) bag fitted with a large star nozzle.

3 Heat the oil in a wok or deep-fryer to 190°C/375°F. Pipe loops of the mixture, two at a time, into the hot oil. Cook the loops for 3–4 minutes until they are golden.

4 Lift out the churros with a wire skimmer or slotted spoon and drain them on kitchen paper. Dredge them with caster sugar and serve warm.

LECHE FLAN

SERVE THIS DELICIOUS DESSERT HOT OR COLD WITH WHIPPED CREAM OR CRÈME FRAÎCHE. THE USE OF EVAPORATED MILK REFLECTS THE 50 YEARS OF AMERICAN PRESENCE IN THE PHILIPPINES.

SERVES 8

INGREDIENTS
5 large (US extra large) eggs
30ml/2 tbsp caster (superfine) sugar
few drops vanilla extract
410g/141/2oz can evaporated milk
300ml/1/2 pint/11/4 cups milk
5ml/1 tsp finely grated lime rind
strips of lime rind, to decorate

For the caramel
225g/8oz/1 cup sugar
120ml/4fl oz/1/2 cup water

1 Make the caramel. Put the sugar and water in a heavy pan. Stir to dissolve the sugar, then boil without stirring until golden. Quickly pour into eight ramekins, rotating them to coat the sides. Set aside to set.

2 Preheat the oven to 150°C/300°F/Gas 2. Beat the eggs, sugar and vanilla extract in a bowl. Mix the evaporated milk and fresh milk in a pan. Heat to just below boiling point, then pour on to the egg mixture, stirring all the time. Strain the custard mixture into a jug (pitcher), add the grated lime rind and cool. Pour into the ramekins.

3 Place the ramekins in a roasting pan and pour in enough warm water to come halfway up the sides of the dishes.

4 Transfer the roasting pan to the oven and cook the custards for 35–45 minutes or until they just shimmer when the ramekins are gently shaken.

5 Serve the custards in their ramekin dishes or by inverting on to serving plates, in which case break the caramel and use as decoration. The custards can be served warm or cold, decorated with strips of lime rind.

COOK'S TIP
Make extra caramel, if you like, for a garnish. Pour on to lightly oiled foil and leave to set, then crush with a rolling pin.

JAPAN AND KOREA

Japanese food is unique. The 200-year ban on foreigners from 1640 meant that food
in Japan remained true to its origins and exquisitely refined. Artistry is evident in
even the simplest dish. Eating out is the norm, and restaurants specialize in dishes such
as Sushi, Sukiyaki, Sashimi or Tempura. Korean food features seven basic flavours —
garlic, ginger, pepper, soy sauce, spring onions, sesame oil and toasted sesame seeds.

SASHIMI

THIS JAPANESE SPECIALITY — SLICED RAW FISH — EMPLOYS THE CUTTING TECHNIQUE KNOWN AS HIRA ZUKURI. THE PERFECTLY CUT FISH CAN BE ARRANGED IN MANY ATTRACTIVE WAYS AND IS THEN SERVED WITH WASABI — JAPANESE HORSERADISH — AND SOY SAUCE.

SERVES 4

INGREDIENTS
    2 fresh salmon fillets, skinned and
    any stray bones removed, total
    weight about 400g/14oz
    Japanese soy sauce and wasabi
    paste, to serve

For the garnish
    50g/2oz mooli (daikon), peeled
    shiso leaves

1 Put the salmon fillets in a freezer for 10 minutes to make them easier to cut, then lay them skin side up with the thick end to your right and away from you. Use a long sharp knife and tilt it to the left. Slice carefully towards you, starting the cut from the point of the knife, then slide the slice away from the fillet, to the right. Always slice from the far side towards you.

2 Finely shred or grate the mooli and place in a bowl of cold water. Leave for 5 minutes, then drain well.

3 Arrange the salmon in an attractive way on a serving platter, or divide the salmon among four serving plates.

4 Give guests their own platter, together with a garnish of mooli and shiso leaves. The fish is eaten dipped in soy sauce and wasabi paste.

COOK'S TIP
Salmon and tuna are among the most popular choices for sashimi, although almost any type of fish can be used. If you are making sashimi for the first time, choose salmon or tuna and make sure you buy from a reputable fishmonger where you can be sure the fish is absolutely fresh.

YAKITORI CHICKEN

THESE ARE JAPANESE-STYLE KEBABS. THEY ARE EASY TO EAT AND IDEAL FOR BARBECUES OR PARTIES.
MAKE EXTRA YAKITORI SAUCE IF YOU WOULD LIKE TO SERVE IT WITH THE KEBABS.

SERVES 4

INGREDIENTS
   6 boneless chicken thighs
   bunch of spring onions (scallions)
   shichimi (seven-flavour spice),
      to serve (optional)

For the yakitori sauce
   150ml/¼ pint/²⁄₃ cup Japanese
      soy sauce
   90g/3½oz/scant ½ cup sugar
   25ml/1½ tbsp sake or dry
      white wine
   15ml/1 tbsp plain (all-purpose) flour

3 Cut the spring onions into 3cm/
1¼in pieces. Preheat the grill or light
the barbecue.

4 Thread the chicken and spring
onions alternately on to the drained
skewers. Grill (broil) under medium
heat or cook on the barbecue, brushing
generously several times with the sauce.
Allow 5–10 minutes, until the chicken
is cooked but still moist.

5 Serve with a little extra yakitori
sauce, offering shichimi with the kebabs
if available.

COOK'S TIP
Paprika can be used instead of shichimi,
if that is difficult to obtain.

1 Soak 12 bamboo skewers in water
for at least 30 minutes to prevent them
from scorching under the grill (broiler).
Make the sauce. Stir the soy sauce,
sugar and sake into the flour
in a small pan and bring to the boil,
stirring. Lower the heat and simmer the
mixture for 10 minutes, until the sauce
is reduced by a third. Set aside.

2 Cut each chicken thigh into bitesize
pieces and set aside.

ROLLED OMELETTE

*THIS IS A FIRMLY SET, ROLLED OMELETTE, CUT INTO NEAT PIECES AND SERVED COLD. THE TEXTURE
SHOULD BE SMOOTH AND SOFT, NOT LEATHERY, AND THE FLAVOUR IS SWEET-SAVOURY. PICKLED
GINGER, SOMETIMES CALLED GARI, MAKES AN ATTRACTIVE GARNISH.*

SERVES 4

INGREDIENTS
8 eggs
60ml/4 tbsp sugar
20ml/4 tsp Japanese soy sauce,
  plus extra, to serve
90ml/6 tbsp sake or dry white wine
vegetable oil, for cooking
wasabi and pickled ginger, to garnish

COOK'S TIP
Wasabi, which can be bought from Asian
stores, is a very hot and peppery, bright
green paste. Use it sparingly.

1 Put the eggs in a large bowl and
stir them together, using a pair of
chopsticks and a cutting action.

2 Mix the sugar with the soy sauce and
sake or wine in a small bowl. Lightly stir
this mixture into the eggs. Pour half the
mixture into another bowl.

3 Heat a little oil in a frying pan, then
wipe off the excess. Pour a quarter of
the mixture from one bowl into the pan,
tilting the pan to coat it thinly. When the
edge has set, but the middle is moist,
roll up the omelette towards you.

4 Moisten kitchen paper with oil and
grease the empty side of the pan. Pour
a third of the remaining egg into the
pan. Lift the rolled egg up with your
chopsticks and let the raw egg run
underneath it. When the edge has set,
roll up in the opposite direction, tilting
the pan away from you.

5 Slide the roll towards you, grease
the pan and pour in half the remaining
mixture, letting the egg run under.
When set, insert chopsticks in the side
of the rolled omelette, then flip over
towards the opposite side. Cook the
remainder in the same way. Slide the
roll so that its join is underneath. Cook
for 10 seconds.

6 Slide the roll out on to a bamboo mat
and roll up tightly, then press neatly
into a rectangular shape. Leave to cool.
Cook the second batch in the same way.
Slice the cold omelettes into 2.5cm/1in
pieces, arrange on a platter and garnish
with a little wasabi and with a pickled
ginger flower. Serve with soy sauce.

FIVE-FLAVOUR NOODLES

THE JAPANESE NAME FOR THIS DISH IS GOMOKU YAKISOBA, *MEANING FIVE DIFFERENT INGREDIENTS; HOWEVER, YOU CAN ADD AS MANY DIFFERENT INGREDIENTS AS YOU WISH TO MAKE AN EXCITING AND TASTY NOODLE STIR-FRY.*

SERVES 4

INGREDIENTS

    300g/11oz dried Chinese thin egg
      noodles or 500g/1¼lb fresh
      yaki-soba noodles
    200g/7oz lean boneless pork,
      thinly sliced
    22.5ml/4½ tsp sunflower oil
    10g/¼oz grated fresh root ginger
    1 garlic clove, crushed
    200g/7oz green cabbage,
      roughly chopped
    115g/4oz/2 cups beansprouts
    1 green (bell) pepper, seeded and
      cut into fine strips
    1 red pepper, seeded and cut into
      fine strips
    salt and ground black pepper
    20ml/4 tsp ao-nori seaweed,
      to garnish (optional)

For the seasoning mix
    60ml/4 tbsp Worcestershire sauce
    15ml/1 tbsp Japanese soy sauce
    15ml/1 tbsp oyster sauce
    15ml/1 tbsp sugar
    2.5ml/½ tsp salt
    ground white pepper

1 Cook the noodles according to the instructions on the packet. Drain well and set aside.

2 Cut the pork into 3–4cm/1¼–1½in strips and season with salt and pepper.

3 Heat 7.5ml/1½ tsp of the oil in a large wok or frying pan. Stir-fry the pork until just cooked, then remove it from the pan.

4 Wipe the wok with kitchen paper, and heat the remaining oil in it. Add the ginger, garlic and cabbage and stir-fry for 1 minute.

5 Add the beansprouts, stir until softened, then add the peppers and stir-fry for 1 minute more.

6 Return the pork to the pan and add the noodles. Stir in all the ingredients for the seasoning mix and stir-fry for 2–3 minutes. Serve immediately, sprinkled with ao-nori seaweed (if using).

CHICKEN AND EGG WITH RICE

OYAKO-DON, *THE JAPANESE NAME FOR THIS DISH MEANS PARENT* (OYA), *CHILD* (KO) *AND BOWL* (DON); *IT IS SO CALLED BECAUSE IT USES BOTH CHICKEN MEAT AND EGG. A CLASSIC DISH, IT IS EATEN THROUGHOUT THE YEAR.*

2 Place the onion, dashi, sugar, soy sauce and mirin in a pan and bring to the boil. Add the chicken pieces and cook over medium heat for about 5 minutes, or until cooked. Skim off any scum that rises to the surface of the liquid.

3 Ladle a quarter of the chicken and stock mixture into a frying pan and heat until the liquid comes to the boil.

4 Pour a quarter of the beaten egg over the mixture in the frying pan and sprinkle over 15ml/1 tbsp of the peas.

5 Cover and cook over medium heat until the egg is just set. Slide the egg mixture on to a large plate and keep it warm while cooking the other omelettes in the same way. Transfer to serving dishes and serve with boiled rice.

SERVES 4

INGREDIENTS
300g/11oz skinless chicken
    breast fillets
1 large mild onion, thinly sliced
200ml/7fl oz/scant 1 cup freshly
    made dashi (kombu and bonito
    stock) or instant dashi
22.5ml/4½ tsp sugar
60ml/4 tbsp Japanese soy sauce
30ml/2 tbsp mirin
4 eggs, beaten
60ml/4 tbsp frozen peas, thawed
boiled rice, to serve

1 Slice the chicken fillets diagonally with a sharp knife, then cut the slices into 3cm/1¼in lengths.

COOK'S TIP
Ideally use either Japanese rice or Thai fragrant rice for this meal and allow 50–75g/2–3oz raw rice per person.

RICE TRIANGLES

PICNICS ARE VERY POPULAR IN JAPAN AND RICE SHAPES — ONIGIRI — ARE IDEAL PICNIC FARE.
YOU CAN PUT ANYTHING YOU LIKE IN THE RICE, SO YOU COULD INVENT YOUR OWN ONIGIRI.

SERVES 4

INGREDIENTS
  1 salmon steak
  15ml/1 tbsp salt
  450g/1lb/4 cups freshly cooked
    sushi rice
  4 umeboshi (plum pickles)
  ½ sheet yaki-nori seaweed,
    cut into four equal strips
  white and black sesame seeds,
    for sprinkling

1 Grill the salmon steak for about
4–5 minutes on each side, until the
flesh flakes easily when it is tested with
the tip of a sharp knife. Set aside to
cool while you make other *onigiri*. When
the salmon is cold, flake it, discarding
any skin and bones.

2 Put the salt in a bowl. Spoon a
quarter of the warm cooked rice into
a small rice bowl. Make a hole in the
middle of the rice and put in one
umeboshi. Smooth the rice over to cover.

3 Wet the palms of both hands with
cold water, then rub the salt evenly on
to your palms.

4 Empty the rice and umeboshi from
the bowl on to one hand. Use both
hands to shape the rice into a triangular
shape, using firm but not heavy
pressure. Make three more rice
triangles in the same way.

5 Mix the flaked salmon into the
remaining rice, then shape it into
triangles as before.

6 Wrap a strip of yaki-nori around each
of the umeboshi triangles. Sprinkle
sesame seeds on the salmon triangles.

COOK'S TIP
Always use warm rice for the triangles.
Allow them to cool completely and wrap
each in foil or clear film (plastic wrap).

MISO SOUP

THIS SOUP IS ONE OF THE MOST COMMONLY EATEN DISHES IN JAPAN, AND IT IS USUALLY SERVED WITH EVERY MEAL THAT INCLUDES RICE.

SERVES 4

INGREDIENTS
- ½ packet silken tofu, drained weight about 150g/5oz
- 1 litre/1¾ pints/4 cups freshly made dashi (kombu and bonito stock) or instant dashi
- 10g/¼oz dried wakame seaweed
- 60ml/4 tbsp white or red miso paste
- 2 spring onions (scallions), shredded, to garnish

COOK'S TIP
Reduce the heat when the stock boils, as the delicate flavour of the soup will be lost if it is boiled for too long.

1 Cut the tofu into 1cm/½in cubes. Bring the dashi to the boil, lower the heat and add the wakame seaweed. Simmer for 1–2 minutes.

2 Pour a little of the soup into a bowl and add the miso paste, stirring until it dissolves. Pour the mixture back into the pan.

3 Add the tofu and heat through for 1 minute. Pour the soup into warmed serving dishes and serve immediately, garnished with the shredded spring onions.

VARIATION
Wakame is a young, dark-coloured seaweed that can be found dried and in Japanese supermarkets. Nori seaweed could be used instead.

SWEET ADUKI BEAN SOUP WITH RICE CAKES

DON'T ASSUME FROM THE WORD SOUP THAT THIS IS A SAVOURY DISH – ZENZAI IS ACTUALLY A CLASSIC AND POPULAR JAPANESE DESSERT, SERVED WITH THE READY-TO-EAT RICE CAKES (MOCHI) THAT ARE SOLD IN JAPANESE SUPERMARKETS. JAPANESE GREEN TEA MAKES A GOOD ACCOMPANIMENT.

SERVES 4

INGREDIENTS
- 165g/5½oz/scant 1 cup dried aduki beans
- 225g/8oz/1 cup sugar
- pinch of salt
- 4 ready-to-eat rice cakes (mochi)

1 Put the aduki beans in a strainer, wash them under cold running water, then drain them and transfer them into a large pan. Add 1 litre/1¾ pints/4 cups water and bring to the boil. Drain the aduki beans and return them to the rinsed out pan.

2 Add a further 1.2 litres/2 pints/5 cups water to the pan and bring to the boil, then add a further 1.2 litres/2 pints/5 cups water and bring to the boil again. Lower the heat and simmer for 30 minutes until the beans are soft.

3 Skim the surface of the broth regularly to remove any scum. If left, it would give the soup an unpleasant bitter taste.

4 When the beans are soft enough to be mashed between your fingers, add half the sugar and simmer for a further 20 minutes.

5 Add the remaining sugar and the salt to the pan, stirring until the sugar has completely dissolved.

6 Heat the grill (broiler), then cook both sides of the rice cakes until softened, but not browned. Add the rice cakes to the soup and bring to the boil. Serve the soup immediately in deep warmed bowls.

SIMPLE ROLLED SUSHI

THESE SIMPLE ROLLS, KNOWN AS HOSOMAKI, ARE AN EXCELLENT WAY OF LEARNING THE ART OF ROLLING SUSHI. THEY ARE VERY GOOD FOR PICNICS AND CANAPÉS AND ARE ALWAYS SERVED COLD. YOU WILL NEED A BAMBOO MAT (MAKISU) FOR THE ROLLING PROCESS.

MAKES 12 ROLLS OR 72 SLICES

INGREDIENTS
400g/14oz/2 cups sushi rice, soaked
 for 20 minutes in water to cover
55ml/3½ tbsp rice vinegar
15ml/1 tbsp sugar
2.5ml/½ tsp salt
6 sheets yaki-nori seaweed
200g/7oz tuna, in one piece
200g/7oz salmon, in one piece
wasabi paste
½ cucumber, quartered lengthways
 and seeded
pickled ginger, to garnish (optional)
Japanese soy sauce, to serve

1 Drain the rice, then put in a pan with 525ml/18fl oz/2¼ cups water. Bring to the boil, then lower the heat, cover and simmer for 20 minutes, or until all the liquid has been absorbed. Meanwhile, heat the vinegar, sugar and salt, stir well and cool. Add to the hot rice, then remove the pan from the heat and allow to stand (covered) for 20 minutes.

2 Cut the yaki-nori sheets in half lengthways. Cut the tuna and salmon into four long sticks, each about the same length as the long side of the yaki-nori, and about 1cm/½in square if viewed from the side.

3 Place a sheet of yaki-nori, shiny side down, on a bamboo mat. Divide the rice into 12 portions. Spread one portion over the yaki-nori, leaving a 1cm/½in clear space at the top and bottom.

4 Spread a little wasabi paste in a horizontal line along the middle of the rice and lay one or two sticks of tuna on this.

5 Holding the mat and the edge of the yaki-nori nearest to you, roll up the yaki-nori and rice into a cylinder with the tuna in the middle. Use the mat as a guide – do not roll it into the food. Roll the rice tightly so that it sticks together and encloses the filling firmly.

6 Carefully roll the sushi off the mat. Make 11 more rolls in the same way, four for each filling ingredient, but do not use wasabi with the cucumber. Use a wet knife to cut each roll into six slices and stand them on a platter. Garnish with pickled ginger, if you like, and serve with soy sauce.

ASSORTED TEMPURA

TEMPURA IS ONE OF JAPAN'S MOST FAMOUS AND DELICIOUS DISHES. FISH, RATHER THAN MEAT, IS TRADITIONALLY USED, BUT CHOOSE ANY VEGETABLE YOU LIKE. THE ESSENCE OF GOOD TEMPURA IS THAT IT SHOULD BE COOKED AND SERVED IMMEDIATELY.

SERVES 4–6

INGREDIENTS
    1 small sweet potato, about 115g/4oz
    8 large tiger prawns (shrimp)
    1 small squid, cleaned
    vegetable oil, for deep-frying
    flour, for coating
    1 small carrot, cut into matchsticks
    4 shiitake mushrooms, stems removed
    50g/2oz green beans, trimmed
    1 red (bell) pepper, seeded and
        sliced into 2cm/³⁄₄in thick strips

For the dip
    200ml/7fl oz/scant 1 cup water
    45ml/3 tbsp mirin
    10g/¹⁄₄oz bonito flakes
    45ml/3 tbsp Japanese soy sauce

For the batter
    1 egg
    90ml/6 tbsp iced water
    75g/3oz/³⁄₄ cup plain (all-purpose) flour
    2.5ml/¹⁄₂ tsp baking powder
    2 ice cubes

2 Peel the prawns, leaving the tail shells intact, and devein. Lay a prawn on its side. Make three or four diagonal slits, about two-thirds of the way in towards the spine, leaving all the pieces attached. Repeat with the rest. Flatten with your fingers. Cut the body of the squid into 3cm/1¹⁄₄in thick strips.

3 Put the egg in a large bowl, stir without beating and set half aside. Add the water, flour and baking powder. Stir two or three times, leaving some flour unblended. Add the ice cubes.

4 Heat the oil in a deep-fryer to 185°C/365°F. Dust the prawns lightly with flour. Holding each in turn by the tail, dip them into the batter, then carefully lower them into the hot oil; cook until golden. Fry the remaining prawns and the squid in the same way. Keep warm.

5 Reduce the temperature of the oil to 170°C/340°F. Drain the sweet potato and pat dry. Dip the vegetables into the batter and deep-fry (see Cook's Tip). Drain well, then keep warm. As soon as all the tempura are ready, serve with the dip.

1 Mix the dip ingredients in a pan. Bring to the boil, cool, then strain. Divide among 4–6 bowls. Slice the unpeeled sweet potato thinly. Put in a bowl with cold water to cover.

COOK'S TIP
Batter and deep-fry the carrots and beans in small bunches. The mushrooms look best if only the undersides are dipped. Cut a cross in the upper side of the mushroom cap, if you like.

GREEN AND YELLOW LAYERED CAKES

THIS COLOURFUL TWO-TONE DESSERT IS MADE BY MOULDING CONTRASTING MIXTURES IN A SMALL POUCH. THE JAPANESE TITLE IS DERIVED FROM THE PREPARATION TECHNIQUE: CHAKIN-SHIBORI, IN WHICH CHAKIN MEANS A POUCH SHAPE AND SHIBORI MEANS A MOULDING ACTION.

MAKES 6

INGREDIENTS
For the yolk mixture (kimi-an)
    6 small hard-boiled eggs
    50g/2oz/¼ cup sugar

For the pea mixture (endo-an)
    200g/7oz/1¾ cups frozen peas
    40g/1½oz/3 tbsp sugar

1 Make the yolk mixture. Shell the eggs, cut them in half and scoop the yolks into a strainer placed over a bowl. Using a wooden spoon, press the yolks through the strainer. Add the sugar and mix well.

2 To make the pea mixture, cook the peas in lightly salted boiling water for about 3–4 minutes, until softened. Drain and place in a mortar, then crush with a pestle. Transfer the paste to a pan. Add the sugar and cook over low heat until thick. Stir constantly so that the mixture does not burn.

3 Spread out the pea paste in a shallow dish so that it cools as quickly as possible. Divide both mixtures into six portions.

COOK'S TIP
Use a food processor instead of a mortar and pestle if preferred. Process for a few seconds to make a coarse paste.

4 Wet a piece of muslin (cheesecloth) or thin cotton and wring it out well. Place a portion of the pea mixture on the cloth and put a similar amount of the yolk mixture on top. Wrap the mixture up and twist the top of the cloth to join the mixtures together and mark a spiral pattern on the top. Unwrap and place on a plate. Make five more cakes in the same way. Serve cold.

SUKIYAKI

YOU WILL NEED A SPECIAL CAST-IRON SUKIYAKI PAN (SUKIYAKI-NABE) *AND BURNER OR A SIMILAR TABLE-TOP COOKER FOR THIS DISH. IT IS GREAT FUN BECAUSE GUESTS CAN COOK THEIR OWN DINNER IN FRONT OF THEM, AND THEN HELP THEMSELVES TO THE DELICIOUS MORSELS OF FOOD.*

SERVES 4

INGREDIENTS

1kg/2¼lb beef topside, thinly sliced
lard or white cooking fat
4 leeks or spring onions (scallions),
 sliced diagonally into
 1cm/½in pieces
bunch of shungiku leaves, stems
 removed, chopped (optional)
bunch of enoki mushrooms, brown
 roots cut off (optional)
8 shiitake mushrooms,
 stems removed
300g/11oz shirataki noodles, boiled
 for 2 minutes, drained and halved
2 pieces grilled tofu, about 10 × 7cm/
 4 × 2¾in, cut into 3cm/1¼in cubes
4 fresh eggs, to serve

For the sukiyaki stock
100ml/3½fl oz/scant ½ cup mirin
45ml/3 tbsp sugar
105ml/7 tbsp Japanese soy sauce

For the seasoning mix
200ml/7fl oz/scant 1 cup dashi
 (kombu and bonito stock) or
 instant dashi
100ml/3½fl oz/scant ½ cup sake
 or dry white wine
15ml/1 tbsp Japanese soy sauce

1 Make the sukiyaki stock. Pour the mirin into a pan and bring to the boil. Stir in the sugar and soy sauce, bring to the boil, then remove from the heat and set aside.

2 To make the seasoning mix, heat the dashi, sake or wine and soy sauce in a small pan. As soon as the mixture boils, remove from the heat and set aside.

3 Fan out the beef slices on a large serving plate. Put the lard for cooking on the same plate. Arrange all the remaining ingredients, except the eggs, on one or more large plates.

4 Stand the portable cooker on a suitably heavy mat to protect the dining table and ensure that it can be heated safely. Melt the lard, add three or four slices of beef and some leeks or spring onions, and then pour in the sukiyaki stock. Gradually add the remaining ingredients, except the eggs.

5 Place each egg in a ramekin and beat lightly with chopsticks. Place one before each diner. When the beef and vegetables are cooked, diners help themselves to whatever they fancy, dipping their chosen piece of meat, vegetable or grilled tofu in the raw egg before eating.

6 When the stock has thickened, gradually stir in the seasoning mix and carry on cooking until all the ingredients have been eaten.

CHAP CHAE

A KOREAN STIR-FRY OF MIXED VEGETABLES AND NOODLES GARNISHED ATTRACTIVELY WITH THE YELLOW AND WHITE EGG SHAPES THAT ARE SO TYPICALLY KOREAN.

SERVES 4

INGREDIENTS

225g/8oz rump (round) or
   sirloin steak
115g/4oz cellophane noodles, soaked
   for 20 minutes in hot water to cover
4 Chinese dried mushrooms, soaked
   for 30 minutes in warm water
groundnut (peanut) oil, for stir-frying
2 eggs, separated
1 carrot, cut into matchsticks
1 onion, sliced
2 courgettes (zucchini) or
   1/2 cucumber, cut into sticks
1/2 red (bell) pepper, seeded and
   cut into strips
4 button (white) mushrooms, sliced
75g/3oz/1 1/2 cups beansprouts,
   washed and drained
15ml/1 tbsp light soy sauce
salt and ground black pepper
sliced spring onions (scallions)
   and sesame seeds, to garnish

1 Put the steak in the freezer until it is firm enough to cut into thin slices and then into 5cm/2in strips.

2 Mix the ingredients for the marinade in a shallow dish (see Cook's Tip), stir in the steak strips. Drain the noodles and cook them in boiling water for 5 minutes. Drain again, then cut into short lengths. Drain the mushrooms, cut off and discard the stems; slice the caps.

3 Prepare the garnish. Heat the oil in a small frying pan. Beat the egg yolks together and pour into the pan. When set, slide them on to a plate. Add the egg whites to the pan and cook until set. Cut both yolks and whites into diamond shapes and set aside.

COOK'S TIP
To make the marinade, blend together 15ml/1 tbsp sugar, 30ml/2 tbsp light soy sauce, 45ml/3 tbsp sesame oil, 4 finely chopped spring onions (scallions), 1 crushed garlic clove and 10ml/2 tsp crushed toasted sesame seeds.

4 Drain the beef. Heat the oil in a wok or large frying pan and stir-fry the beef until it changes colour. Add the carrot and onion and stir-fry for 2 minutes, then add the other vegetables, tossing them until just cooked.

5 Add the noodles and season with soy sauce, salt and pepper. Cook for 1 minute. Spoon into a serving dish and garnish with egg, spring onions and sesame seeds.

KIMCHI

NO SELF-RESPECTING KOREAN MOVES FAR WITHOUT THE BELOVED KIMCHI. IN THE PAST, LARGE STONE POTS WERE FILLED WITH THIS PICKLED CABBAGE, AND BURIED IN THE GROUND FOR THE WINTER.

SERVES 6–8

INGREDIENTS

675g/1 1/2lb Chinese leaves (Chinese
   cabbage), shredded
1 large or 2 medium yam beans,
   total weight about 675g/1 1/2lb or
   2 hard pears, peeled and thinly sliced
60ml/4 tbsp salt
200ml/7fl oz/scant 1 cup water
4 spring onions (scallions),
   finely chopped
4 garlic cloves, crushed
2.5cm/1in piece fresh root ginger,
   peeled and finely chopped
10–15ml/2–3 tsp chilli powder

1 Place the Chinese leaves and yam beans or pears in a bowl and sprinkle evenly with salt. Mix well, then press down into the bowl.

2 Pour the water over the vegetables, then cover the bowl and leave overnight in a cool place. Next day, drain off the brine from the vegetables and set it aside. Mix the brined vegetables with the spring onions, garlic, ginger and chilli powder (use rubber gloves if you have sensitive hands). Pack the mixture into a 900g/2lb jar or two smaller ones. Pour over the reserved brine.

3 Cover with clear film (plastic wrap) and place on a sunny windowsill or in an airing cupboard for 2–3 days. Thereafter store in the refrigerator, where the mixture can be kept for several weeks.

MARINATED BEEF STEAKS

Bulgogi is a very popular dish for outdoor entertaining. Traditionally it would have been cooked on a Genghis Khan grill, which is shaped like the crown of a hat, but a ridged heavy frying pan or wok works almost as well.

SERVES 3–4

INGREDIENTS
    450g/1lb fillet of beef or rump
      (round) steak, in the piece
    sesame oil, for frying

For the marinade
    150ml/¼ pint/⅔ cup dark soy sauce
    30ml/2 tbsp sesame oil
    30ml/2 tbsp sake or dry white wine
    1 garlic clove, cut into thin slivers
    15ml/1 tbsp sugar
    30ml/2 tbsp crushed roasted
      sesame seeds
    4 spring onions (scallions), cut into
      long lengths
    salt and ground black pepper

1 Put the meat into the freezer until it is firm enough to slice very thinly and evenly. Arrange the slices of beef in a shallow glass dish.

2 Make the marinade. Mix the soy sauce, oil, sake or wine, garlic, sugar and sesame seeds in a bowl and add the spring onions. Season to taste.

3 Pour the marinade over the slices of beef and mix well. Cover the dish and transfer to the refrigerator. Chill for at least 3 hours or overnight.

4 Heat the merest slick of oil in a ridged heavy frying pan or wok. Drain the beef slices and fry over high heat for a few seconds, turning once. Serve immediately.

PORK AND SPRING ONION PANCAKES

BINDAEDUK IS SOMETIMES REFERRED TO AS KOREA'S ANSWER TO THE PIZZA, ALTHOUGH IT IS REALLY A BEANCAKE. THE FILLING CAN INCLUDE KIMCHI, CARROT AND GINGER, BUT PORK AND SPRING ONIONS ARE MORE TRADITIONAL INGREDIENTS.

2 Add the soy sauce, sesame seeds and bicarbonate of soda and process briefly to mix. When ready to cook, transfer the batter into a bowl and add the beansprouts, garlic, spring onions and pork. Season to taste.

3 Heat about 10ml/2 tsp of the sesame oil in a large frying pan. Spoon or ladle in half the batter, and, using the back of a spoon, spread it into a thick pancake.

4 Drizzle a little more sesame oil over the surface of the pancake, cover and cook over medium heat until the underside is cooked. Invert a lightly oiled plate over the pan. Remove the pan from the heat and, holding both plate and pan tightly together, turn both over carefully so that the pancake is transferred to the plate. Slide it back into the pan and cook on the other side for 3–4 minutes more. Keep this first pancake hot while cooking a second pancake in the same way. Place the pancakes on serving plates and garnish with chives. Cut into wedges and serve with soy sauce.

SERVES 4–6

INGREDIENTS
225g/8oz/1¼ cups skinned, split mung beans
50g/2oz/⅓ cup glutinous rice
15ml/1 tbsp light soy sauce
15ml/1 tbsp roasted sesame seeds, crushed
2.5ml/½ tsp bicarbonate of soda (baking soda)
115g/4oz/½ cup beansprouts, blanched and dried
1 garlic clove, crushed
4 spring onions (scallions), chopped
115g/4oz cooked lean pork, shredded
30ml/2 tbsp sesame oil, plus extra for drizzling
salt and ground black pepper
fresh chives, to garnish
light soy sauce, to serve

1 Pick over the mung beans and put them in a bowl. Add the glutinous rice and pour in water to cover. Leave to soak for at least 8 hours. After this time, transfer the beans and rice into a strainer, rinse under cold water, then drain. Put the mixture into a food processor and process to a batter with the consistency of double (heavy) cream.

SHOPPING FOR ASIAN FOODS

UK

General
Bart's Spices
York Road
Bedminster
Bristol BS3 4AD
Tel: 0117 977 3474

Chinese
Good Harvest Fish
  Market
14 Newport Place
London WC2H 7PR
Tel: 020 7437 0712

Golden Gate Cake Shop
13 Macclesfield Street
London W1V 7LH
Tel: 020 7287 9862

Golden Gate Supermarket
16 Newport Place
London WC2H 7JS
Tel: 020 7437 6266

Golden Gate
  Hong Kong Ltd
14 Lisle Street
London WC2 7BE
Tel: 020 7437 0014

Hong Kong Supermarket
62 High Street
London SW4 7UL
Tel: 020 7720 2069

Loon Fung Supermarket
42–44 Gerrard Street
London W1V 7LP
Tel: 020 7437 7332

New Peking Supermarket
59 Westbourne Grove
London W2 4UA
Tel: 020 7928 8770

Newport Supermarket
28–29 Newport Court
London WC2H 7PQ
Tel: 020 7437 2386

Rum Wong Supermarket
London Road
Guildford
Surrey GU1 2AF
Tel: 01483 451 568

S. W. Trading Ltd
Horn Lane
Greenwich
London SE10 0RT
Tel: 020 8293 9393

Wang Thai Supermarket
101 Kew Road
Richmond
Surrey TW9 2PN
Tel: 020 8332 2959

The Good Earth
  Express
335 West End Lane
West Hampstead
London NW6 1RS
Tel: 020 7433 3111

Wing Tai
11a Aylesham Centre
Rye Lane
London SE15 5EW
Tel: 020 7635 0714

Wing Yip
395 Edgware Road
London NW2 6LN
Tel: 020 7450 0422

South-east Asian
Hopewell Emporium
2F Dyne Road
London NW6 7XB
Tel: 020 7624 5473

Manila Supermarket
11–12 Hogarth Place
London SW5 0QT
Tel: 020 7373 8305

Miah, A. and Co.
20 Magdalen Street
Norwich NR3 1HE
Tel: 01603 615 395

Sri Thai
56 Shepherd's Bush
  Road
London W6 7PH
Tel: 020 7602 0621

Talad Thai Ltd
320 Upper Richmond
  Road
London SW15 6TL
Tel: 020 8789 8084

Tawana
18–20 Chepstow Road
London W2 5BD
Tel: 020 7221 6316

Japanese
Arigato
48–50 Brewer Street
London W1F 9TG
Tel: 020 7287 1722

Miura Japanese Foods
44 Coombe Road
Nr Kingston KT2 7AF
Tel: 020 8549 8076

Natural House
Japan Centre
212 Piccadilly
London W1V 9LD
Tel: 020 7434 4218

Oriental City
399 Edgware Road
London NW9 0JJ
Tel: 020 8200 0009

T.K. Trading
Unit 6/7
The Chase Centre
Chase Road
London NW10 6QD
Tel: 020 8453 1001

Thai
Rum Wong Supermarket
London Road
Guildford
Surrey GU1 2AF
Tel: 01483 451568

Talad Thai Ltd
320 Upper Richmond
  Road
London SW15 6TL
Tel: 020 8789 8084

Tawana Supermarket
18 Chepstow Road
London W2 4BD
Tel: 020 7221 6316

Equipment
Neal Street East
5–7 Neal Street
London WC2H 9PU
Tel: 020 7240 0135

Obhrai Cash and Carry
168 Ealing Road
Wembley
Middlesex HA0 4DQ
Tel: 020 8903 4450

Popat Store
138 Ealing Road
Wembley
Middlesex HA0 4PY
Tel: 020 8903 6797

USA

General
99 Ranch Market
5150 Buford Highway
B-199, Doraville, GA 30340
Tel: (770) 458-8899

Asian Food Market
6450 Market Street
Upper Darby, PA 19082
Tel: (610) 352-4433

Asian Foods, Etc.
1375 Prince Avenue
Atlanta, GA 30341
Tel: (404) 543-8624

Asian Foods Ltd.
260–280 West Lehigh
  Avenue
Philadelphia, PA 19133
Tel: (215) 291-9500

Asian Market
2513 Stewart Avenue
Las Vegas, NV 89101
(702) 387-3373

Asian Market
18815 Eureka Road
South Gate, MI 48195
www.asianmarket.qpg.com

Augusta Market Oriental
  Foods
2117 Martin Luther King
  Jr. Boulevard
Altanta, GA 30901
Tel: (706) 722-4988

Bharati Food & Spice Center
6163 Reynolds Road
Suite G, Morrow, GA 30340
Tel: (770) 961-9007

First Asian Food Center
3420 East Ponce De Leon
  Avenue
Scottsdale, GA 30079
Tel: (404) 292-6508

The House of Rice Store
3221 North Hayden Road
Scottsdale, AZ 85251
Tel: (480) 947-6698
www.houserice.com

Han Me Oriental Food
  & Gifts
2 E. Derenne Avenue
Savannah, GA 31405
Tel: (912) 355-6411

Hong Tan Oriental Food
2802 Capitol Street
Savannah, GA 31404
Tel: (404) 233-9184

Huy Fong Foods Inc.
5001 Earle Avenue
Rosemead, CA 91770
Tel: (626) 286-8328
www.huyfong.com

Khanh Tam Oriental Market
4051 Buford Highway, NE
Atlanta, GA 30345
Tel: (404) 728-0393

May's American Oriental
  Market
422 West University Avenue
Saint Paul, MN 55103
Tel: (651) 293-1118
www.maysamoriental.
  qpg.com

Norcross Oriental Market
6062 Norcross-Tucker
  Road
Chamblee, GA 30341
Tel: (770) 496-1656

Oriental Grocery
11827 Del Amo Boulevard
Cerritos, CA 90701
Tel: (310) 924-1029

Oriental Market
670 Central Park Avenue
Yonkers, NY 10013
(212) 349-1979

The Oriental Pantry
423 Great Road
Acton, MA 01720
Tel: (978) 264-4576
www.orientalpantry.com

Saigon Asian Market
10090 Central Avenue
Biloxi, MS 39532
Tel: (228) 392-8044
www.saigonor.qpg.com

Siam Market
27266 East Baseline
  Street
Highland, CA 92346
Tel: (909) 862-8060

Unimart American and
Asian Groceries
1201 Howard Street
San Francisco, CA 94103
Tel: (415) 431-0362

Chinese
Chinese Oriental
Market
300 South Bruce Street
Las Vegas, NV 89101
(702) 382-7295

DIHO Market
655 Pasquinelli Drive
Westmont, IL 60559
Tel: (630) 323-1668
www.pcmax.net/Chinese/
food/diho.html

Pearl River Chinese
Products Emporium
277 Canal Street
New York, NY
Tel: (212) 431-4770

Indian
Alhambra, CA 91801
Tel: (626) 576-2455
kajala@GTE.net

Bombay Sweets
1401 University
Boulevard
Langley Park, MD 20783

Cherian Indian Groceries
1707 Church Street
Decatur, GA 30030
Tel: (404) 299-0842

Indian Asian Bazaar
159 North 72nd Street
Omaha, NE 68127
Tel: (402) 556-3309

Indian Grocery
4535 Fredricksburg Road
San Antonio, TX 78200
Tel: (210) 737-0556

Indian International Mart
6391 S. Sheridan Road
Tulsa, OK 74133

Indian Spices and Gifts
3901 Wilson Boulevard
Arlington, VA 22203
Tel: (703) 522-0149

Indo-Pak Spices
422 Elden Street
Herndon, VA 22070

Kajala Imports
23 East Main Street
Alhambra, CA 91801
Tel: (626) 576-2455
kalaja@GTE.net

Patel Brothers
2080 University Boulevard
Langley Park
MD 20783
Tel: (301) 422-1555

Spice & Sweets Mahal
431 South Frederick
Avenue
Gaithersburg, MD 20877

Spice Mahal
3621 Kirkwood
Highway
Wilmington, DE
Tel: (302) 994-8144

Subzi Mandi
Twin Oaks Center
757 Hungerford Drive
Rockville, MD 20850

Sushma Emporium
480-A Blossom Hill
Road
San Jose, CA
Tel: (408) 281-0392
www.indolink.com/SFO/
sushma.html

TAJ International
Foods
7334 Lee Highway
Chattanooga, TN 37421
Tel: (423) 892-0259

Indonesian
Bachri's Chili & Spice
Gourmet
5617 Villa Haven
Pittsburgh, PA 15236
Tel: (412) 831-1131

Japanese
Daido
1385 16th Street
Fort Lee, NJ 07024
Tel: (201) 944-0020

Katagiri Speciality
224 East 59th Street
New York, NY 10022
Tel: (212) 755-3566
www.katagiri.com

Maruwa Foods Company
of America
1737 Post Street
San Francisco, CA 94115
Tel: (415) 563-1901
www.maruwa.com

Sea Rance
3223 West Lake Avenue
Wilmette, IL 60091
(708) 256-4404

Suruki Super Market
71 East 4th Avenue
San Maleo
CA 94401
Tel: (415) 347-5288
www.americandreams.com

Yaohan
595 River Road
Edgewater, NJ 07020
Tel: (201) 941-9113

Korean
Lotte
2030 Will Ross Court
Chamblee, GA 30341
Tel: (770) 454-7569

Thai/Laos
Ai Hoa
860 North Hill Street
Los Angeles, CA 90026
Tel (213) 482-48

Bangkok Market
4757 Melrose Avenue
Los Angeles, CA 90029
Tel: (203) 662-7990

Modern Thai Incorporated
135 Yacht Club Way #210
Hypuluxo, FL 33462
Tel: (888) THAI-8888

Thai Market
3297 Las Vegas
Boulevard
Las Vegas, NV 89030
Tel: (702) 643-8080

Thai Market
916 Harrelson Street
Fort Walton Beach
FL 32547
Tel: (904) 863-2013

Thai Number One
Market
5927 Cherry Avenue
Long Beach, CA 90805
Tel: (310) 422-6915

Thai-Lao Market
1721 West La Palma
Avenue
Anaheim, CA 92801
Tel: (714) 535-2656

AUSTRALIA

Asian Supermarkets
Pty Ltd
116 Charters Towers Road
Townsville
QLD 4810
Tel: (07) 4772 3997

PK Supermarkets
Pty Ltd
369 Victoria Avenue
Chatswood
NSW 2067
Tel: (02) 9419 8822

Kongs Trading
Pty Ltd
8 Kingscote Street
Kewdale
WA 6105
Tel: (08) 9353 3380

Duc Hung Long Asian
Foodstore
95 The Crescent
Fairfield
NSW 2165
Tel: (02) 9728 1092

Exotic Asian Groceries
Q Supercentre
Cnr Market and Bermuda
Streets
Mermaid Waters
QLD 4218
Tel: (07) 5572 8188

Saigon Asian Food Retail
and Wholesale
6 Cape Street
Dickson
ACT 2602
Tel: (02) 6247 4251

The Spice and Herb
Asian Shop
200 Old Cleveland Road
Capalaba
QLD 4157
Tel: (07) 3245 5300

Sydney Fish Market
Pty Ltd
Cnr Pyrmont Bridge Road
and Bank Street
Pyrmont
NSW 2009
Tel: (02) 9660 1611

Harris Farm Markets
Sydney Markets
Flemongton
NSW 2140
Tel: (02) 9746 2055

Burlington Supermarkets
Chinatown Mall
Fortitude Valley
QLD 4006
Tel: (07) 3216 1828

**Author's
Acknowledgements**
Sallie Morris would like to
thank her family: Johnnie,
Alex and James for their
support; Beryl Castles
for her help in typing the
manuscript; Beth Ware
for advice on recipes from
the Philippines; Rupert
Welchman for his advice
on Japanese recipes; John
Phengsiri at the Wang
Thai Supermarket in
Richmond; Bart's Spices
Ltd; Cherry Valley Farms
(Tel: 01472 371 271),
who supplied ducklings
for recipe testing; Ken the
Fishman from Grimsby
(Tel: 0860 240 213), and
Magimix (Tel: 01483 427
411) for supplying a food
processor, ice cream
maker and electric
steamer for recipe testing.
Deh-ta Hsiung would
like to thank Sallie Morris
and Emi Kazuko for
their advice and help in
writing about South-east
Asian and Japanese foods.

INDEX

Picture
Acknowledgements

All pictures are by
Nicki Dowey and Janine
Hosegood, except:
p8 Tony Stone/Glen
Allison, Cephas/Nigel
Blythe; p9 Cephas/Alain
Proust, Cephas/Nigel
Blythe; p10 Tony
Stone/Ron Dahlquist.